W9-ACN-656

# The Evolution of
# American Secondary School
# Textbooks

❖─◇─◇─◇─◇─◇─◇─◇─◇─◇─◇─◇─◇─❖

## J. A. NIETZ

# THE EVOLUTION OF
# AMERICAN
# SECONDARY SCHOOL
# TEXTBOOKS

Rhetoric & Literature
Algebra, Geometry
Natural History (Zoology), Botany
Natural Philosophy (Physics), Chemistry
Latin and Greek
French, German, & World History
as taught in American
Latin Grammar Schools
Academies
and early High Schools
before 1900

by JOHN A. NIETZ
EMERITUS PROFESSOR OF EDUCATION
UNIVERSITY OF PITTSBURGH

CHARLES E. TUTTLE COMPANY
RUTLAND, VERMONT

St. Mary's College Library
Winona, Minnesota

REPRESENTATIVES

*for Continental Europe*
Boxerbooks, Inc., Zurich

*for the British Isles*
Prentice-Hall International, Inc., London

*for Australasia*
Paul Flesch & Co., Pty. Ltd., Melbourne

PUBLISHED BY THE
Charles E. Tuttle Company, Inc.
*of Rutland, Vermont & Tokyo, Japan*
*with editorial offices at*
*Suido 1-chōme, 2-6, Bunkyo-ku, Tokyo*

*Copyright in Japan, 1966*
*by Charles E. Tuttle Co., Inc., all rights reserved*
*First printing 1966*

LIBRARY OF CONGRESS CATALOG CARD NO. 65–20613

PRINTED IN JAPAN

PETER BROGREN, THE VOYAGERS' PRESS, TOKYO

373.132
N67

# PREFACE

72818

D URING the teaching of graduate courses in the history of education it soon became evident to the writer that to determine what was really taught in the schools of the past one would have to know what was the content in the old textbooks used. This led the writer to begin collecting old textbooks for analysis. Since it would be a forbidding task to collect the old textbooks from many countries, he has attempted to obtain as complete a collection as reasonably possible of texts used or published in America. It is known that many of the earliest textbooks used in America were brought here from Europe, particularly from England. Thus an attempt has been made to include such books in the collection. Too, many of the earliest texts published here were largely reprints of European books. No international copyright laws were in effect then.

The collection contains more than 8,000 volumes published before 1900. The textbooks of the fields or subjects most commonly taught in the elementary schools were dealt with in the writer's other book, *Old Textbooks*. It is the purpose of this book to be a companion volume dealing with the evolution of texts most commonly used in the American Latin grammar schools, academies, and early high schools. However, to include an analysis of the texts used in all the subject fields taught in these schools would make this volume unduly large. So treatment of the texts in certain fields will be omitted. Since books relating to English grammar, arithmetic, physiology, geography, American history, civil government (civics), music, and art, were covered in the other book, even though they were often taught in secondary schools. Their treatment will be omitted here. Though trigonometry, surveying, navigation, mental philosophy (psychology), and pedagogy were often taught in academies and some early high schools, they will be omitted since they are not commonly taught in secondary schools today. On the other hand, such business subjects as bookkeeping, shorthand, typing, and business correspondence are commonly taught today, they were not commonly taught in academies or high schools before 1900. Before 1900 they were most commonly taught in private commerical or business schools. A separate work could be written about their books.

The collection contains between 150 and 500 old textbooks in each of the thirteen fields dealt with in this book. Then, too, the students who wrote doctoral dissertations at the University of Pittsburgh involving analysis of old textbooks in various fields visited other well known libraries for additional books. Among these were the Library of Congress, the Plimpton and Smith Collections at Columbia University, the New York City Public Library, the Harvard Library, the Antiquarian Society Library at Worcester, Massachusetts, the Univeristy of Michigan Library, and many others. Thus the findings of these studies reflect the nature of old American school textbooks. Ample use has been made of these studies, as well as of other studies made elsewhere known to the writer.

Everyone who has attended or is attending a secondary school ought to understand something about the past struggles and development of our evolving civilization. The molders of our American civilization were the products of the schools of the past. The thinking and ideals of these leaders evidently were greatly influenced by textbooks they studied in the schools. Thus an understanding of the textbooks of the past should throw considerable light upon the evolution of our culture and civilization. Both students and teachers of our secondary schools may profit by gaining such understanding.

The writer is keenly aware that in dealing with thousands of textbooks of the past it is easy to commit errors of statement. Such errors may relate to the dates of their first publication, whether particular books were the first to appear in the field, whether the nature and characteristics of certain textbooks were the first to have them, or when and where the particular subjects were first taught in a secondary school in America. The writer merely claims that he has attempted to be as accurate in his statements as research known to him reasonably warrants.

The writer acknowledges his debt to many persons and libraries. He is grateful to his colleagues and library staff at the University of Pittsburgh for their encouragement and cooperation in the development of the collection and in the pursuance of the many studies involving the textbooks; to the thousands of students in his history of education classes who manifested interest in the old textbooks, and in many cases contributed old books to the collection; to the many other librarians who generously aided the students conducting researches of old textbooks; to the editors of professional journals who published articles relating to old textbooks studies; and to news reporters who helped publicize the collection, which in turn resulted in locating additional books. He is also grateful to his wife, Florence, for her patience with the inconveniences attending the writing of the book; and to my colleagues, Doctors Benjamin W. Haseltine, Ruth Kuschmierz, Vernon C. Lingren, Robert E. Mason, Erston V. Miller, Karl C. H. Oermann, and Arthur M. Young, for reading chapters for correction and criticism.

# Contents

# List of Illustrations

# Old Textbooks

Most authorities agree that in the United States the old textbooks in use in any particular place at any particular time largely constituted the course of study of its school. This was true because the teachers in the early days of our country were so meagerly trained and educated that their dependence on the textbooks was very strong, both for what and how to teach. This was particularly true of the textbooks in the secondary schools, where the subject matter was much more difficult than in the common schools. Thus an analysis of the old secondary school textbooks should reflect the evolution of the American secondary school curriculum, and to some extent the teaching and learning methods as well.

An attempt is here made to show the development of the most commonly taught subjects as reflected in the more popular textbooks used in American secondary schools up to 1900. There are several reasons for selecting this terminal date. First, many persons reading this book will be more or less versant with the more recent textbooks. Second, the scientific influence on American education began to take hold about 1900. It was then that objective studies began, national committees began to make reports, and national associations were formed for various subject matter fields, which soon began to influence the content and methods in those fields. Thus whatever studies will be made involving textbooks after 1900 may require somewhat different analyses than here employed. The content of the books will not be determined so much by individual authors, as was true in the past, as by the reports of the national associations in the various subject fields.

Historically there have been three types of secondary schools in America: the Latin grammar school, the academy, and the high school. The pattern of the Latin grammar school was brought from Europe, and it was established here later to prepare youth for the colonial colleges. The pattern for the academy was somewhat originally molded by Benjamin Franklin in his *Proposals*, though he may have gotten some ideas from certain non-conformist schools in England. The academy aimed to fulfill broader purposes. The high school definitely was an American creation, originally preparing students for life rather than for college. Both the academy and the high school changed considerably with the changing times. In time, both aimed to prepare students both for college, if desired, and for life.

Throughout this study the writer encountered difficulty in determining just which books were used in secondary schools in distinction from those used in the upper grades of the so-called grammar school (elementary) and from those in the colleges. The chief reason for this difficulty was that most early secondary schools were not carefully graded, particularly most academies and high schools. Secondary schools were in a state of confusion roughly until the standardizing and accrediting associations were formed shortly before 1900. A subject was taught every day in one school, or only two or three times per week in another; taught for a year in one school, but only for a semester in another. This variation meant that books of different scope and difficulty were needed. Thus books of greatly varying types and difficuloty will need to be analyzed. Comments will be made about many books regarding their probable grade placement. It is very clear that a great number of the same textbooks were used both in secondary schools and colleges, for statements on the title pages of numerous books were as follows: "For schools and colleges," "For Academies and Colleges," "For Schools and Academies," and later "In High Schools and Colleges."

### A. *Characteristics of Old Textbooks*

*Bindings and Paper.* Unlike old elementary school textbooks, which even from the beginning were usually bound in paper covers, nearly all secondary school books were bound in brown leather until about the middle of the nineteenth century. Many of these were even trimmed and lettered in gold. Lardner's 1832 edition of his *Outlines of Universal History* was even bound in green leather. A few were bound in home spun linen. After about 1840 many texts began to appear bound either in colth-covered stiff paper backs or in plain paper board covers. However, the spines often continued to be leather.

Nearly all of the older textbooks were printed on rag paper. Thus the paper in books even over 400 years old may still be in good condition, except possibly slightly yellowed. Since about 1870 books have been more commonly printed on less durable pulp paper, which ultimately disintegrates. Future textbook collectors may find the more recent books difficult to preserve.

*Pictures, Figures, and Print.* There was great variation in the use of pictures and figures in the old secondary school textbooks. In the Latin, Greek, French, and German textbooks very few pictures appeared. In the general field of mathematics, the books in arithmetic and algebra rarely contained pictures, but, as could be expected, most geometries contained figures to illustrate the more important theorems.

It was in the science books where the most generous use of pictures was developed. An average of 233 pictures per book appeared in 57 analyzed natural histories (zoologies), although five of the six oldest contained none. Two books included 590 each, and Sanborn Tenny's *Elements of Zoology* (1875) contained 750 engravings. Most texts in botany included pictures. Alphonso Wood's *Object Lessons in Botany* (1860) contained 665 illustrations. Several other botanies contained 500 each. The texts in natural philosophy (physics) likewise used cuts or picutures freely. The average per book of the 45 analyzed was 246. The later books used more than the earlier. Sidney A. Norton's *Elements of Natural Philosophy* (1870) contained 350 pictures or illustrations, and Elroy M. Avery's *Elements* used 400 engravings. Nearly one half of the illustrations in the natural philosophy books related to mechanics. Chemistry textbooks did not use illustrations so freely as in the other sciences. However, an analysis of 69 books revealed that an average of 65 illustrations were used per book. Thus

TABLE I: *Comparison in Size of Old and Recent
Textbooks in Several Fields*

| SUBJECT FIELD | BEFORE 1900 | | RECENT BOOKS | |
|---|---|---|---|---|
| | NUMBER OF BOOKS ANALYZED | AVERAGE PAGES PER BOOK | NUMBER OF BOOKS | AVERAGE PAGES PER BOOKS |
| GEOMETRY *(Plane & Solid)* | 61 | 306 | 3 *(plane only)* | 449 |
| RHETORIC | 86 | 281 | 4 *(9th Gr. Eng.)* *(10th Gr. Eng.)* | 436 455 |
| WORLD HISTORY | 95 | 439 | 6 | 730 |
| PHYSICS *(To 1880)* | 45 | 334 | 8 | 705 |
| CHEMISTRY *(To 1890)* | 69 | 332 | 10 | 673 |
| NAT. HISTORY | 37 | 360 | 10 *(Biology)* 11 *(Gen. Sci.)* | 607 659 |

TABLE II: *Number of Textbooks in Certain Fields*
*Containing Learning and Teaching Aids**

| | ALGEBRA (King) | ZOOLOGY (Casle) | PHYSICS (Shank) | CHEMISTRY (Mangery) | RHETORIC (Hess) | WORLD HIST. (Stewart) | WORLD HIST. (Dawson) | TOTAL |
|---|---|---|---|---|---|---|---|---|
| NUMBER OF BOOKS ANALYZED | 119 | 57 | 45 | 69 | 86 | 45 | 95 | 516 |
| 1 PREFACES | 119 | 50 | 44 | 64 | 68 | 38 | 79 | 453 |
| 2 INTRODUCTIONS | 117 | 28 | 16 | 39 | 43 | 29 | 57 | 329 |
| 3 TABLE OF CONTENTS | 112 | 51 | 37 | 66 | 69 | 40 | 80 | 455 |
| 4 QUESTIONS | 19 | 13 | | 39 | 41 | 20 | 44 | 176 (471 books) |
| 5 NOTES OR FOOTNOTES | 44 | 27 | | 59 | | 14 | | 144 (290 books) |
| 6 SUMMARIES | | 8 | | | 6 | | | |
| 7 TABLES | 60 | 12 | 41 | 59 | | 28 | | 200 (335 books) |
| 8 INDEXES | 4 | 46 | 27 | 55 | 24 | 18 | 34 | 208 |
| 9 GLOSSARIES | | 15 | 7 | 12 | 5 | | | 39 (257 books) |
| 10 APPENDIXES | 15 | 12 | 37 | 43 | 8 | | | 115 (376 books) |
| 11 PICTURES AND ILLUSTRATIONS | 42 | 50 | 45 | 65 | | | | 225 (335 books) |
| 12 SUGGESTIONS TO TEACHERS OR STUDENTS | 14 | | | 23 | | 23 | | |

*For the sources of the data in this table see the chapters dealing with these subject fields.

it is clear that it was in the textbooks of science where illustrations and pictures were most freely used.

In general, the print was smaller than in present-day textbooks. Most old textbooks published before 1850 used 7 or 8 point type, except the foreign language and mathematics books, which often used type of varied sizes. The rules or definitions would be printed in one size, the examples in another, and the textual matter even in another size. Most modern secondary school texts are printed with 10 or 12 point type.

*Size of Texts.* In general the texts published before 1900 were considerably smaller than the more recent ones. The data in Table I show that in several fields the number of pages per book more than doubled in the recent texts. This does not necessarily prove that the amount of content has doubled. The type was smaller in the old books, and the number of pages devoted to learning aids, such as a table of contents, questions, indexes, and so on, were not so common in the earlier books. Often the earlier books were adapted to schools which were open only three, four, or five months per year. In the earlier years greater emphasis was placed on the mere memorization of the content, while today an exposure to a greater amount of material is common. The fund of knowledge in most fields has greatly increased with time, so larger textbooks are needed to deal with it. Likewise the recommendations of professional and learned councils and societies have resulted in the increase in the size of the books in a number of fields. Incidentally it may be mentioned that recent American textbooks are considerably larger than in most European countries.

*Teaching and Learning Aids.* The aids found in the old textbooks analyzed are presented in Table II. It can be seen that the inclusion of pictures in all of the old natural philosophy (physics) books was the only instance in which any aid was in all of the old books of a field. Tables of contents and prefaces were the aids most commonly included. These plus introductions and pictures were the only aids found in more than half of the books. To us today it is surprising that fewer than half of the texts included indexes. Tables were rather frequently included in the fields where their use was feasible. Unfortunately it would require a too extensive and complex table to show how the very earliest texts differed from the later ones in this regard. However, a detailed analysis of the studies from which this table is constructed would show that the earliest books rather commonly would only contain either a preface or an introduction or both, and some times a table of contents and pictures in some subject fields. Other aids gained common usage only in the later books.

*Methods and Teaching Approaches.* Since early American teachers were generally poorly prepared for teaching, many old textbooks included teaching suggestions. It should be kept in mind that the earliest popular pedagogical textbook, *Lectures on Schoolkeeping,* was not published until 1829; and that the first public normal school, at Lexington, Massachusetts, did not open until 1839. The teaching suggestions most commonly appeared in the preface, the introduction, or in a section addressed "To the Teacher" or "To the Student."

It may be stated that at no time before 1900 did all the authors of textbooks favor the same single one method or approach for the teaching of their books. In addition to the suggestions made in the beginning of books, the methods or approaches were usually implicit in the arrangement of the materials in the books. Whenever the lessons or sections began with rules, tables, vocabulary lists, or declensions and conjugations, to be followed by their application, memorization was implied. This was the deductive approach. By far the larger fraction of old textbooks largely used this approach. On the other hand, even among the oldest American used books, a considerable number of authors favored the pure or modified inductive approach. Many textbooks used the analytical method in which the authors claimed to use a combination of the inductive and deductive approaches. This was particularly true in mathematics and foreign language books.

A number of texts were written in conversational form. Mrs. Marcet wrote popular texts in the fields of physics, chemistry, and political economy in such form. Physics texts by Comstock, Joyce, and Blake followed the same procedure.

In general, the earlier texts did not require much pupil activity except memorization and the formal application of rules. The earliest rhetoric books required little writing, physics and chemistry texts did not require pupil experimentation until after 1875, and rarely did zoology texts imply laboratory work. Botany books asked for student activities earlier than was true in the other sciences. Usually it was suggested that students gather and analyze plants and flowers and keep the samples in books.

### B. *Some Peculiarities*

*Testimonials.* It was a rather common practice during the middle of last century for textbooks to contain testimonials regarding the book or for other books by the publisher. The 1831 edition of Comstock's *Natural Philosophy* contained eight testimonials written by leading educators. Boyd's *Rhetoric*

(1846) contained seven pages of testimonials in fine print. The last 24 pages of Greenleaf's *Algebra* (1852) were devoted to listing the schools in which his mathematics books were used and to recommendations. Many other books had similar lists. In fact, some books contained both testimonals and advertisements. This was true of Rolfe and Gillet's *Natural Philosophy* (1870) in devoting 18 pages to them.

*Advertisements.* Even more textbooks included advertisements of the publisher's books than those having testimonials. Jacobs and Doering's *Latin Reader-Part Second* (1825) contained 30 pages of advertisements of other textbooks. The Harkness revision of Arnold's *First Latin Book* (1851) devoted 26 pages to books for sale by the publisher, and Bullions' *Greek Grammar* also used 26 pages with advertisements. Many other texts could be mentioned which used many pages for the same purpose. One of the extreme examples was the 1819 edition of the *Latin Tutor* published by Cummings and Hilliard, which listed more than 300 books for sale by the publisher.

*Printers and Publishers.* In the early years there were no large publishing houses serving the entire country. For one thing, easy mailing and shipping facilities were not available. So nearly all textbooks were both printed and sold by local printers. The 14 copies of my Blair's *Lectures on Rhetoric* were published by 13 different printers. The books would be printed in the back of the shop and sold in the front. In the larger towns more than one printer often would publish the same book. For example, the writer has Murray *Readers* published by nine different Philadelphia printers. The same occurred in Boston and New York. This could occur because there seemingly were no effective copyright laws until in the late 1820's. A few writers succeeded in securing certain states to enact copyright laws to protect their royalty rights. Among these was Noah Webster.

Before the Revolution Boston was the leading printing center. From the Revolution until about 1815 Philadelphia also became a prominent printing center. Soon after about 1815 New York gradually became the leading printing center, and has remained so until the present time. The writer has Latin texts published before 1815 by five different Boston printers, by eight different Philadelphia printers, and by only two New York printers; but after 1850 only a few were published in Philadelphia, while most of the others were published in Boston or New York.

The two best known printing houses during the colonial period were Isaiah Thomas in Worcester, Massachusetts, and Christopher Sower in Philadelphia.

Shortly after 1800 rather often two or more printers began to form partner-ships to publish books. Even then their book sales apparently were still largely local or regional. Book publishers wanting a wider market either had to make cooperative arrangements with printers in other parts of the country or wait until the more common use of steam boats and the railorads for mailing and shipping the books. However, a few publishing companies were formed before 1850 which still exist.

*Author and Authorship.* Nearly all the secondary school textbooks first used in America were written in Europe. Most of these were first written in England, except that some in the fields of the sciences and foreign languages. Some were first written in Germany and a few in France. A good fraction of those written in England were by Scotch authors, many of them professors at the University of Edinburgh or by ministers.

Since there were no early international copyright laws, American authors and printers soon freely reprinted many of these books here. The more popular ones would even be reprinted here in a number of cities. However, it soon be-came the American practice to revise them slightly or to add such features as questions, indexes, outlines, and other features. Thus the books became more teachable. Even after American writers began to write their own texts, they continued to borrow heavily from European books. This was particularly true in fields involving detailed and technical knowledge, such as the foreign languages and the sciences. In many of these books the American authors even listed the foreign authors to whom they were indebted. In some fields this indebtedness continued until about 1850.

Most textbooks until shortly before 1900 were written by single authors, except when some books would be revised after the author's decease by some-one engaged by the publisher. Today a large fraction of the secondary school textbooks have two or more authors. Likely this is true because the textbooks are generally much larger, require a longer time to write, and because the body of knowledge involved in most fields is now so extensive that highly specializ-ed knowledge is required to write the different parts or aspects of the books.

In contrast to the above, many American writers not only would write a book alone, but would write texts in many fields. Such prolific textbook writers were common in the languages, mathematics, and the sciences. Anthon, Arnold, Bullions, Harkness, Kelsey, and others wrote both Latin and Greek textbooks. Brooks, Davies, Greenleaf, Olney, Robinson, Wentworth, and others, wrote texts in arithmetic, algebra, and geometry. Even a much greater number wrote texts in two of these fields. Comstock wrote texts in mineralogy, natural philosophy (physics), chemistry, botany, and geology. Steele produced texts in physics, chemistry, geology, astronomy, and physiology. A large number of authors wrote texts in at least two science fields. Space does not permit the enumeration of the many prolific textbook writers of the past. Many textbook authors specialized as textbook writers rather than as specialists in a particular field of knowledge.

Another peculiar feature, or was it peculiar, regarding textbook authors of the past was the great number of ministers who wrote texts. Among the ministers, many of them were Scotch. To be mentioned were the Reverends Blake, Blair, Campbell, Genung, Joyce, Priestly, Whately, and others. The likely reason why so many ministers wrote textbooks was due to the fact that in the past ministers as a class were more highly educated than those in most other so-called professional groups. In fact, numerous groups now considered professional in nature were not considered so until more recent times. In other words, ministers as a group were among the first to professionalize.

Women were not commonly textbook authors until well into the 19th century. Among the prominent women authors may be mentioned Mary Swift, Mrs. Marcet, Mrs. Willard, and Mrs. Phelps. Mrs. Willard wrote texts in the fields of history and geography, while the other three wrote mostly elementary science books. Near the end of the 19th century a number of other women began to write texts, particularly in the fields of reading and English.

Since the writing of secondary school textbooks required certain specialized knowledge in particular subject fields, by far a great majority of the texts were written by professors of colleges and universities rather than by secondary school teachers. More recently the reverse is true.

*Book Titles.* In a number of fields the practice of using similar titles, in whole or part, became rather common. In Geometry 37 of the 61 books analyzed used "Elements" in the title, apparently because this word was used by Euclid. A large fraction of the world history texts used either the word "Elements" or "Outlines" in the title. During the middle of last century many arithmetics used the word "Analytical" in the title, and many grammars used "Progressive" or "Analytical."

*Omnibus Character of Books.* The earliest American used texts in several fields were rather omnibus in character. A number of advanced arithmetic books included some geometry, trigonometry, logarithms, book-keeping, and algebra. Bookkeeping was treated most often. Early natural philosophy (physics) books included considerable treatment of astronomy and other unusual content. Many of the algebras treated logarithms, and even a larger fraction of the geometry texts included trigonometry, usually both plane and spherical. A number of the earliest chemistry books were virtually general books on science, often dealing with heat, electricity, and atmosphere (air), belonging to physics, and some matters of biology.

*Longevity of Books.* The better textbooks written during the last century enjoyed a longer continued use than has been true of books published since 1900. Many older texts continued in circulation for more than 50 years, particularly if they were revised from time to time. Of course, the science and history books needed revision oftener than those in the foreign languages and mathematics. However, no secondary school texts enjoyed the long popularity of the McGuffey *Readers* (over 100 years) and the Ray's *Arithmetics.* Changes were needed less often in the past, since developments in science, economics, and the nature of society, were less rapid than during the twentieth century. Not only that, but textbook authors apparently did not always seriously attempt to incorporate the latest discoveries and developments in their texts. Advanced arithmetics often used the English monetary system long after the American Congress adopted the American system of dollars and cents. Zoology and biology textbook writers procrastinated a long time before including the findings of Darwin and others.

*Oddities.* Most early natural philosophy books contained anecdotes about certain scientists of the past and/or about certain peculiar applications of physics. Early chemistry texts often contained suggested uses of chemical elements, together with the use of heat and electricity, for entertaining purposes. Some books even contained pictures of scientists entertaining audiences.

## C. *Concluding Comment*

FROM the foregoing analyses it can be said that many and interesting changes have taken place in the development of American secondary school textbooks. Any fair-minded student of education must admit that our modern textbooks are a great improvement over those of the past. The remainder of the book will deal with the more popular textbooks used in the more commonly taught subjects in American secondary schools of the past.

# CHAPTER ONE

# English Subjects

THROUGH the years three types of secondary schools developed in America; namely, the Latin grammar school, the academy, and the high school. In the early Latin grammar schools the emphasis was largely on Latin and Greek rather than on vernacular English. Thus the study of the English subjects received little attention.

In the academies much more stress was given the study of English, even though most larger academies also offered a classical curriculum in which Latin and Greek were offered. Then when high schools were established, the study of English rather than Latin and Greek was given major attention. In fact, the first high school in the United States was entitled the English Classical School. It was opened in Boston in 1821. A considerable part of its curriculum consisted of English grammar, composition, English criticism, and literature.

In this chapter an attempt will be made to discuss the appearance and development of the more popular textbooks used in the past in the study of English in the academies and the high schools in America. Textbooks in the following fields will receive attention: English grammar composition and rhetoric, English literature, and American literature. Although advanced English grammar was offered in many academies and early high schools, a chapter dealing with it is included in my other book, *Old Textbooks*, further treatment of it will be omitted here.

# COMPOSITION AND RHETORIC

*Examine well, ye writers, weigh with care,*
*What suits your genius, what your strength will bear*

HORACE

## Introduction

*Concepts of rhetoric.* Rhetoric has often been defined as the theory of composition. Although commonly the terms rhetoric and composition have become synonymous, yet the principles of rhetoric as applied to composition have varied in emphasis from time to time. For example, the ancient Greeks soon made a distinction between the useful art of words and the finer literary art of poetics. They emphasized the useful art as it applied to oratory. Aristotle wrote a book on *Rhetoric*. It emphasized effective oral composition or oratory.

Later when the Romans conquered the Greeks and absorbed many aspects of Greek culture, they even more fully emphasized the rhetorical principles that applied to oratory. Cicero's *De Oratore* stressed oratory. Too, the higher schools among the Romans were known as Rhetorical Schools, where these aspects were stressed. In these schools Quintilian's *De Institutione Oratoria* became the chief textbook.

During the Renaissance the rediscovery of the classics of the ancient Greeks and Romans led to a study of the diction and style of the ancient writings rather than the useful art of functional oratory. With the acceptance of the Seven Liberal Arts as the core of the classical curriculum, *rhetoria* was considered one of its most important subjects.

This emphasis on the correctness and elegance of style and diction continued into more modern times. In fact, this emphasis was evident in Hugh Blair's *Lectures on Rhetoric and Belles Lettres* written at the University of Edinburgh in 1783, and which later was often reprinted and became the first widely used rhetoric book in America. Later, however, in American rhetoric books various aspects of rhetoric and composition received attention. These aspects will become more clear when the most popular textbooks will be described.

These aspects even became evident when one surveys the varying titles of some of these textbooks in the writers collection. Among the titles are: Composition and Rhetoric, Rhetoric and Belles Lettres, Composition and Grammar, English Composition and Analysis, Grammar of Rhetoric and Polite

Literature, Elements of Criticism, Rhetoric and Literary Criticism, Forms of Discourse, Our Language, Modern English, Lessons in English, Expressive English, Prose Composition, Art and Science of Conversation, Introduction to the English Tongue, and then such as the Elements of, Philosophy of, Manual of, Principles of, Handbook of, Art of, Outlines of, and Grammar of Rhetoric.

*Rhetoric in the curriculum.* Apparently English composition received very meager attention in the early American Latin grammar schools. On the other hand, rhetoric was soon given considerable attention in the academies. It is definitely known that the Philadelphia Academy, Phillips Academy, and the New Ipswich Academy taught rhetoric before 1800. It was also taught in some early private schools. After 1800 it was taught in most academies. Since public speaking was considered important in a growing democracy, the study of composition and rhetoric was thought to contribute much in that respect.

When the first high school in the United States, the Boston English Classical School, was opened in 1821, plans called for the teaching of composition, declamation, and exercises in criticism. Likewise when the Girls' High School of Boston was opened in 1826 composition was included in the curriculum. Composition was taught in the high school at Hartford in 1848 and in Middletown in 1850. Stout's[1] study of the high schools of the middle west between 1860 and 1918 reveals that nearly all of these taught either composition, or rhetoric, or their combination during those years. Thus it is fitting that a chapter be devoted to the evolution of the textbooks most commonly used in the teaching of composition and rhetoric.

## A. *Rhetorics from England*

As WAS true of the textbooks in most fields, the earliest rhetoric textbooks were brought here from England, and then often reprinted here, apparently without any copyright obligations. In fact, American authorship of rhetorics was slower in developing than in most fields. No rhetoric originally written in America gained wide usage until after 1825. So in this section treatment will be given to those rhetorics originally written in England but which gained common usage in America.

*Hugh Blair* (1718–1800). The first rhetoric textbook to gain popularity in America was written by Hugh Blair at the University of Edinburgh. He was graduated from Edinburgh in 1739, and was licensed to preach in 1741. After serving several churches, he was invited in 1759 to teach at the University. He prepared a careful set of lectures on rhetoric. These seemed so excellent that some students began to publish them in part. Eventually in 1783 he published them as his *Lectures on Rhetoric and Belles Lettres*. In the preface he stated:

"The following Lectures were read in the University of Edinburgh, for Twenty-four years. The publication of them, at present, was not altogether a matter of choice. Imperfect copies of them, in manuscript, from notes taken by students who heard them read, were first privately handed about; and afterwards frequently exposed to public sale."

So he thought it high time to publish them to prevent them appearing in "very defective and erroneous from."

In 1784 his book was reprinted in Philadelphia. It was a large book of 466 pages, 8 by 10 inches in size, bound in leather. The writer's collection contains fourteen copies of Blair's *Lectures* printed by thirteen different printers in America all bound in leather. The latest copy was printed in 1853. Most of them appeared with the title of *An Abridgment of Lectures on Rhetoric* by Hugh Blair. Many of these copies had questions added in the back. These reprints varied greatly in size. The smallest contained 202 pages and the largest 557. The size of the pages varied from 3 1/2 by 5 1/2 inches to 8 by 10. In other words, each printer would decide the size and the amount of the content to be included. Apparently the larger books were intended for use in colleges and universities, while the title pages of some of the smaller ones stated them to be for "Schools and Academies." The larger ones were usually *verbatim* reprints of the original, with questions added, while the smaller ones were digested reprints, omitting numerous sentences and paragraphs of the original. The topics treated were more or less the same in all of the copies.

Next, attention should be given to the content of these *Lectures*. Attention was given to the finer theories of style, *Belles Letters*, as illustrated in fine literary selections as well as to their application to public speaking, writing, and drama. The first part of the book dealt with such topics as taste, criticism, beauty, style, structure of sentences, figurative language, and the critical examination of various types of writing and speaking. The latter part dealt with types of eloquence, as the bar, the pulpit, and the conduct of discourse; and with types of writing, as historical, philosophical, and various kinds of poetry and drama. Extracts from the great writers of the Hebrews, Greeks, Romans, and moderns were used to illustrate the best principles and practices of rhetoric.

Not only were the Blair books the most commonly used rhetorics in America for many years, they set the pattern for most other authors of rhetorics for many decades. Naturally other authors would attempt to follow the pattern of a successful book.

*John Walker* (1732–1807). Walker became known as an actor, philologist, and lexicographer. In 1791 his famous *Dictionary* was published. It gained much acceptance both in England and America. Later he published *The Teacher's Assistant in English Composition*. This was reprinted in Boston in 1810. This book was mainly composed of extracts of various types of literary models. These extracts were classified as, narratives, regular subjects, themes, and easy essays. The last section was entitled, "Hints for Correcting and Improving Juvenile Composition."

*Alexander Jamieson.* In 1818 his *Grammar of Rhetoric and Polite Literature* was reprinted here, which later appeared in a number of editions. It was divided into Books. Book I dealt with "Language and Style as the Foundation of Eloquence"; Book II with "Structure of Language"; Book III with "Nature and Structure of Sentences"; Book IV with "Figures"; Book V with "Nature of Taste, and the Sources of Its Pleasures"; Book VI with "General Characteristics of Style"; and Book VII with "Poetry." Then the Books were divided into chapters, each dealing with a particular topic. For example, in Book IV, "Of Figures," the chapters dealt with metaphor, simile, personification, allegory, apostrophe, hyperbole, climax, antithesis, and the last chapter with interrogation, repetition, exclamation, irony, and vision. The topics were first defined or explained and then illustrated by literary extracts.

*George Campbell* (1719–1796). He was born in Aberdeen, Scotland. In 1746 he was licensed to preach, and in 1759 was made principal of Marischal College. In 1776 he wrote his *Philosophy of Rhetoric*. Long after his death it was reprinted in America by several printers, one as late as 1849. In the main it covered the same general aspects of rhetoric as Blair's *Lectures*, except it omitted treatment of literary criticism.

*Henry Home of Kames* (1696–1782). Like several other authors of rhetorics from across that were reprinted in America Kames lived in Scotland. By profession he was a lawyer and judge. However, he wrote books on such subjects as agriculture, morality, religion, and the art of thinking. In 1762 he wrote the *Elements of Criticism*. During the 19th century several publishers reprinted it for use in American academies and seminaries. More than half of the book was devoted to such psychological matters as emotions, passions, appreciation of beauty, novelty, custom and habit, and wit. The latter part treated matters commonly dealt with in rhetorics, such as comparisons, figures, narration, style, and taste. One of these reprints appeared as late as 1859.

*Richard Whately* (1787–1863). He was born in London, educated at Oxford, and entered the field of religion. Eventually he was appointed to be the Archbishop of Dublin. As was true of so many ministers in the British Isles during that period, he wrote books in various fields. His *Elements of Logic* had wide usage both in England and America. What concerns us here was the *Elements of Rhetoric,* "comprising an analysis of the laws of moral evidence and of persuasion with rules for argumentative composition and elocution." It was reprinted in Cambridge, (Mass.) in 1834, and later by other printers.

After an extensive definitive introduction, the book was divided into parts: Part I, "Of the Address to the Understanding, with a view to produce conviction"; Part II, "Of the Address to the Will, or Persuasion"; Part III, "Of Style"; and Part IV, "Of Elocution, or Delivery." The Appendix of 90 pages contained extracts from authors with comments.

*Alexander Bain.* The last English author of rhetorics to be discussed here was Bain. He was a professor of logic at the University of Aberdeen. Several reprints of his *English Composition and Rhetoric* appeared here beginning in 1866. Since this book was written much later than those heretofore discussed, it represented a departure from the others in stressing composition. He claimed to have omitted many technical terms as of little practical use which were in previous rhetorics. Part I pertained to composition in general, and Part II dealt with the five leading kinds of composition; namely, "Description, Narration, Exposition, Oratory, and Poetry." It certainly was a more modern and functional book than those previously mentioned.

## B. *American Rhetorics before 1870*

No early American rhetoric textbook gained wide acceptance. English and Scottish culture and literary attainments were considered so superior during the 18th and early 19th centuries that even American schools believed the rhetorics written in England to be better than any produced here. The writer's collection contains more than thirty different rhetorics written by American's between 1825 and 1870, but the books of only a few went through several editions. These will now be discussed.

*Samuel Newman* (1797–1842). As a boy Newman attended Phillips Academy, where previously his father had been principal. Then he studied at Andover

# LECTURES

ON

## RHETORIC

AND

## BELLES LETTRES.

By HUGH BLAIR, D. D.

ONE OF THE MINISTERS OF THE HIGH CHURCH, AND PROFESSOR OF
RHETORIC AND BELLES LETTRES IN THE UNIVERSITY,
OF EDINBURGH.

PHILADELPHIA:

PRINTED AND SOLD BY ROBERT AITKEN, AT POPE's HEAD IN
MARKET STREET.
MDCCLXXXIV.

1  A first American edition of the most popular early rhetoric textbook

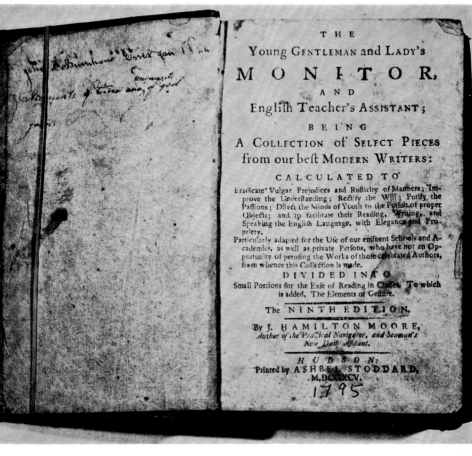

THE

Young GENTLEMAN and LADY's

MONITOR,

AND

English Teacher's ASSISTANT;

BEING

A COLLECTION of SELECT PIECES
from our best MODERN WRITERS:

CALCULATED TO

Eradicate Vulgar Prejudices and Rusticity of Manners; Im-
prove the Understanding; Rectify the Will; Purify the
Passions; Direct the Minds of Youth to the Pursuit of proper
Objects; and to facilitate their Reading, Writing, and
Speaking the English Language, with Elegance and Pro-
priety.

Particularly adapted for the Use of our eminent Schools and A-
cademies, as well as private Persons, who have not an Op-
portunity of perusing the Works of those celebrated Authors,
from whence this Collection is made.

DIVIDED INTO

Small Portions for the Ease of Reading in Classes. To which
is added, The Elements of Gesture.

The NINTH EDITION.

By J. HAMILTON MOORE,
Author of the Practical Navigator, and Seaman's
New Daily Assistant.

HUDSON:
Printed by ASHBEL STODDARD,
M,DCC,XCV.
1795

2 J. Hamilton Moore's *Young Gentleman and Lady's Monitor*

Theological Seminary. However, most of his adult life was spent at Bowdoin College. There he taught in several fields, but most of the time held the Chair of Rhetoric and Oratory.

In 1827 he published *A Practical System of Rhetoric*. In the preface he stated that, "The complaint is often heard, that the study of Rhetoric is of little practical advantage. Many who have learned its rules, do not become good writers, or good critics"; and many who write well do not acknowledge "much assistance from the study of the art." Then he stated the instructions of rhetoric to be twofold: first, pointing out the excellencies of style; and secondly, give cautions against its most frequent faults.

The five chapters dealt with: (1) On thought as the foundation of good writing, (2) On taste, (3) On the nature and objects of a literary taste, (4) On skill in the use of language, and (5) On style. Newman's *Rhetoric* was one of the first to place considerable stress on original writing and composition. The English written books discussed the principles and rules of good writing, but did not provide practice in composition. This book went through many printings. The one printed in 1856 was the "Sixtieth Edition." Thus it appeared to be the first successful American written rhetoric.

*Richard Green Parker* (1798–1869). The second somewhat popular American rhetoric was written by Parker. He was the son of the Rector of the famous Trinity Church of Boston. He attended the Boston Latin Grammar School and Harvard. Most of his life was spent as principal of six different Boston schools. Soon he became a prolific textbook author, writing textbooks on natural philosophy (physics), grammar, a series of readers, and composition books. All of these became rather popular. As a hobby he became an authority as a music critic for Boston newspapers and a builder of hand organs.

In 1832 Parker's *Progressive Exercises in English Composition* was published. This was a small book of 106 pages. This was planned to be a Sequel to Parker's *Grammar*. He mentioned that two obstacles beset pupils when attempting composition: First, obtaining ideas to express, and secondly, expressing them properly. He claimed the use of this book would help overcome both difficulties. Practice in the use of words and phrases was given first attention. Then attention was given to their arrangement. Throughout, the work consisted of exercises. It is not certain whether its use was common in secondary schools. It went through many editions until about 1880.

In 1844 Parker published his *Aids to English Composition*, which was a large book of 429 pages bound in leather. In it he defined composition as "the art of

B

forming ideas, and expressing them in language." As in his earlier book, the emphasis was on exercises in composition rather than on principles of rhetoric. The contents were presented in 99 lessons. Essential explanations and models accompanied the exercises. Even a cursory examination of the book shows that it differed widely in approach from the rhetorics written by the authors of England. It continued to appear for two decades, but not as long as his *Progressive Exercises.*

*James Robert Boyd.* In 1844 Boyd published his *Elements of Rhetoric and Literary Criticism.* The 1846 edition was its fifth, and one edition appeared as late as 1873. Seven pages of testimonials in fine print appeared in the beginning of the book. Part I dealt with spelling, punctuation, use of words, structure of sentences, and arrangement of sentences; Part II with style and figurative language; Part III with the different kinds of composition; Part IV with original composition; Part V with the history of the English language; Part IV with original composition; Part V with the history of the English language; Part VI with modern British literature; Part VII with American literature; and in the 1846 edition a Part VIII was added consisting of supplementary matters. He claimed that this book presented in more convenient form the most useful matters of rhetoric than the works of Blair, Whately, Beattie, Campbell, and Watts.

*G. P. Quackenbos.* He, like Parker and others, wrote textbooks in several fields. For years he was the principal of the Collegiate School in New York. His *First Lessons in Composition* was published in 1851. The 1865 edition mentioned that 169,000 copies had been printed. Since it contained only 182 pages it may have been used oftener in the upper grades of the elementary school than in the secondary school.

The first fifty pages inductively introduced the use of the different parts of speech. Then the kinds of sentences and clauses were discussed, together with punctuation. This done, "the scholar is prepared to express thought in his own language, and he is now required to write sentences of every kind, a word being given to suggest an idea for each," and so on. The lessons were simply and clearly presented.

In 1854 Quackenbos published an *Advanced Course of Composition and Rhetoric.* This was a book of 451 pages and was suggested for "Colleges and Higher Academies." It was divided into five parts, as follows: Part I, History of the English Language; Part II, Punctuation; Part III, Rhetoric; Part IV, Prose Composition; and Part V, Poetical Composition. Parts I and III were somewhat like the English rhetorics, while the other parts were more like other American written rhetorics. This book continued to appear without revision for at least two decades.

*David B. Tower and Benjamin F. Tweed.* These authors jointly wrote *A Grammar of Composition* in 1855. They noted the inconsistency of pupils excelling "in grammar and 'parsing,' as taught in our schools, and yet be unable to form grammatical sentences, either orally or in writing." They held the ability to write well to be an *art*, which cannot be acquired without practice. This was a rather attractive book of 131 short lessons. In the back a list of 150 miscellaneous subjects for composition appeared. It went through several printings.

*Other rhetorics.* Many other American written rhetorics besides these five appeared during this period, but none attained wide adoption. Among them may be mentioned rhetorics by John Andrews (1813), J. L. Blake (1822), Samuel Willard (1830), Ebenezer Porter (1830), William B. Lacey (1834), Charles Morley (1838), John Frost (1839), Charles Northend (1848), Henry N. Day (1850), F. Knighton (1853), Dr. Brewer (1853), F. Brookfield (1855), Henry Coppee (1859), M. E. Lilienthal and Robert Allyn (1862), Levi Branson (1863), W. W. Davis (1864), T. S. Pinneo (1864), J. M. Bonnell (1867), Augustus Layres (1867), H. J. Zander and T. E. Howard (1868), E. O. Haven (1869), and Simon Kerl (1869).

## C. *Rhetorics 1870–1900*

SO-CALLED English subjects came into their own in secondary schools during this period. As a consequence many new rhetorics were published, of which a goodly number became rather popular. This was in contrast to grammars, when not many new popular books were written in this period. One reason that gave the study of rhetoric an impetus was that about 1870 most colleges began to require credit in composition and rhetoric for admission. Up to this time writings in English were considered "vulgar" by many classical scholars. Writings in Latin and Greek were reversed.

*John S. Hart* (1810–1877). After graduation from the College of New Jersey (Princeton) Hart held a number of positions. For a while he was principal of Philadeplhia Central High School, then taught at New Jersey State Normal School, and eventually taught at Princeton. While in Philadelphia he was founder and editor of the *Sunday School Times.* Since he was primarily interested in English and writing, he soon began writing English language textbooks.

In 1870 he published *A Manual of Composition and Rhetoric.* He stated that this book was written "for learners, not for the learned." Thus he spent little space with theoretical principles of rhetoric, but rather stressed their application in practice. The chapters in Part I dealt with punctuation, diction, sentences, figures, special properties, versification, kinds of poetry, and prose composition. Part II dealt concretely with different kinds and applications of writing. With only meager revision this book continued to be reprinted as late as 1892.

*Adams S. Hill.* He was for many years the Boylston Professor of Rhetoric and Oratory in Harvard College. In 1878 he published *The Principles of Rhetoric and Their Application.* Rhetoric was defined "as the art of efficient communication by language." Furthermore, he said, "It is an *art,* not a science." Since rhetoric was the art of communication by language, he held that it applied to any subject-matter that can be treated in words. Thus it had no subject-matter peculiar to itself.

These principles he applied in his book. This book contained fewer topics, especially theoretical topics, than any of the rhetorics thus far discussed. The main parts dealt with grammatical purity, choice and use of words, and several kinds of composition. Punctuation and capital letters were treated in the appendix. Interestingly, the book had three indexes: an index to the book proper, an index to the appendix, and an index of 1400 words and phrases. It appeared in a number of editions.

*Brainerd Kellogg.* For years he was Professor of English in Brooklyn Collegiate and Polytechnic Institute. In 1880 he wrote *A Textbook on Rhetoric.* The preface began with a quotation by Portia in the *Merchant of Venice,* in saying:

> If *to do* were as easy as *to know what were good to do,* chapels had been churches, and poor men's cottages princes' palaces.

Thus Kellogg stressed that the study of rhetoric was not merely learning what was best in writing, but how to do it. He claimed his plan to be simple, standing under three heads: Invention, Qualities of Style, and Productions. Under invention stress was placed upon finding the thoughts to be expressed. Under qualities of style "the six, grand, cardinal ones" were stressed: perspicuity, imagery, energy, wit, pathos, and elegance. Under productions the discourse was divided into oral and written, and the written into prose and poetry. Special attention was given to conversation, debates, orations, and letters. This book was revised and recopyrighted in 1891 and 1892, and continued to appear in reprintings even later.

*Miss L. A. Chittenden.* Miss Chittenden was one of the first women to write a rhetoric. She was an English teacher in the Ann Arbor High School. Too, the *Elements of English Composition* was published in Chicago rather than in the East. Although it was a rather small book of 174 pages, she intended it to be used in the lower grades of high school. Her object was to furnish, with as little theory as possible, set of directions and exercises to help the student to "become a correct composer."

Her view was that after covering the exercises in punctuation, transformation of elements, and rhetorical principles, the student should have attained a certain degree of accuracy. If further exercises were necessary, these would be provided in the "Reproductions." Then original writing would be provided in the "Developments." This was considered half way between the wholly reproductive and the wholly original. Also, considerable attention was given to paraphrasing. It was simply and clearly organized. An examination of the book impresses one with the fact that Miss Chittenden was pedagogically conscious of what the average high student could master in English composition. This book appeared in a number of editions.

*John F. Genung* (1850–1919). After graduation from Union College he attended Rochester Theological Seminary preparing to become a minister. In 1884 he left the ministry to teach rhetoric and Bible at Amherst. In 1886 he published *The Practical Elements of Rhetoric.* This was a book of 488 pages, which apparently was intended mainly for college use. Part I, Style, dealt with style in general, diction, figures of speech, and composition. Part II, Invention, dealt with the basis in mental aptitudes and habits, general processes in the ordering of material, reproduction of the thought of others, and invention dealing with observed objects, events, generalizations, truths, and practical issues. It appeared in a number of editions.

In 1893 Genung published his *Outlines of Rhetoric,* which was a much smaller book and which likely was mostly used in high schools. Part I, Mastery of Materials, had chapters on choice of words, phraseology, and special objects in style. This part dealt with the theoretical phases of rhetoric. Part II, Organization of Materials, contained chapters dealing with the sentence, the paragraph, and the whole composition. In this part the rhetorical principles were to be applied. The appendix contained a digest of rules, illustrative extracts, and a fine glossary of words and forms. Editions of this book continued to be reprinted even after the turn of the century.

*Sarah E. H. Lockwood.* She was a teacher of English in the New Haven High

School, and the second woman author of a rhetoric book to become somewhat popular during the latter part of the 19th century. In 1888 her *Lessons in English* was published. It was particularly adapted to be studied in conjunction with American classics. Her plan was to present in her lessons in English during the first year, the following: History of the English Language, Saxon and Classical Elements, Figures of Speech, Common Errors in the Use of English, Punctuation and Capitals, and Letterwriting and Composition. The literature to be taught simultaneously dealt with the chief writings of Irving, Longfellow, and Whittier. During the second year diction, a critical study of words, rules for the construction of sentences, and letter-writing and composition, were to be taught, together with the chief writings of Hawthorne, Holmes, Lowell, and Bryant. Miss Lockwood's book was one of the first definitely to combine the teaching of composition and rhetoric with literature. This book appeared in a number of reprintings.

*Fred N. Scott and Joseph V. Denny.* Scott for many years taught English at the University of Michigan, while Denny taught at Ohio State University. In 1893 they began to combine their talents in writing several textbooks in composition. Their first was *Paragraph Writing*. Then in 1897 they produced their *Composition-Rhetoric*. This book soon attained wide usage. Three considerations influenced the nature of this book. First, there should be a closer union between composition and rhetoric. Hence the hyphenation of the terms in the title. Second, greater stress should be placed on paragraph writing. Third, attention should be given the concept of growth. A composition should be the product of an "active, creative mind." It is clear that these authors stressed the development of the ability to write rather than the understanding of the principles of rhetoric. In 1902 these authors wrote a *Composition-Literature*.

*Other authors of rhetorics, 1870-1900.* Many other composition and rhetoric textbooks appeared during this period, but most of them failed to gain wide adoptions, although some of these books appeared in more than one edition. Among the authors of these were: William Swinton (1874), David Hill (1878), John Nichol (1878), Calvin Patterson (1882), T. Whiting Bancroft (1884), C. W. Bardeen (1885), J. E. Murray (1886), Eliphalet Lyte (1886), G. A. Southworth and E. B. Goddard (1887), Virginia Waddy (1888), H. I. Strang and J. A. Eaton (1889), Wm. Williams (1889), C. C. Long (1890), Harriet L. Keeler and Arthur Beatly (1891), E. S. Buckheim (1893), William Mead (1894), William B. Cairns (1896), Robert Herrick and L. T. Damon (1899). No attempt has been made to cover books published after 1900.

## D. *Characteristics of Composition & Rhetoric Textbooks*

IN addition to the descriptions given book by book of the more commonly used rhetoric textbooks, it may be well to present some summary characteristics of these books as a whole. Naturally there have been wide variations among them. Some of these variations were individual by authors, while others were due to the changing times.

*Aims.* The aims expressed or implied in early rhetoric books were a far cry from the thirteen aims proposed by a committee of the National Council of Teachers of English in 1942. The following were some of the aims most frequently mentioned in rhetorics of the past.

Cultural aims. The chief aim stressed in the earliest rhetorics, particularly those first written in England and then reprinted here, was cultural. Blair aimed to "cultivate their Taste, to form their Style," and to present a "comprehensive view of what relates to these subjects." In fact, part of the title of Blair's book (1784) was to teach *Belles Lettres,* which meant something related to fine literature and aesthetic writings. Jamieson's book (1821) stressed the "perusal of the best models of literary composition." Boyd (1860) designed to "cultivate the taste, the judgment, the imagination." These values were not so fully stressed by the later American authors of rhetorics.

Writing skill. Only Bain of the English authors, and to some extent Whately, provided exercises for actual composition. On the other hand, nearly all of the American authors, even the early ones, began to provide writing exercises for the students. In the main, this stress increased with time. Brewer's book (1853) wanted to raise composition into an "art which has for its object the analysis, illustration, and expression of solid thought." Boyd (1860) said, "Its object is to train the young mind to think, and be able to give a perspicuous, forcible, and elegant expression to thought in written form." While these authors definitely meant the development of writing skill, yet Kerl (1869) was the only author before 1870 actually to stress the word, skill. He "designed to develop skill in the use of words, skill in the construction of sentences, and skill in finding thoughts." Others aimed to develop skill in writing different types of writing, such as description, narration, exposition, argumentation, and poetry.

Correlation. Various forms of correlation were mentioned as aims. Even many titles indicated this purpose, such as rhetoric and *belles-lettres,* rhetoric and composition, rhetoric and literary criticism, and so on. Nearly all books printed before 1850 recognized the importance of correlating reading with speaking and writing activities. Too, good composition required a background knowledge of grammar, spelling, and punctuation. Again, themes for composition were in literature, geography, history, science, music, and art. Even though only a few books actually mentioned correlation as an aim, yet nearly all suggested certain matters that implied correlation.

Provision for individual differences. Little recognition of individual differences was evident in early rhetoric books. In the 1830's such recognition began to appear in one of two forms. One way was to write more than one book with varying difficulty. The other way was to suggest different activities for children of differing interests and ability. Many of the later books contained long lists of topics from which the students could choose to write compositions.

*Content.* The nature of some of the content has already been indicated in the descriptions of the more popular rhetorics. However, it may be even more meaningful if more specific data were presented for a greater number of rhetorics. Hess[2] analyzed the contents of 86 rhetoric and composition textbooks. He found that their contents could be classified under eight categories. These follow together with the average percentage of space devoted to each category: (1) Development of taste, 5.5; (2) Origin, progress, and structure of language, 4.8; (3) Style, 18.1; (4) Figurative language, 9.3; (5) Oratory and eloquence, 16.0; (6) Original composition, 16.8; (7) Literary criticism, 4.6; and (8) Related subject matter, 24.9. Table II of his dissertation gives the percentage of space devoted to each topic for each of the 86 textbooks. An examination of this table shows great variations both according to authors and to the period when the books were written. For example, 18 of the 19 oldest rhetorics scarcely paid any attention to original composition. On the other hand, the 23 latest books all suggested original writing. In a number of books more than 50% of the space related to composition exercises. Next, brief treatment will be given to the nature of the content of these categories.

Development of taste. Forty of the books specifically dealt with "taste." This topic was given much more attention in the earlier books than in the later. In fact, two-thirds of the later authors totally omitted special treatment of this topic. In the main, the texts that were first written in England and then reprinted here greatly emphasized the development of taste, while even the earlier American authors gave it little attention. Blair, who greatly emphasized taste, defined it as "the power of receiving pleasure or pain from the beauties

A

# GRAMMAR OF RHETORIC,

AND

# POLITE LITERATURE:

COMPREHENDING THE

## PRINCIPLES OF LANGUAGE AND STYLE,

THE

## ELEMENTS OF TASTE AND CRITICISM:

WITH

## RULES

FOR THE

## STUDY OF COMPOSITION AND ELOQUENCE;

ILLUSTRATED

## BY APPROPRIATE EXAMPLES,

Selected chiefly from the

## BRITISH CLASSICS,

FOR THE USE OF SCHOOLS, OR PRIVATE INSTRUCTION.

## BY ALEXANDER JAMIESON.

The Second American, from the last London Edition.

New-Haven:
PUBLISHED BY A. H. MALTBY AND CO.
Glebe-Building, Chapel-Street.

1821.

3  One of the earlier American written rhetorics

or deformities of Nature and of Art." Only Quackenbos of the American authors stressed the development of taste.

Origin, progress, and structure of language. As was true of taste, the texts before 1830 paid much more attention to this general category than those written later. Again Blair set the pattern for the earlier books. He considered "Language" to be "the foundation of the whole power of eloquence." He further stated that "an adequate idea of the origin of language" can be formed if "we .... contemplate the circumstances of mankind in their earliest and rudest state." He then commented how the word order in sentences has changed between the ancient and modern tongues. Jamieson, also an English author, devoted Book I of his text to this general topic. Of the American writers, Quackenbos gave this topic most attention. Boyd in dealing with this topic showed how changes in language depended "partly upon the political changes occasioned by war and conquest, and partly upon the progress of knowledge and of civilization."

Style. On an average, style was given more space than any topic except related subject matter. Only six of the 86 books failed to give it attention. The most common sub-topics of style were: qualities of style, kinds of style, and directions for using a proper style. Blair mentioned the following properties as relating to quality of style: (1) Clearness, (2) unity, (3) strength, and (4) harmony. Campbell (1818) mentioned perspicuity, vivacity, elegance, animation, and music, as the chief qualities. Pinneo (1864) mentioned the following: Purity, propriety, precision, unity, clearness, strength, and harmony. Some writers also mentioned euphony, rhythm, and melody.

In regard to kinds of style, Blair identified the diffuse, concise, nervous, feeble, dry, plain, neat, elegant, flowery, simple, affected, and vehement. The first four depended partly on clearness, the next five on the degree of ornament employed, and the last three on the nature of the ideas themselves. These or similar kinds of style were referred to in more than half of the books. Newman (1836) used the following additional kinds of style: Idiomatic, easy, labored, barren, luxuriant, elevated, pedantic, and ornamented. Twenty-eight of the 86 texts failed to discuss kinds of style. However, Kerl (1869) mentioned 42 kinds of style.

Many authors concluded their treatment of style by suggesting direction for attaining a good style. Blair suggested that first one must have clear ideas of the subject to be treated, follow careful and frequent practice, keep in mind the style of great authors, be cautious about servile imitation, and lastly, observe that attention to style should not detract one from the thoughts to be expressed. Most later authors suggested these or similar directions for the attainment of good writing style.

Figurative language. All rhetoric texts before 1848 gave this topic attention. Only eight failed to give it treatment. Blair in his treatment of figures of speech mentioned and illustrated the following: Metaphor, allegory, hyperbole, personification, apostrophe, simile, antithesis, interrogation, exclamation, vision, and climax. The book that gave figurative language most technical treatment was written by Andrews in 1813. He listed metaphor, metonymy, synecdoche, and irony as primary tropes; and antonomasia, communication, extenuation, euphemism, catachresis, and hyperbole as secondary tropes. Then he mentioned the following "as important figures—Allegory, Prosopopeia, Apostrophe, and Parabole, or Similitude to which may be added Antithesis or Opposition, Interrogation, Exclamation, Vision, Amplification, Climax, Correction, and Suppression."

In all, fifteen different figures of speech were used by more than five authors. The most frequently mentioned figures were: Metaphor in 78 books, personification in 77, simile in 76, allegory in 71, hyperbole in 63, apostrophe in 63, interrogation in 55, vision in 55, antithesis in 54, climax in 53, exclamation in 50, irony in 35, metonymy in 25, and synecdoche in 23. These data clearly indicate that the rhetoric textbooks of the past stressed the use of figures of speech.

Oratory or eloquence. All rhetoric textbooks before 1830 gave oratory considerable attention. After 1830 about one-third failed to give it space. In all 67 of the 86 texts gave it treatment. Most of the books before 1830 gave about 20% of the space to oratory. After 1830 there was great variation in the space devoted to oratory, varying from zero to 71.9%.

Blair defined eloquence as the "Art of Speaking in such a manner as to attain the end for which we speak." He further stated that the "three great scenes of Eloquence," to be "Popular Assemblies, the Bar, and the Pulpit." Jamieson (1821) mentioned four requisites for good eloquence: Loudness of voice, distinctness, slowness, and propriety of pronunciation. Many of the later books more or less followed the suggestions for the development of oratory as presented in books by Blair, Newman, Whately, and Jamieson.

Original composition. The one of the first rhetoric texts to provide for original composition exercises was written by Willard. He claimed that it was prepared as early as 1821, but for fear that the public was not prepared for such innovation he did not publish it until 1830. Thereafter most texts written by American authors dealt with it. In all, 56 of the rhetorics dealt with it. In some texts more than 50% of the space dealt with matters relating definitely to composition. In fact, many of the later books failed to use the word, rhetoric, in the titles. Instead, such words as composition, discourse, writing, English lessons, language, and so on, were used. Parker's text (1832) gave practice for writing simple themes, complex themes, essays, and letters. A list of 302 suggested topics were also included. The text by Quackenbos (1856) suggested prose composition under five types: Letters, descriptions, narrations, essays, and argumentative discourses. Other texts suggested similar exercises.

Literary criticism. Less attention was given this type of work than any other. The very earliest rhetorics gave it more attention than the later ones. In fact, only a few texts dealt with it extensively after 1835. Its purpose was to apply literary criticism to the great writings of the past. For example, Blair's book gave space to critical examination to the works of such men as Homer, Virgil, Voltaire, Milton, and Addison. After courses in literature entered the secondary school curriculums this topic was largely dropped from rhetoric books.

Related subject matter. Nearly all books contained considerable material not belonging to the seven most common aspects of rhetoric. On an average, nearly one-fourth of the space of the books was devoted to material classified under this heading. Of this space 26.2% was given to grammar, 43.5% to literature, 11.4% to punctuation, and much less to spelling, vocabulary, and so on.

In conclusion, it can be said that the contents of composition and rhetoric textbooks changed greatly from the earliest, especially those written in England, to the later ones. The earliest texts particularly stressed attention to the principles of rhetoric, often specifically as they applied to the great writings of the past. The later ones stressed the application of only the more basic principles to the more common types of writing. Practice in writing was then considered most important.

# LITERATURE

## *Introduction*

THE study of literature has a very long history, even though its entrance into the American secondary school curriculum has been very slow. Nearly every ancient country that had a written language built up at least a limited store of writings, these in addition to the legends and folklore which were passed on orally from generation to generation. For example, the Homeric epics were passed on long before the ancient Greeks accumulated written literature. By the Age of Pericles (490–429 B.C.) the teaching of literature had found a definite place in the higher schools. The students of Isocrates (436–338 B.C.) studied literature in the rhetorical school. The purpose was to direct the thoughts of his pupils toward the example of noble lives through the study of history and literature.

When the Romans conquered the Greeks much of the latter's culture was absorbed to form a Graeco-Roman culture. Soon the rhetorical school was highly developed among the Romans. In them the study of grammar, rhetoric, and literature became very important to help the learner become a great orator, the highest attainment of a Roman. Quintilian (c. 35–97 A.D.), in his famous *Institutio Oratoria*, favored wide reading of the great writers, particularly such as Cicero, for those who seek to become great orators.

Presumably a wide study of literature suffered a set-back during the Middle Ages. Although literature was not one of the seven Liberal Arts, during the Renaissance considerable literature was studied in connection with grammar, rhetoric, and dialectic. In fact, the revival of the study of the great writings of the ancient Greeks and Romans helped develop the Renaissance into the great movement that it became. The ancient classics became known as the *humanities*.

Coming to the more modern times mention should be made of the advocacy by several men in this regard. Joseph Priestly (1733–1804) strongly advocated the study of literature in the secondary schools of England. Johann Friedrich Herbart (1776–1841), a great German educator, greatly emphasized the study of history and literature as means for the development of moral character. Thus the study of literature is not something solely of recent development.

## (Ch.I: §2) A. *Literature Stages*

Roughly, the teaching of literature in American secondary schools has developed in four stages. The first was to present classical readings, commonly composed of extracts from great writings. At first this was not done through regular literature textbooks, but rather through textbooks in other fields. For example, most early rhetoric textbooks contained numerous literary extracts as models for good composition. Blair's *Rhetoric,* which was very popular in early academies, contained many such selections.

Likewise, most advanced readers contained literary pieces to serve as reading lessons. A number even classified these selections according to the different types of literature. For example, the popular *English Reader* written by Lindley Murray in 1799 classified the selections, as narrative, didactic, argumentative, descriptive, pathetic, dialogues, public speeches, and promiscuous pieces. John Pierpont's *American First Class Book* (1823), which was an advanced reader, used a similar classification for his selections. The most publicized readers ever to appear in America were written by McGuffey. The upper *Readers* contained many selections written by famous English and American authors. Even today many older people, who studied the McGuffey books, can recite these selections. Many early advanced readers were often called *Speakers.* These contained literary selections suitable for elocutionary presentation. These *Speakers* were often used in academies.

The second stage was characterized by teaching the history of literature. Some of the earliest textbooks taking this approach dealt with literature of the Greeks and the Romans. A little later they dealt mainly with the history of English literature. Finally, the history of American literature also received treatment. These commonly dealt with the biographies of leading authors by periods, together with brief comments about their chief literary works.

The third period stressed the use of whole classic works. Generally, however, some history of literature was taught in conjunction with the classics. This practice continued until about 1900.

During the fourth stage literature has been taught largely from large anthologies. These would contain rather long selections from many authors, both of the past and the present. Thus it is clear that the teaching of literature in secondary schools has taken various forms. It is very evident that literature as a subject field has never been fully standardized, as has been true of many other fields.

## B. *European Written Literature Books*

As HAS been true in most fields, the earliest literature textbooks used in America were brought here from Europe, usually England, and often reprinted here. In literature, most of these books were large and dealt with past writings of the ancients as well as of later authors.

*John Dunlop* (d. 1842). The oldest books dealing with the history of literature in the writer's collection were written by Dunlop. By profession he was a lawyer in Scotland, but like many other lawyers and ministers in Scotland, he was also a scholar and writer in the more purely literary pursuits. In 1814 he began publishing *The History of Fiction* in two volumes. These were later reprinted in Philadelphia, and likely were used in some academies and colleges here. It was a "critical account of the most celebrated prose works of fiction, from the earliest Greek romances to the novels of the present day." Each volume contained more than 400 pages. In order, he dealt with the origin of fictitious narrative, Greek romances, Latin romances, romances of chivalry (a long treatment), Italian tales (also extended treatment), spiritual romance, comic romance, political romance, pastoral romance, heroic romance, French novels, and English novels. These books appeared in several editions.

In 1823 Dunlop began publishing a *History of Roman Literature* from its earliest period to the Augustan Age in several volumes. The writer's copy was printed in Philadelphia in 1827 consisting of two volumes in one book of 702 pages of rather fine print. Dunlop said that a perusal of Henry Bankes' *Civil and Constitutional History of Rome, from its Foundation to the Age of Augustus* (1818) led him to believe that a literary history of Rome, for the same period, "might prove not uninteresting." The topics and authors treated in the two volumes were: Etruria, Latin language, Ennius, Plautus, Terence, Pacuvius, Roman drama, satire, Lucilius, Lucretius, Catullus, Mimes, agriculture, Varro, Roman history, Fabius Pictor, Sallust, Caesar, the Gracchi, Crassus, Hortensius, Calvus, and lastly a very extended treatment of Cicero. In defense of the value of the history of literature Dunlop quoted Dr. Johnson in saying, "There is no part of history so useful, as that which relates to the human mind—the gradual improvement of reason—the successive advances of science—. . . . the extinction and resuscitation of arts, and the revolutions of the intellectual world." In 1838 Dunlop also prepared a *Latin Anthology* translated into English verse. Just how widely these books were studied in our academies and colleges is not now certain, but likely they were used in some.

*Sir Walter Scott* (1771–1832). It is interesting to learn that such a great literary genius as Sir Walter should have written a book that could well be used as a literature textbook. In all, Scott wrote about sixty literary works plus editing many others. In 1825 he wrote a book of more than 300 pages entitled, *Biographical and Critical Notices of Eminent Novelists*. Its purpose was to serve as a preface to *Ballantyne's Novelists Library*, an enterprise of that great Edinburgh bookseller, John Ballantyne. Scott's book was republished in Boston in 1829. It could well have been used in American schools as a literature textbook. It contained biographical sketches of Samuel Richardson, Henry Fielding, Tobias Smollett, Ricard Cumberland, Oliver Goldsmith, Samuel Johnson, Laurence Sterne, Henry Mackenzie, Horace Walpole, Clara Reeve, Anne Radcliffe, Alain Rene Le Sage, Charles Johnstone, and Robert Bage.

*J. J. Eschenburg* (1743–1820). He was a distinguished professor in the Carolinum at Brunswick, Germany. He became a great authority on Shakespeare. Eventually he was asked to write the *Handbuch der Classischen Literatur* (*Manual of Classical Literature*). This book was definitely prepared as a textbook of literature. After his death N. W. Fiske, a professor at Amherst, translated it into English in 1836. The seventh edition appeared in Germany by 1825, and later was republished several times in English here. In America it was a large book of 753 pages bound in leather. It contained five parts, as follows: Part I, Archaeology of Literature and Art; Part II, History of Ancient Literature, Greek and Roman; Part III, Mythology of the Greeks and Romans; Part IV, Greek and Roman Antiquities; and Part V, Classical Geography and Chronology. It was the best organized book of literature with which we have dealt thus far. Its organization well lent itself to be used as a textbook. Our only question here is whether it was used at all on the secondary level. It certainly was well adapted to college use.

*Henry Nelson Coleridge.* Coleridge, late fellow of King's College, Cambridge, was deeply devoted to the ancient classics, particularly in his late years. In an attempt to pass on this interest, he wrote a book entitled, *Introductions to the Study of the Greek Classic Poets*. It was "designed principally for the use of young persons at school and college." In 1842 it was republished in Boston. In the introduction he bewailed the fact that so few young people could read the ancient poets in the original Greek. He claimed that poetry very often loses its rhythm and charm in translation. The book dealt with: History of the Origin and Preservation of the Iliad, The Iliad, Odyssey, Margites, Batrachomyomachia, Hymns, Epigrams, Fragments, and Conclusion.

*Comments.* Apparently the five literature books written by the above discussed European authors, and then reprinted here, were among the first general literature books studied in America. Too, the contents of them dealt largely with the ancient classics. The one exception was a few selections in Dunlop's *History of Fiction.* Evidently the European scholars were hesitant to recognize contemporary writings as important literature. Beginning in the 1840's, however, certain American textbook writers began to change this attitude, when they began dealing with more modern writings. These will be discussed next.

### C. *American Written General Literature Books*

SOME of the first literature books written in the U.S. dealt with a mixture of selections and authors. Most of these were concerned mainly only with English and American literature, with the predominant emphasis on the English.

*Peter Parley (S. G. Goodrich).* In 1845 Parley published in leather a *Literature, Ancient and Modern, with Specimens.* This book was an exception to the above statement in that it dealt with literature of all ages and with writers of various peoples, such as the Hebrews, Greeks, Romans, Chinese, Persian, Italians, Spanish, French, Scandinavian, German, English, and only two pages on Americans. In the main, a brief history of the development of the literature of each of these national groups was given, and then in some instances brief specimens of important writings. This book likely was used in some schools.

*Truman Rickard and Hiram Orcutt.* In 1847 these authors published their *Class Book of Prose and Poetry,* "consisting of selections from the best English and American authors." Although it was a book of only 120 pages, the 1850 edition listed many academies and normal schools where it was in use. It presented fourteen brief prose and 43 poetry selections. The authors of the selections were identified, but no biographical facts regarding them mentioned. Only a few of these were written by American authors. These were by W. Irving, Longfellow, Bryant, and Daniel Webster.

*William Smith and Henry Tuckerman.* In 1870 these writers published *A Smaller History of English and American Literature.* This was really a condensation of Shaw's *A Complete Manual of English Literature,* with about 60 pages added dealing with American literature. It dealt historically with the development of English and American literature by periods. The lives and works of the more important writers were discussed rather than presentating specimens of their writings, as was true of Rickard and Orcutt's text. It contained 374 pages of rather fine print.

OF

# CLASSICAL LITERATURE:

FROM THE GERMAN OF

J. J. ESCHENBURG,

PROFESSOR IN THE CAROLINUM, AT BRUNSWICK.

## WITH ADDITIONS.

BY

## N. W. FISKE,

PROFESSOR OF MORAL AND INTELLECTUAL PHILOSOPHY (FORMERLY OF THE LATIN AND GREEK LANGUAGES) IN AMHERST COLLEGE.

Entered according to Act of Congress, in the year 1836,
BY EDWARD C. BIDDLE,
in the Clerk's Office of the District Court for the Eastern District of Pennsylvania.

THIRD EDITION.

## PHILADELPHIA:

FREDERICK W. GREENOUGH, 23 MINOR-STREET.
1839.

4  One of the earliest literature textbooks. At first classical literature received more attention than English literature

*George Cathcart.* In 1874 Cathcart wrote a *Literary Reader*, which was a manual of literature. He acknowledged that in the "catalogue of school studies, literature then held but a humble place." The intention was that this book would help popularize literature as a school subject. It discussed the development of literature under four periods: The Elizabethan Literature, The Literature of the Commonwealth and the Restoration, The Literature of the Eighteenth Century, and Literature of the Nineteenth Century. In the first two periods only English authors were discussed, but during the last two periods about one-third of the space was given to American writers. In treatment Cathcart combined the features of the two above mentioned books. In most cases, it dealt first with the life and works of the author, and then presented rather long extracts, or even whole poems, of their writings. Pictures of the important writers were included. The 1892 edition contained 541 pages. The last 15 pages consisted of thumb-nail sketches of "Notable Contemporary Writers," including numerous pictures of them. It was an attractive appearing textbook.

*Truman J. Backus and T. B. Shaw.* A number of American writers produced literature textbooks largely based on Shaw's *Manual*, but adding some treatment of American literature. One of these books first appeared in 1875. Part I of 400 pages dealt chronologically with the lives and works of the most important English writers, while the last 85 pages dealt with the American. Part I was largely borrowed from Shaw's *Manual*, and Part II was written by Backus. This book was revised and reprinted in numerous editions, and apparently became one of the most widely used literature textbooks in U.S.

*J. Willis Westlake.* He believed that smaller textbooks were in demand, so he prepared a *Common-School Literature—English and American* (192 pages) in 1876. It was revised in 1898. Part I briefly discussed the lives and works of English authors, together with brief extracts of their writings; and Part II in similar manner dealt with American writers. Furthermore, Westlake believed, "The memorizing of extracts has long been recognized by educators as one of the most efficient means of culture," so in Part III be presented "A Casket of Thought-Gems." He expected the teachers to require the pupils to memorize many of these gems. These consisted of more than 200 brief quotations from great English and American writings.

*Harriet B. Swineford.* In 1883 Miss Swineford wrote the *Literature for Beginners*, which was a little larger but very similar in treatment and arrangement to Westlake's book. Likewise many gems were included for memorization.

*Esther J. Trimble.* Also in the 1880's Miss Trimble prepared two literature

C

textbooks: *Handbook of Literature* (1882–1897), and *A Short Course in Literature, English and American* (1883–1885). The *Short Course* text was really larger than those by Westlake and Swineford. She too dealt with the great English and American writers chronologically, briefly discussing their lives and works, but incorporating their extracts and gems with the treatment of the writers. Interestingly, Westlake, Miss Swineford, and Miss Trimble were instructors in three different normal schools in Pennsylvania. Evidently these schools favored the teaching of Enlgish and American literature as a combined course.

Other authors who wrote textbooks combining a treatment of English and American literature were: O. L. Jenkins (1876), A. N. Raub (1882), H. H. Morgan (1889), and Frank V. Irish (1896).

Among the eight books discussed above several approaches were taken. Rickard's included only literary selctions; the books by Goodrich, Smith and Shaw, and Backus and Shaw dealt with the lives and works of great authors chronologically; those by Cathcart and by Trimble also dealt with the lives and works, but incorporated short excerpts of past authors; and the texts by Westlake and by Swineford discussed the lives and works of past great writers, and then added short literary gems to be committed in the back of their books.

### D. *English Literature Textbooks*

TEXTBOOKS that dealt with English writers only were used more commonly and earlier than those with American writers only or that combined the treatment. Thus in this section brief treatment will be given some of the more popular English literature textbooks.

*Robert Chambers.* Apparently Chambers was the first to write a history of English literature suitable for school use, although earlier voluminous treatments had been written. He first prepared the *Cyclopaedia of English Literature*, which too was voluminous. Later he prepared a shortened version of this for school use in Scotland and England. In 1837 it was revised by Royal Robbins and printed in Hartford for American school use. It contained the names and works of many English authors, dealing briefly with each work according to its origin, design, and character. The text was not interesting to read. Shaw referred to the book as being "dry list-like."

*John S. Hart.* In 1844 Hart published a *Class Book of Poetry*. After dealing very briefly with the lives of many great English poets, beginning with Chaucer, he reproduced some of their poems. These were arranged chronologically. Incidentally, Bryant's "Thanatopisis" was included.

*Thomas B. Shaw* (1813–1862) The books by Shaw more fully dominated the field of the history of English literature in American schools than any other. He was born in London, attended Shrewsbury and St. John's College, became a tutor, and was later induced to go to Russia. Soon he was appointed to teach English literature at the Imperial Alexander Lyceum in St. Petersburgh. His lectures were eagerly attended. After some miscellaneous writing, he began writing his *Outlines of English Literature in* 1846. Later he wrote *A Complete Manual of English Literature,* and a book entitled *Choice Specimens of English Literature* to accompany the study of his *Outlines.* All of these books were soon republished in U.S., where they became very popular.

Shaw's original works were very scholarly and represented a thorough treatment of English writers by chronological periods. A chapter was devoted to each period. Each period was characterized, together with a detailed discussion of the lives and works of each important writer in the period. Most editions contained more than twenty chapters. While these books were scholarly, he used a highly Latinized vocabulary and a heavy style. His sentences were often long, intricate, and detailed. Apparently, these books were intended mainly for college use, but it was not long before academies and high schools began using them. However, to make them more palatable to secondary schools, revisions and refinements were necessary.

One of the first revisions of Shaws's *Manual* was made by William Smith, University of London, with "A Sketch of American Literature" of 55 pages added by Henry T. Tuckerman and printed in New York in 1867. This book had 540 pages of very fine print. The treatment of Shakespeare in 28 page was as follows: Parentage and education, early life, in London with Globe Theatre, turning author, his acting, his success, return to Stratford and death, classification and sources of his dramas, and his sonnets. A smaller revised edition was published here in 1870.

A more popular revision was made by Truman J. Backus, Professor of English Literature at Vassar, which was entitled *Shaw's New History of English Literature* in 1875. This was a very much simpler and more appealing book and appeared in numerous editions. For example, the chapter on Shakespeare began with ten fine tributes written by other great writers. Less space was given to his life, but a clearer treatment of his activities. A fine historical table was included listing Shakespeare's writings and their sources under plays, semi-historical or legendary, and fictional. The revision also included "A Sketch of American Literature." Shaw's books, and their revisions, greatly influenced the nature of the purely American written histories of English literature.

*Charles D. Cleveland.* Apparently he was one of the first Americans to see a serious need for teaching English literature in secondary schools. He claimed that as early as 1834, soon after he opened a school for young ladies, he began to prepare short accounts of the best English writers. "Accordingly, in 1838, I printed, solely for the use of my pupils, a small syllabus of the names of most of the British authors, with the dates of their birth and death, arranged under the different sovereigns." From this outline he delivered series of lectures. Then in 1847 he published *A Compendium of English Literature.* This was a large book of 700 pages. The next year he revised it by adding 76 pages and treatment of 35 new authors. Too, it appeared in finer print and larger pages, so that the enlargement was equivalent to 150 additional pages. Several editions even were printed in the 1870's.

The contents began with writings of Sir John Mandeville and continued to Cowper. In Cleveland's words the contents consisted of "biographical sketches of the authors, selections from their works, with notes, explanatory, illustrative, and directing to the best editions and to various criticisms." Although it was used in some secondary schools, it was best adapted for college classes. In 1852 he wrote another large book of nearly 800 pages entitled *English Literature of the Nineteenth Century,* which was "designed for colleges and advanced classes in schools." It appeared in several editions.

*William Spalding.* Spalding's *The History of English Literature* was published in 1853. It really was a literary history. Part First covered "Literature in the Dark and Middle Ages"; Part Second, "The Origin and Growth of the English Language"; and Part Third, "The Literature of Modern Times." In several ways it was different than most other books of similar title. It contained very few biographical notes of the great writers, but definitely played up the evolution of the English language and the nature of great English writings. It emphasized the intellectual currents of the various ages, explaining the philosophy, moral concepts, and other influences that dominated the thinking of the writers of England. His style was logical but heavy. It appeared in numerous editions, even as late as the 1880's.

*Henry Reed.* While he was Professor of Rhetoric and Literature at the University of Pennsylvania Reed prepared a series of twelve lectures for his classes. While returning from a trip to Europe, due to a collision at sea, the boat and its passengers sank on September 20, 1854. His brother William knew about these lecture notes. So in 1855 he published the *Lectures on English Literature*. Since these *Lectures* were prepared primarily for oral delivery, the style is rather peculiar. Many sentences were long and often involved and filled with emotional outbursts. The treatment seemed to have been designed to develop appreciations, and to show trends and relationships. The titles of the lectures were: Principles of literature, application of literary principles, the English language, early English literature, literature of the 16th century, literature of the 17th century, the 18th, the 19th, contemporary literature, tragic and elegiac poetry, literature of wit and humour, and the literature of letter writing. Only meager attention was given to the biographies of writers and only occasionally quotations fom their writings. The 1866 edition was the fifth.

*Francis H. Underwood.* In 1871 he published *A Handbook of English Literature* containing 646 pages. It was considerably different than most literature books of that date. The first 38 pages were introductory, which were largely historical, and which contained tabular lists of well-known writers for six periods, together with their literary classification and their dates of birth and death. The remainder of the book was virtually an anthology, long before this type of book was common. It began with Chaucer, giving first a brief biographical sketch in fine print, and then reproduced several of his poems. This approach continued throughout the book, dealing with dozens of authors. Another edition was printed in 1883.

*Henry Coppée.* In 1872 Coppée published his *English Literature*, which he "considered as an Interpreter of English History." His objective was to present "prominently the historic connections and teachings of English litereture, to place great authors in immediate relations with great events in history." His style and presentation was vivid. In commenting upon *The Canterbury Tales*, he said, "It may be clearly shown that the work of Chaucer informs us of a wholesome reform in religion." In referring to the change from the literature of the "barren" fifteenth century to the "fresh" and "beautiful" writing of the Elizabethan period, which "fills the reader with a delight" like the "joy" of a "traveler in a desert" who, after a day of "scorching" and "breathless heat," arrives at a "splendid palace" where he may enjoy "perfumed baths," "soothing music," and "rare dishes." With similar language he bitterly condemned the private life of Henry VIII, and the early life of Lord Byron. The 1881 edition was the seventh, and in 1895 a revised edition appeared. Very little was given of the lives of most authors, and not many quotations were included.

*Augustus S. Brooke*. His *English Literature*, as edited by John R. Green, was published in 1879. Other editions continued to appear until 1898. It was a rather simple treatise, the different editions ranging from 159 to 247 pages. It briefly discussed the history, literary trends, biographies and principal works of authors, criticism, and evaluation of eight literary periods. The popularity of the book apparently led Brainard Kellogg to use it as a framework for a revised and much enlarged *Textbook on English Literature* in 1882. Kellogg divided his edition into "lessons." He added many excerpts. It was slightly revised and republished in 1889.

*Henry Pancoast*. In 1893 he published *Representative English Literature*, and the next year *An Introduction to English Literature*. These dealt more fully with critical material than most preceding texts. They emphasized matters which had influenced certain authors in their writings. The writer divided the treatment into "the period of preparation," "period of Italian influence," "period of French influence," and "modern English period." Philosophical, historical, and literary influences were given attention. Biographies and works of the principal authors were discussed. Sixteen portraits of authors were included. The first book also contained excerpts of writings. Both books gained wide usage, even into the twentieth century.

*Others*. Other textbooks which dealt with the history of English literature were written by: William F. Collier (1861?), Arthur Gilman (1870), H. A. Taine (1873), Henry Morley (1875), William Swinton (1880), Abby Sage Richardson (1881), Anna Buckland (1882), J. Scherr (1882), Albert P. Southwick (1883), Theodore Hunt (1887), Maude Phillips (1890), Thomas Arnold (1891), Mrs. Oliphant (1892), J. Logie Robertson (1894), F. V. N. Painter (1894), Sister Mary Lambatine (1896), and Rueben P. Halleck (1900). It can be seen that the study of English literature did not become a widely accepted subject in American secondary schools until after 1870. It was not until then that colleges began to require a knowledge of or credit in literature for admission.

### E. *American Literature Textbooks*

TEXTBOOKS in this field were even later to appear than those in English literature. In fact, Stout's[3] study of the courses of study of mid-western high schools shows that very few of them taught American literature as a separate subject until in the late 1880's, and then only in about one-third as many high schools as English literature. In some schools the subject was merely referred to as literature. In those cases part of the work could have dealt with American literature. Too, many of the advanced readers commonly used, such as Mc-Guffey's, included many selections written by American authors. Apparently, no acceptable textbook dealing with American literature alone appeared before 1872, although a number of books heretofore discussed dealt with both English and American literature, such as the Backus-Shaw books.

*John S. Hart.* In 1872 Hart, the same author who had published a *Class Book of* (English) *Poetry* in 1844, published *A Manual of American Literature.* This was a large book of 641 pages and intended for "schools and colleges." He believed that the study of English literature had so well established itself as a secondary school subject, that it was time for American literature also to be taught. This view prompted the writing of this textbook. Beginning with the Colonial Period he covered American literature in five periods. In all, he dealt, more or less encyclopedically, with more than 500 Americans who had done some writing. In most cases, these were dealt with biographically with mention of their writings. Excerpts of some of the writers were included. The print was very small, and the make-up rather forbidding.

*Henry A. Beers.* In 1878 Beers wrote *A Century of American Literature, 1776–1876*, and in 1887 *An Outline Sketch of American Literature.* The latter was published by the Chautauqua Press, and apparently was intended as required reading for Chautauqua's Study Circle. However, the make-up of the book was such that it could well have been used as a school textbook. Since Beers was a Professor of English at Yale, it can be said that it was a scholarly treatment under five periods of American literature.

*Charles F. Richardson.* His *Primer of American Literature* appeared in 1878. The 1884 edition claimed that 26 thousand had already been printed. This was a small book of 116 pages. It dealt with most American writers very briefly in four periods, and included portraits of twelve. It likely was used in the upper grades of the elementary school or as a supplementary book to be used as a companion to an English literature book in secondary schools.

*Albert H. Smyth.* As a teacher in Philadelphia Central High School, Smyth believed that not many of the literature books were very teachable. So in 1889 he published his *American Literature*, in which he said: "In the present work I have tried to make a book from which teachers can teach, and from which students cannot 'cram.' Its purpose is to exhibit the process of American literature as an evolution." More than half of the book dealt with this evolution, chiefly by dealing briefly with the lives and works of the more important

American writers by periods. The latter part of the book consisted of readings written by American writers. These included both prose and poetry. In a sense this part was a small anthology, the form of literature textbook which later became popular after 1900. This book soon appeared in numerous printings. The 1895 edition contained an appendix of 24 pages, which consisted of popular poems and songs expected to be familiar to those taking the New York Regents' examinations.

*F. V. N. Painter.* The last author to be discussed was Painter. In 1897 he produced an *Introduction to American Literature.* This book, like Smyth's, was very carefully prepared. The first part of the book dealt with the lives, works, and influencing backgrounds of the chief American writers by periods. The material under each period was uniquely organized. First, thumb nail biographies in fine print were given of the writers of the period. Then more extensive treatment was given only to the most important writers, and how and why their works were produced. A number of portraits were included. The latter part of the book consisted of Illustrative Selections, with notes. The selections were from the writings of Captain John Smith, Mather, Franklin, Jonathan Edwards, Jefferson, Hamilton, Irving, Cooper, Bryant, Poe, Emerson, Hawthorne, Longfellow, Lowell, Whittier, and Holmes. It was popular at the turn of the century.

*Other authors.* Other textbooks which dealt with the history of American literature were written by: Moses Tyler, N. K. Royse (1872), Eugene Lawrence (1880), Julian Hawthorne and Leonard Lemmon (1891), Houghton Mifflin Company (1891), Mildred C. Watkins (1894), Katharine L. Bates (1897), Charles Noble (1898), Henry S. Pancoast (1898), Mary Fisher (1899), and Walter Bronson (1900). After 1900 the appearance of new American literature textbooks was very frequent, many of which were anthologies.

## F. *Characteristics of English Literature Textbooks*

THUS far only the nature of the most frequently used texts in this field have been discussed. Now a more summary view of a greater number of textbooks needs to be taken. In 1954 Mrs. Neel[4] analyzed 44 textbooks. Space permits the presentation only of a few of her findings.

*Aims of Textbooks.* Apparently most authors did not have too clear a conception of the chief aims for teaching English literature. Four books mentioned the developing of an appreciation of great literary master pieces, nine the enjoyment of reading good literature, twelve building foundations for future study, eight mental discipline, sixteen tracing literary changes, and twenty-six learning to choose the best reading materials. On the other hand nearly all 44 authors mentioned as an aim to provide a suitable or needed literature textbook or to provide a systematic guide for the study of English literature.

*Excerpts.* Nearly all of the books included some literary excerpts, but there was great variation how this was done, how many, and how long. Forty-eight per cent incorporated them in the text, 20% following the treatment of the author, 9% at the end of chapters, 2% in footnotes, 5% in a separate section of the book, and 16% in a companion book. In the earlier books the excerpts were usually very brief, but after the mid-seventies they commonly were longer. Some later books devoted nearly half the book to excerpts. In other words some later ones were approaching the form of an anthology.

*Subject matter.* The presentation of details about the great writers of the past varied greatly. One book dealt only with six major authors, while several presented at least something about more than a hundred. The most common topics treated were: Historical background; ideas and customs of the people by periods; biographical sketches, works, and evaluations of major authors; minor authors; literary changes and influences; types of writing; and literary extracts.

*Style.* Most of the texts were written in a rather formal style. Since 26 of the 44 books were written by educators, usually college professors of English, they too often thought in terms of advanced students. In general, the later books were much more readable and attractively written. Too, the later ones usually contained many more learning aids, such as tables of contents, charts, outlines, questions, and bibliographies.

## G. *Characteristics of American Literature Textbooks*

AN analysis of American literature textbooks shows some similarities with those of English literature, but also many differences. Dunmire[5] analyzed 66 of these, 19 published before and 47 after 1900. Some of the findings are now presented.

*Authorship.* Nearly all of the texts published before 1900 were written by college professors or presidents, while after 1900 more than one-third were written by high school teachers of English. Apparently this field had not been sufficiently established as a subject before 1900 to have attracted high school teachers competent to write literature textbooks.

*Aims.* In most subject fields the authors of textbooks used the preface to state the aims and purposes of the book, and often also directions to teachers. However, five of the 19 books before 1900 stated no aims. In the remaining books five mentioned culture as an aim, and three an understanding of the development of literature. Of the 47 books after 1900, nine mentioned culture; nine the relationship of literature, life, and history; nine the enjoyment of good literature; and six the development of critical thinking.

*Content.* Roughly, the texts before 1900 devoted 22% of the space to selections, those after 1900 nearly 54%; to biographical material 25%, and 14.5%; to background material 12%, and 14.7%; to material dealing with selections 22%, and 13.7%; and to combinations of types 19%, and 3.3%. Clearly there was a change of emphasis from the lives and works of great writers to that of actually reading their works.

Only 10% of the space of the texts before 1900 was devoted to prose excerpts, while about 40% was given to them after 1900. Poetry excerpts were given 13% of the total pages before 1900, and 17% after. Roughly an average of the space given to prose in all the books 23% was given to excerpts relating to biography and history, 29% to short stories, 24% to essays, 10% to fiction, 8% to drama, and 6% to miscellaneous selections. Of the poetry selections about 75% were lyric in nature, and 25% narrative. In general, the lyric type increased slightly, while the narrative decreased after 1900.

The authors whose writings were most frequently quoted in the 66 texts were; Longfellow in 52; Bryant, 52; Whittier, 52; Emerson, 51; Holmes, 49; Lowell, 49; Poe, 47; Franklin, 43; Whitman, 43; Freneau, 41; Irving, 41; Hawthorne, 39; Lanier, 39; Thoreau, 36; Timrod, 34; Sandburg, 31; Lincoln, 31; Frost, 31; and Harte, 30. Thirteen others were mentioned in 25 or more books.

## H. *Concluding Statement*

IT IS evident from the foregoing findings that the literature books used in American secondary schools have gone through definite evolutionary stages: from the study of the ancient classics; to the history of literature by discussing chiefly the lives and works of English, and later also American, writers; to dealing with authors, but including excerpts or outside readings from their writings; and finally to the use of large anthologies composed of their writings, with less attention to their lives.

1  John E. Stout, *The Development of High School Curricula in North Central States from 1860 to 1918,* University of Chicago, 1921

2  Glenn C. Hess, "An Analysis of Early American Rhetoric and Composition Textbooks from 1784 to 1870." (Unpublished doctor's dissertation. University of Pittsburgh, 1949)

3  John E. Stout, *ibid.*

4  Helen McDonnell Neel, "An Analysis of English Literature Textbooks Used in American Secondary Schools Before 1950." (Unpublished doctoral dissertation, University of Pittsburgh, 1954.)

5  Burt Lewis Dunmire, "The Development of American Literature Textbooks Used in the United States from 1870 to 1952." (Unpublished doctoral dissertation, University of Pittsburgh, 1954)

# CHAPTER TWO

# Mathematics

THE subjects constituting mathematics are among the oldest in history. They were given attention by the ancient Egyptians, Babylonians, Hindus, Greeks, and Romans. Developing the number systems and discovering the reasons or proofs for mathematical truths occupied many centuries. Eventually the identification or classification of certain aspects of mathematics into subject fields resulted. During the middle ages arithmetic and geometry became parts of the Seven Liberal Arts. The more common divisions now are arithmetic, algebra, geometry, trigonometry, calculus, surveying, and possibly navigation and astronomy. All of these subjects have been taught in the past in at least some American secondary schools.

It is the purpose here to trace the evolution of the most popular textbooks used in American secondary schools before 1900. Too, only the textbooks of the most commonly taught subjects will be traced; namely, algebra, and geometry. Some mention will be given trigonometry, since it was usually dealt with in connection with geometry in the past. Although advanced arithmetic was offered in the later Latin grammar schools, academies, early high schools, and even some colleges, a chapter in my other book, *Old Textbooks*, deals rather extensively with arithmetic, so treatment of it will be omitted here.

## SECTION ONE

## ALGEBRA

### *Introduction*

HISTORICALLY algebra has borne numerous meanings. At first it referred largely to the science of equation. Then with the development of symbolism it was more commonly referred to as that aspect of mathematics that dealt with the use of letters to represent numbers, or quantities, not merely when dealing with equations but with more advanced operations of mathematics.

Epigrammatical definitions of algebra have been given by certain scholars. For example, Newton characterized it as "universal arithmetic;" and Comte as "calculus of functions," as distinguished from "calculus of values" as in arithmetic. Higher algebra has gradually taken on additional functions and characteristics.

Although it is thought that the early Babylonians developed certain aspects of algebra, but apparently the Egyptians developed it more fully. Ahmes, a scribe, prepared a manuscript on papyrus about 1700 B.C., which was copied from an even earlier work. The Greeks developed further use of symbols. Diaphantus about 275 A.D. used special symbols for the unknown quantity. For sometime thereafter apparently algebra was used more commonly in the east than in the west. Algebra seemed to have flourished in India, China, and among the Arabs and Persians. In fact, some think that the first writing to contain the word algebra appeared in Bagdad about 830 A.D. During the late middle ages and during the Renaissance certain scholars of Italy, Germany, and France became interested in algebra. The symbols as currently used in algebra largely date from 1550 to 1650. René Descartes (1596–1650), a French scholar, has been credited with developing the use of $x$ and $y$ for unknowns and $a$ and $b$ for knowns. Recent developments in algebra have chiefly been beyond the elementary theories.

### A. *Algebra in Omnibus Mathematics Books*

THE introduction of the teaching of algebra in the American schools was a piecemeal matter or practice. It began through the inclusion of some algebraic content either in the larger arithmetics or in general mathematics books. The earliest algebra teaching was done from such books originally written in England, and later brought to America. The writer's collection contains at least three such books.

#### Imported books

*John Ward.* One of these books was Ward's *The Young Mathematician's Guide,* which was "a Plain and Easie Introduction to Mathematics," in five parts. The third edition was published in London in 1719. The parts were: "I, Arithmetick; II, Algebra; III, Elements of Geometry; IV, Conic Sections; and V, Arithmetick of Infinites." It is very evident that this was an omnibus mathematics book. Pages 143–276 dealt with algebra. The chapters of Part II dealt with such topics as "Method of Noting down Quantities," "Algebraick Arithmetick," "Surds, or Irrational Quantities," "Nature of Aequations," "Proportional Quantities," "Substitution," "Simple Interest," and "Compound Interest." Dealing with interest by means of algebraic rules was a unique feature.

*John Hill.* A second book was Hill's *Arithmetick, Both in Theory and Practice*. Its eleventh edition was printed in London in 1772. Eighteen pages presented "Problems, or Questions in Algebra." No algebraic rules were included. Apparently the pupils were expected to solve these 99 problems by the use of principles used in arithmetic. Incidentally, in the back of the book 98 pages of logarithmic tables also appeared.

*John Gough.* A thirdi mported book, which was later reprinted in Baltimore, was written by Gough in Dublin. The Baltimore reprint appeared in 1798. An appendix of 13 pages presented some basic rules and examples of algebra.

### American omnibus books

*Pieter Venema.* According to Simons[1] the first such book written in America was Venema's *Arithmetica of Cyffer-Konst* in Dutch published in 1730. Forty-five of its 120 pages dealt with algebra. Apparently the author viewed an understanding of some algebra as essential for clearing up some doubtful aspects of arithmetic. The contents of the algebra text dealt with such topics as, signs of operation, general notions, axioms, reduction of fractions, solution of simple equations, simultaneous equations in two unknowns, and problems. The arrangement was to present a rule, work out an example, and prove the result by numerical substitution.

*Nicholas Pike.* The first American book of this type in English was Pike's *A New and Complete System of Arithmetic* first published in 1788. This was a large book of 512 pages bound in leather. Seventy of its pages dealt with plain geometry, trigonometry, mensuration, and conic sections. Thirty-three pages dealt with "An Introduction to Algebra Designed for the Use in Academies." After presenting some basic algebraic definitions, this section presented algebra as applied to the four fundamentals: Involution, evolution, proportion, quadratic equations, and miscellaneous problems. Several later editions of this book continued to include some algebra. However, in 1793 Pike also published *An Abridgement*, which did not include algebraic content. Pike's *Arithmetics* were the first written in America to become at all popular.

*Consider and John Sterry.* In 1790 their book *The American Youth: Being a New and Complete Course of Introductory Mathematics* was published. The last 147 of its 387 pages were devoted to algebra. Its treatment of algebra was more complete than was true in the afore-mentioned books. Among the topics treated were: Infinite series, binomial theorem, several types of proportion, formation of equations, method of approximations, and Diaphantine problems. Apparently it appeared only in one edition.

*L. I. M. Chevigne.* He was a retired sea captain teaching mathematics at St. Mary's College in Baltimore. In 1806 he published a *Mathematical Manual* for his students. Two-thirds of its 276 pages were devoted to algebra. It was republished in 1807. Its circulation was likely limited.

*Charles Vyse.* The last omnibus book to be mentioned here was Vyse's *The Tutor's Guide* published in 1806. It was largely an arithmetic. Its last 25 pages dealt with algebra. It defined algebra as "a kind of specious arithmetic, or an arithmetic in letters." As was somewhat customary in some early mathematics textbooks, several problems were in poetic form. One interesting one was:

> Old John, who had in Credit liv'd,
> > Though now reduc'd, a Sum receiv'd.
> This lucky Hit's no sooner found,
> > Then clam-rous Duns came swarming round.
> To th' Landlord—Baker—many more,
> > John paid, in all, Pounds ninety-four.
> Half what remain'd a Friend he lent;
> > On Joan and self one-fifth he spent;
> And when of all these Sums bereft,
> > One tenth o' th' Sum receiv'd had left.
> Now show your Skill, ye learned youths,
> > And by your work the Sum produce.

Certainly little algebra could have been learned from this book, or from most of the omnibus books thus far discussed. Many others contained some algebra.

## B. *Imported Algebra Textbooks Before 1840*

As was true of most secondary school textbooks, the earliest algebras were imported. In the case of algebras, they were brought here from England, France, and Germany. Then apparently the ones that seemed most satisfactory were often reprinted here. Brief treatment will be given to those which apparently gained widest circulation.

*John Bonnycastle.* Bonnycastle was connected with the Royal Military Academy, Woolwich, England. He wrote *An Introduction to Algebra.* In 1806 it was reprinted in Philadelphia, and a revised edition was reprinted in New York in 1815. Then in 1822 James Ryan revised, corrected, and enlarged the 11th London edition, and published it as the 2nd New York edition. Additional Ryan editions appeared in 1825, 1827, 1829, 1831, 1836, 1837, and 1838. In the 1840's John F. Jenkins, of New York, added original and selected exercises and republished it. It is evident that Bonnycastle's text was the first popular algebra textbook used in American schools.

This was a carefully prepared textbook covering the more important phases of algebra. In the preface he mentioned his indebtedness to such mathematical authorities as Newton, Maclaurin, Saunderson, Simpson, and Emerson among the English, and to Clairant, Euler, Lagrange, and La Croix on the continent. It dealt with the algebraic applications to the four fundamentals, fractions, involution and evolution, surds, proportion, various types of equations, binomial theorem, indeterminate analysis, logarithms, and miscellaneous questions. Commonly the algebraic principles were illustrated with examples, and then followed by exercises. This book to a considerable extent set a pattern for the early algebras to be used in the U.S.

*Thomas Simpson.* A second English algebra to appear here was Simpson's *A Treatise of Algebra* in 1809 reprinted from the 8th London edition. In 1821 David Mc Clure revised and republished it as a second American edition. This book contained larger and nearly 100 more pages than Bonnycastle's, however 15 pages were devoted to trigonometry and 146 to geometry. It devoted much more space to equations than Bonnycastle, but less to fractions, roots and radicals, logarithms, and series. In the various sections the "Problems" were printed in italics and followed by lengthy explanations of their application. The examples were worked out completely, leaving it to the teachers to provide exercises for the students to solve. This was an evident weakness of the book.

*Other English algebras.* In 1832 Bewick Bridge's *A Treatise on the Elements of Algebra* was reprinted in Philadelphia, which was largely copied from the 6th London edition. It was revised and reprinted several times by 1850. Its contents covered the usual algebra of that period. Also in 1832 John R. Young's *An Elementary Treatise on Algebra* was reprinted here. It continued to appear in reprints through the 1840's. Young acknowledged his indebtedness to Lacroix, Bourdon, Hirsch.

*Other Imported algebras.* Several French algebras were translated and then republished here. The earliest of these was *Elements of Algebra* by S. F. Lacroix reprinted here in 1818. The translation has been ascribed to John Farrar of

# THE
## Young Mathematician's Guide.
### Being a PLAIN and EASIE
# INTRODUCTION
## TO THE
# Mathematicks.
### In Five PARTS.
#### Viz.

I. **Arithmetick**, Vulgar, and Decimal, with all the Useful Rules; And a general Method of Extracting the Roots of all Single Powers.

II. **Algebra**, or Arithmetick in Species; wherein the Method of Raising and Resolving Æquations is rendered easie; and Illustrated with Variety of Examples, and Numerical Questions. Also the whole Businefs of Interest and Annuities, &c. perform'd by the Pen, and a small Table, with several new Improvements.

III. The **Elements** of **Geometry**, Contracted, and Analytically Demonstrated; With a New and Easie Method of finding the Circle's Periphery and Area to any assigned Exactness, by one Æquation only; Also a New Way of making Sines and Tangents.

IV. **Conick-Sections**, wherein the Chief Properties, &c. of the Ellipsis, Parabola, and Hyperbola, are Clearly Demonstrated.

V. The **Arithmetick** of **Infinites** Explain'd, and render'd Easie; with its Application to Superficial, and Solid Geometry.

With an
APPENDIX of **Practical Gauging.**

The Third Edition Corrected.

### By JOHN WARD, Philomath.
*Heretofore Chief Surveyor and Gauger-General in the Excise; now Professor of the Mathematicks in the City of Chester.*

LONDON: Printed for *Tho. Horne* at the *South-Entrance* of the *Royal-Exchange, A. Bettesworth* at the *Red Lyon* in *Pater-nester-row*, and *F. Fayram* at the *Bible* in *Scalding-Ally* against *Stocks-Market*, 1719.

5  An early text from which various branches of mathematics were taught

Harvard. It had previously been successfully used in French schools. The algebraic principles and examples were clearly presented. In most sections problems followed the examples, but with the answers given. Apparently the students were to work out their complete solution. It was one of the earliest texts to present a method for the solution of simultaneous equations involving three unknown quantities.

Another French book to gain influence here was Louis P. M. Bourdon's *Elements of Algebra* (1817). One translation was by William Smyth in 1830. Then two separate translations of it were published here in 1831. One was by Lieut. Edward C. Ross, and the other has been ascribed to Prof. Farrar. The Ross translation became the basis of Charles Davies' *Bourdon*. The first edition of *Bourdon* by Davies appeared in 1834. He later revised and recopyrighted it several times. It is apparent that the Davies' editions must have gained wide usage. These editions were attractively printed and bound in leather. They contained more exercises to be solved by the students than was true of Lacroix's *Elements*. These were all abridged editions of the origional text by Bourdon. Lacroix and Bourdon exerted considerable influence upon American algebras. In 1834 Charles Hackley published *A Catechism and Notes upon the Algebras of Bourdon and Lacroix*, in which he pointed to certain weaknesses, but also referred to the French algebras as "Superior as books of instruction."

Several German algebras also were translated and published in America. In 1831 Meier Hirsch's *A Collection of Arithmetical and Algebraic Problems and Formulae* was translated by Francis Grund and published here. It was a good source book of 340 pages for problems. In 1837 F. A. Hegenberg's *Handbibliothek der Reinen, Höhern and Niedern Mathematik* was republished in Baltimore. Evidently it had only meager influence here.

## C. *American Algebras Before 1840*

*Jeremiah Day* (1773–1867). Day was professor of mathematics and later president at Yale. In all, he was connected with Yale for 69 years. As a keen scholar he became versant with the most commonly used algebras of his time. He admitted free use was made of works by Newton, Maclaurin, Saunderson, Simpson, Euler, Emerson, Lacroix, and others. However, he believed that many texts were too technical and difficult for their intended purpose. So in 1814 he published *An Introduction to Algebra*. This was the first well-received algebra written in America. He intended it to be "the first part of a course in mathematics" for use in American colleges. Few colleges then required credit

D

in algebra for admission. Thus beginning algebra was first taught in the colleges. Day's book immediately gained wide acceptance. It continued to appear in edition after edition, the 67th appearing in 1850. The later editions likely were also taught in academies, for by that time most academies and even high schools taught algebra.

The book covered all of the aspects of algebra that had most commonly been accepted as important in his day. It included treatment of positive and negative quantities, the four fundamentals, algebraic fractions, involution and evolution, reduction of equations by several methods, unknown quantities, ratio and proportion, progression, compound quantities, infinite series, and application of algebra to geometry. Each aspect or rule was first explained, then illustrated, and followed by examples for student solution together with their answers. The later editions contained more examples than the first edition. This book evidently exerted considerable influence on later American written algebras.

*Warren Colburn* (1793–1833) Colburn, who previously had written several arithmetics, in 1825 published *An Introduction to Algebra,* "upon the inductive method of instruction." In this approach he was following the general principles of Pestalozzi. His first object was "to make the transition from arithmetic to algebra as gradual as possible." So the book began with practical questions involving simple equations. In defending the inductive approach he said: "The best mode seems to be, to give examples so simple as to require little or no explanation, and let the learner reason for himself." The first 50 pages involved nearly all operations in simple equations, with one or two unknowns. Next, the learner was taught to "generalize particular cases, and to form rules. Then the various algebraic aspects were taken up and discussed. Thereafter, he claimed, there was nothing "peculiar in the arrangement or in the manner of treating them." He claimed new ways of finding the coefficients of the Biominal Theorem, and of treating and demonstrating the "principle of summing *series of differences.*" It appeared in nearly 20 editions by 1848. It represented a rather sharp departure from most other algebras.

*William Smyth.* He was one of the first American authors to make heavy use of Bourdon, as well as of Lacroix. However, this book was written anew, rather than being a mere translation of the French texts. The explanations were more ample than in most early algebras. The 1847 printing was the 6th edition.

*Ebenezer Bailey.* He was the principal of the Young Ladies' High School in Boston. He strongly believed that by making the study of algebra less technical it could be studied earlier in the school curriculum. So in 1833 he published his *First Lessons in Algebra*, "designed for the use of Academies and Common Schools." This was an attractive book of 227 pages. In format and approach it was similar to the better arithmetics of his day. The chapters dealt with the four fundamentals, fractions, powers, equations of the first degree, exercises in generalization, evolution, equations of the second degree, and miscellaneous questions. The fact that the 1847 edition was the 31st attested to its popularity.

*Charles Davies* (1798–1861). Davies taught mathematics at the U.S. Military Academy for 20 years, after which he taught in several colleges, ending his teaching career at Columbia University. He became one of America's most prolific mathematics textbook writers. He wrote at least seven different arithmetics, four algebras, three geometries, a calculus book, a combined geometry and trigonometry, a general mathematics book, and one dealing with surveying and navigation.

As mentioned before, in 1834 Davies abridged the Ross translation of Bourdon's *Elements of Algebra*. With minor revisions and slight enlargements, the Davies' *Elements* continued to appear with a new copyright as late as 1873. Apparently Davies' *Bourdons* gained wider circulation than the translations by Smyth, Farrar, Ross, and Hackley.

In 1838 Davies published his *First Lessons in Algebra*. In this book he intended to form a connecting link between arithmetic and algebra. It appears that he attempted to follow the algebraic principles according to Bourdon, but in his simple presentation the approach of Bailey's *First Lessons*.

This book appeared in several editions until 1842, when a chapter on the Theory of Logarithms was added and the title changed to *Elementary Algebra*. It appeared in numerous reprints, and was somewhat enlarged and recopyrighted in 1852 and 1859, with reprints appearing even in the 1870's. Davies' books were very systematically arranged and contained the basic content of algebra, but they did not show the originality and pedagogical qualities of those by Colburn and Bailey.

*Other algebras before 1840.* A number of other algebras were published before 1840 that appeared in more than one printing, but apparently did not gain wide circulation. Among them were books by Enoch Lewis (1826), Timothy Clowes (1831), Silas Totten (1836), and Richard Green (1839 and 1840).

### D. *Algebras, 1840–1870*

A number of the algebras first written in the previous period continued in use during this period, several even to its end. However, we are now concerned with those that were first written during this period.

*James B. Thomson.* He, like several others, wrote books in arithmetic, geometry, and algebra. When Jeremiah Day wrote his *Introduction to Algebra* in 1814, it was primarily intended for college use. The number of its editions attests to wide usage, mostly in colleges, but also in some academies. However, in the 1840's Day believed that an abridgment of it ought to be written for more suitable use in secondary schools. Impaired health prevented him from doing it, so Day asked J. B. Thomson to do so. Consequently, in 1843 Thomson's *Elements of Algebra*, "being an Abridgment of Day's Algebra," was published. This was an attractive and well organized book of 252 pages. Its success was immediate. The 1853 printing of it was the 19th edition. Thus the books by Day and Thomson provided keen competition for those based on the French books by Lacroix and Bourdon.

In the meantime Thomson wrote several very popular arithmetics. He believed that mathematics books should be practical and concrete in application. Then in 1877 he published a *New Practical Algebra*. It contained many problems involving the practical application of algebra, including many involving commercial formulas. It appeared in several editions.

*Horatio N. Robinson.* In 1844 he published *A Universal Key to the Science of Algebra*. This was not a regular textbook, but which provided a new method in the treatment of problems taken from algebras written by such authors as Day, Ryan, Colburn, Young, and Bourdon. Then in 1846 Robinson published *An Elementary Treatise of Algebra*. In it he made a plea for earlier teaching of algebra. He claimed: "Algebra is elementary Arithmetic, and no one can acquire a knowledge of Arithmetic in an enlarged and scientific sense, without the previous knowledge of Algebra." Some peculiarities he claimed for the book were the abbreviations generally in solving equations, the unusual formation of problems, and the manner at arriving at certain rules. It was an attractive book with many practical problems. This book was revised and recopyrighted in 1850 and again in 1859. The latter edition continued to be reprinted until in the 1880's. Apparently it was widely used in secondary schools.

In 1847 Robinson published *A Theoretical and Practical Treatise on Algebra*, designed for "schools, colleges, and private students." The 1852 printing was the 15th edition. Other printings appeared even in the 1860's. It is not now certain how widely this book was used in academies, but likely in some.

*David B. Tower.* In 1845 Tower published an *Intellectual Algebra*, which was based on oral inductive exercises. One reason for this was because it was originally prepared for instruction of the blind. By 1850 it appeared in its 7th edition, so evidently it was used in other schools as well. Tower believed the inductive method would lead to better understanding of the algebraic principles.

*Elias Loomis.* He was a professor at Yale. He became a prolific writer of textbooks in arithmetic, algebra, geometry, trigonometry, natural philosophy (physics), astronomy, and meteorology. In 1846 his *Treatise on Algebra* appeared. In revised editions this book continued to appear even in the 1880's. Although it was primarily a college text, in the preface of the 1858 edition he stated that it was also used in numerous academies. However, an examination of it reveals that it must have been difficult for secondary school students. In 1851 he published a simpler text entitled, *Elements of Algebra*, which apparently was used in many secondary schools.

*Joseph Ray* (1807–1857). Ray, whose arithmetics were more popular than any written during the 19th century, also wrote texts in algebra. His *Algebra, Part First* was published in 1848, on the "Analytic and Inductive Methods of Instruction." He stated the object of mathematics to be two fold: "the acquisition of useful knowledge, and the cultivation of the mental powers." He claimed that every rule was demonstrated, and every principle analyzed. He aimed to combine the explanatory methods of the French mathematicians with the practical exercises of the English and German, together with his own reflections and experience in the subject. This book was intended for "Common Schools and Academies," and appeared in numerous printings.

In 1852 Ray's *Algebra, Part Second* was published. This was an "Analytical Treatise, designed for High Schools and Colleges." It was one of the earliest algebras to appear in cloth binding rather than leather, and to refer to high schools rather than academies. In addition to dealing with the same topics found in *Part First*, it covered permutations, indeterminate coefficients, logarithms, and the general theory and resolution of numerical equations. After Ray's decease, *Part Second* was revised in 1866 by L. D. Potter with the title *Elements of Algebra*, and then in 1875 it was revised by Del. Kemper. These books appeared in numerous printings. Several *Keys* to Ray's *Algebras* were also published.

*Benjamin Greenleaf* (1786–1864). After his arithmetics had become very popular, Greenleaf turned to writing several algebra texts. His first was *A Practical Treatise on Algebra* in 1852. He particularly mentioned it to be for high schools and academies. Throughout he aimed to give it "a practical character, that those who study it may know how to apply their knowledge to useful purposes." Too, he mentioned that it should provide "mental exercise," quoting John Locke as claiming this to be of great value. The last 24 pages were used in listing the schools in which Greenlleaf's *Arithmetics* and/or *Algebras* were being used and for recommendations. Most secondary schools in New England used it, as well as many elsewhere. Ten of these pages were devoted to testimonials for his books. It is evident that his *Treatise* was very popular in the 1850's. It appeared in 40 editions.

Later Greenleaf apparently saw the need for a two-book series, so in 1862 he with the assistance of H. B. Maglathlin, prepared a *New Elementary Algebra*, "in which the first principles of analysis are progressively developed and simplified for Common Schools and Academies." Then the *New Higher Algebra* was for "High Schools and Colleges." Such suggested flexibility of use for these books was common in those days, for neither schools nor textbooks were then carefully graded. The 1879 edition of the *New Elementary* mentioned only "High Schools and Academies" for its use. The later revisions were made by others after his decease.

*Other algebras, 1840–1870.* In addition to the algebras heretofore discussed, many others were written during this period, a number of them appeared in several editions. Among these may be mentioned texts written by: John H. Harney (1840), based upon the inductive approach; John D. Williams (1840); George Perkins (1842); Thomas Sherwin (1842), it appeared in at least five printings; Davis W. Clark (1843), written for teachers of arithmetic to broaden their knowledge of mathematics; O. M. Mitchel (1845); Samuel Alsop (1846); Charles W. Hackley (1846); Francis H. Smith (1848); Stephen Chase (1849); James B. Dodd (1854); John F. Stoddard and W. D. Henkle (1857); Benjamin Peirce (1864); and William F. Bradbury (1868).

### E. *Algebras, 1870–1900*

A number of the algebras first written in the previous period continued in use in many schools during this period. Thus only those first written after 1870 will be discussed here.

*Edward Olney.* In 1870 Olney published his *Complete Algebra.* In this book he aimed to provide in a single volume of convenient size, a complete elementary treatise of algebra; provide training in methods of reasoning; and present a book convenient for classroom use. In "Part I: Literal Arithmetic," he presented the basic aspects of arithmetic with the use of letters. In "Part II: Algebra," the chapters dealt with simple equations; ratio, proportion, and progression; business rules [of arithmetic]; quadratic equations; and logarithms. Treatment of the binominal theorem and of permutations was omitted. Revised and enlarged editions later appeared even in the 1880's. In 1874 he also published an *Introduction to Algebra*.

*Edward Brooks*. Brooks, like numerous other mathematics authors, wrote texts in the fields of arithmetic, algebra, geometry, and trigonometry. In 1871 he published *The Normal Elementary Algebra*. It was intended for use in "Common Schools, Academies, Seminaries, and Normal Schools." It was interesting to mention seminaries, which meant that by that time girls were studying algebra in female seminaries. Mentioning normal schools, too, was significant. At that time few normal schools were collegiate in character. Mainly they would review the common branches on a higher level, such as English grammar arithmetic, geography, physiology, and American history. Then in addition they would offer such courses as literature, mental philosophy (psychology), methods of teaching, and school room management. Algebra, if taught, likely aimed at developing a better understanding of advanced arithmetic. In fact Brooks favored teaching his *Algebra* before advanced arithmetic.

This was a rather clearly written book, omitting a number of the more technical topics of algebra. Higher and intermediate equations were omitted, and the binomial theorem, logarithms, and permutations were only in the supplement. It apparently was a very teachable book.

*G. A. Wentworth* (1835–1906). After teaching mathematics in Phillips Exeter Academy for thirty years, he resigned to spend full time to textbook writing. He wrote texts in arithmetic, geometry, algebra, and trigonometry. More than one text appeared in all these fields.

Wentworth's *Elements of Algebra* was published in 1881. He claimed that the materials were obtained from English, French, and German sources. He interestingly stated, "To avoid trespassing upon the works of recent American authors, no American textbook has been consulted." This is testimony that algebra changed less in America than most other subjects. To justify adding this book to a crowded market he claimed that its usefulness must be based upon its method of treatment. He included about 4000 examples that had been selected, arranged, and tested in the recitation room. Many examples for practice were provided. The 1888 edition was some smaller. Answers to the problems were bound separately in paper covers and could be obtained.

In 1890 Wentworth published *A School Algebra,* written for high schools and academies. In scope it was similar to his *Elements,* but was a rather completely rewritten book and the material more attractively presented. This book apparently had wide circulation during the 1890's and after, as the *Elements* had in the 1880's. In 1888 he published *A College Algebra,* and in 1906 *An Elementary Algebra.* The Wentworth texts somewhat dominated the mathematics adoptions in American schools during the later decades of the 19th century, and many were still in use after 1900.

*William Milne.* In 1881 Milne published an *Inductive Algebra.* Not many algebras had been written on the inductive plan. In 1892 this appeared in a revised edition as the *High School Algebra.* The various topics of algebra were again first presented inductively. In defense of the inductive approach he said:

"Improvement in methods of teaching has been very great in recent years, and it is necessary, therefore, that new textbooks should keep pace with the noticeable advance in educational science."

It was a very attractive book. Answers were in the back of the book.

*Webster Wells.* He was a professor of mathematics at the Massachusetts Institute of Technology, and so was interested in doing something about improving the mathematical training in secondary schools to provide good college preparation. Therefore, in 1885 he published *A Complete Course in Algebra.* It contained the topics "usually included in an Elementary Algebra." It was a well-organized text of 305 pages, plus 43 pages of answers. Ample practice problems were included. It continued to be published without change even after 1900. In 1897 he wrote the *Essentials of Algebra for Secondary Schools.* This was a larger book. After 1900 he continued his textbook writing, and later several books appeared under the joint names of Wells and Walter W. Hart.

*Other algebras, 1870–1900.* Other algebras were written during this period, but apparently failed to gain wide acceptance, although several appeared in more than one edition. Mention may be made of those written by: A. Schuyler (1870), Joseph Ficklin (1874), Edwin P. Seaver and George A. Walton (1882), the Sheldon Company (1887), David Stensenig (1888), George Smith (1890), George W. Hull (1895), and Arthur Lefevre (1896).

10. Two men, driving their sheep to market, A says to B, give me one of your sheep and I shall have as many as you ; B says to A, give me one of your sheep and I shall have twice as many as you. How many had each?

Let       $x =$ the number A had,

And      $y =$ the number B had.

If B gives A one, their numbers will be

$$x + 1 \text{ and } y - 1.$$

If A gives B one, their numbers will be

$$x - 1 \text{ and } y + 1, \&c.$$

11. If A gives B \$5 of his money, B will have twice as much as A has left ; but if B gives A \$5 of his money, A will have three times as much as B has left. How much has each?

12. A man bought a quantity of rye and wheat for £6, the rye at 4s. and the wheat at 5s. per bushel. He afterwards sold $\frac{1}{5}$ of his rye and $\frac{3}{4}$ of his wheat at the same rate for £2. 17s. How many bushels were there of each?

13. A man bought a cask of wine, and another of gin for \$210 ; the wine at \$1.50 a gallon, and the gin at \$0.50 a gallon. He afterwards sold $\frac{2}{3}$ of his wine, and $\frac{3}{4}$ of his gin for \$150, which was \$15 more than it cost him. How many gallons were there in each cask?

14. A countryman, driving a flock of geese and turkeys to market, in order to distinguish his own from any he might meet with on the road, pulled three feathers out of the tail of each turkey, and one out of the tail of each goose, and found that the number of turkeys' feathers exceeded twice those of the geese by 15. Having bought 10 geese and sold 15 turkeys by the way, he was surprised to find that the number of geese exceeded the number of turkeys in the proportion of 7 to 3. Required the number of each at first.

Let       $x =$ the number of turkeys,

and      $y =$ the number of geese.

1.     ·     ·     ·     ·     ·   $3x = 2y + 15$

2.     ·     ·     ·     ·     ·   $y + 10 = \dfrac{7x - 105}{3}$

3. Freeing the 2d from fractions, $3y + 30 = 7x - 105$

Instead of the method employed above for eliminating one of the unknown quantities, we may find the value of one of them in one equation, as if the other were known ; and then

### F. *Characteristics of Algebra Textbooks*

THUS far our treatment has been to discuss some of the more popular algebras used in American schools before, 1900. Details of their content were mentioned only in a few instances. Next a more detailed treatment of the actual nature of more books needs to be made. For this treatment the writer will depend heavily on the findings of a study made by Mrs. King.[2] Her study involved an analysis of 119 algebras. Other than a few English and French books that were reprinted here, all were both written and published in America. It is assumed that the imported books that were reprinted here were also used in America. So the findings should reflect rather accurately what algebraic content was studied by American students before 1900.

*General characteristics.* The earliest algebra taught in America was mainly from omnibus mathematics books, some of them entitled, arithmetic. Usually only the latter part of the book dealt with algebra. It is doubtful whether many students acquired a very functional knowledge of algebra in the colonial period. Then later when separate algebra textbooks appeared they were most commonly studied only in colleges. However, some of the better academies gradually began to teach algebra also. In fact, during the early national period in many instances academies and colleges used the same texts, not only in algebra but also in other fields as well. The title pages of many algebras contained such statements as, "For Schools and Colleges," "For Academies and Colleges," "For Schools and Academies," and Sherwin's in 1842 "In High Schools and Colleges." One reason for such statements was to sell more books in more kinds of schools. Another reason was because schools were not carefully graded or standardized. It is quite evident that there must not have been much difference between what was taught in the better academies and in some colleges.

Nearly all algebra textbooks published before 1850 were bound in leather. This was true because they were used in the schools attended mostly only by students coming from the wealthier homes. Ray's *Algebra's* were among the first to appear both in leather in cloth binding. One reason may have been that they were published in the mid-west, where not so many students came from wealthy homes.

Nearly all popular algebras, even to 1900, were written by authors who wrote textbooks in several branches of mathematics. They commonly wrote texts in arithmetic, algebra, geometry, trigonometry, and even navigation, and astronomy. Among the prolific mathematics textbook writers were Colburn, Davies, Thomson, Robinson, Tower, Loomis, Ray, Greenleaf, Olney, Brooks, Milne, and Wentworth.

A number of authors believed that the basic principles of algebra should be taught before the study of arithmetic, at least before advanced arithmetic. In fact, some claimed that advanced arithmetic could not be mastered without a knowledge of algebra. Among these authors were Robinson, Clark, and Brooks.

*Aims.* The most frequently mentioned aim in the older algebras was the training of the mind or mental discipline. The stress was upon developing the reasoning powers. It was not until the latter part of the 19th century before many texts emphasized the problem solving and functional thinking aims. Few texts included among its exercises problems involving life situations.

*Approaches.* Throughout until 1900 nearly all algebras were patterned on the deductive approach. That is, each topic would be presented with definitions, rules, or principles, which would be followed by a few illustrative examples. Then commonly what was learned or committed was to be applied to exercises. A few of the old algebras did not even contain exercises. Only a few algebras were written wholly or in part on the inductive approach. The first of these was by Colburn in 1825. It began with practical questions involving simple equations. Another was by Tower in 1845. It was largely based on oral inductive exercises. Ray's popular *Algebra, Part First* (1848) was presented on the "Analytic and Inductive Methods of Instruction." However, Ray's later books were largely deductive in approach. The chief difference in the presentations was in the number and nature of the working exercises.

*Content.* The earliest algebras used in America were either reprints of English or French texts or were largely patterned after them. Not only was the European influence strong in the earlier books, which was also true of the textbooks in many other subject fields, but this influence continued rather strong in algebra texts even to 1900. Wentworth, whose texts were very popular during the latter part of the 19th century, acknowledged his debt to the French for the theoretical aspects of algebra and to the English for the practical. All of which means that algebraic content did not change much during last century. This fact is shown in Table III, which has been constructed from data derived from Mrs. King's study. It shows that at least two-thirds of the 119 algebra textbooks analyzed dealt with the fundamental operations, first degree and quadratic equations, factors and factoring, fractions, proportion and pro-

TABLE III: *Number of Textbooks*
*Dealing with Algebraic Topics by Periods*

| TOPICS TREATED IN ALGEBRA BOOKS | PERIODS | 1814 −29 | 1830 −9 | 1840 −9 | 1850 −9 | 1860 −9 | 1870 −9 | 1880 −9 | 1890 −9 | TOTAL |
|---|---|---|---|---|---|---|---|---|---|---|
| | BOOKS ANALYZED | 9 | 13 | 13 | 21 | 10 | 13 | 12 | 28 | 119 |
| Fundamental operation | | 9 | 13 | 13 | 21 | 10 | 13 | 12 | 27 | 118 |
| Equations: | | | | | | | | | | |
| First degree | | 9 | 13 | 13 | 21 | 10 | 13 | 12 | 28 | 119 |
| Quadratic | | 9 | 12 | 13 | 21 | 10 | 13 | 12 | 26 | 116 |
| Radical | | 4 | 3 | 3 | 3 | 3 | 5 | 7 | 11 | 39 |
| Higher | | 6 | 5 | 6 | 10 | 6 | 4 | 3 | 5 | 45 |
| Intermediate | | 2 | 5 | 3 | 4 | 4 | 1 | 5 | 11 | 35 |
| Factors & factoring | | 3 | 5 | 7 | 10 | 9 | 12 | 11 | 27 | 84 |
| Fractions | | 9 | 13 | 13 | 20 | 10 | 13 | 12 | 26 | 116 |
| Proportion & Progression | | 9 | 11 | 13 | 19 | 10 | 12 | 12 | 24 | 110 |
| Roots & radicals | | 9 | 12 | 13 | 21 | 10 | 13 | 12 | 27 | 117 |
| Binomial theorem | | 7 | 10 | 9 | 13 | 8 | 9 | 8 | 15 | 79 |
| Logarithms | | 6 | 9 | 9 | 14 | 7 | 9 | 10 | 18 | 82 |
| Permutations | | 1 | 3 | 7 | 8 | 6 | 4 | 5 | 7 | 41 |
| Probability & Chance | | 0 | 3 | 1 | 2 | 2 | 1 | 2 | 4 | 15 |
| Series | | 8 | 8 | 8 | 13 | 9 | 7 | 4 | 11 | 68 |
| Theory of Equations | | 4 | 4 | 5 | 10 | 6 | 6 | 5 | 12 | 52 |
| Imaginaries | | 2 | 1 | 2 | 4 | 6 | 3 | 2 | 9 | 29 |
| Inequalities | | 0 | 1 | 4 | 6 | 1 | 4 | 8 | 15 | 39 |
| Theory of numbers | | 0 | 1 | 2 | 1 | 2 | 2 | 1 | 6 | 15 |
| Differentiation | | 0 | 0 | 0 | 0 | 0 | 1 | 1 | 1 | 3 |
| Parentheses | | 0 | 0 | 0 | 0 | 2 | 1 | 8 | 16 | 27 |

gression, roots and radicals, the binomial theorem, and logarithms. It can also be seen that six of the last nine topics listed in the table were dealt with in less than one-third of the texts. In the main, the topics that appeared in the algebras of the first period consistently continued to appear throughout the century. On the other hand, the topics which began to appear in later algebras never gained consistent acceptance, except that treatment of inequalities and parentheses received considerable attention after 1880.

In conclusion it can be noted that algebraic content had become fairly well standardized in France and England before it was seriously introduced in America, and that the content had not changed very much even by 1900.

# GEOMETRY

## *Introduction*

THE word geometry etymologically came from two Greek words literally meaning earth measure. Later it came to mean the general science of form, rather than applied merely to the measure of land such as surveying.

Old records of the application of geometry have been found among the clay tablets of the Babylonians and in papyrus manuscripts among the ancient Egyptians. Too, the existence of the pyramids is further evidence that the Egyptians knew how to apply certain geometric principles in their construction. A surviving papyrus written by Ahmes about 1700 B.C., which was copied from one written about 2300 B.C., dealt with certain principles of algebra and mensuration, including the measurement of the isosceles triangle and the circle. Later they developed the use of a rope with which to make a right triangle by the use of knots at 3, 4, and 5, to erect a perpendicular. They also used this principle to resurvey land after the overflow of the Nile.

The greatest development of the principles of geometry, however, took place among the ancient Greeks. One of the first to develop certain propositions of geometry was Thales (640–546 B.C.). Even greater contributions were made by Pythagoras, a pupil of Thales. One contribution was to prove why the square of the hypotenuse is equal to the sum of the squares of the other two sides of a right triangle. The Egyptians had used this principle but never proved why it was true. Numerous other principles were proven by Pythagoras. Other Greeks who made contributions in the development of goemetry as a science were Hippocrates, Antiphon, Hippias, and several pupils of Plato. Several of these either studied or taught at the University of Alexandria in Egypt.

The first good textbook in geometry was written by Euclid, a Greek scholar, while working in the Museum of Alexandria about 300 B.C. In his book he arranged all of the leading propositions then known in logical order. The sequence set by Euclid to a large extent has been followed in geometries ever since. In regard to this, Playfair in the preface of his *Elements of Geometry* (1819) said:

"It is a remarkable fact in the history of science, that the oldest book of Elementary Geometry is still considered as the best, and that the writings of Euclid, at the distance of 2,000 years, continue to form the most approved introduction to the mathematical sciences."

The mathematical writings of the Greeks, particularly of Euclid, were translated by the Hindus and the Arabs. Thus after Alexandria ceased to be a center of learning, these works were preserved in the East. Eventually it was from the Arabic that Euclid's work was brought to Europe in full form and translated into Latin during the 12th century. The first printed edition of Euclid appeared in Latin in 1482, and the first one in English in 1570. However, some meager elements of geometry had been taught in European schools in connection with the *seven liberal arts* during the middle ages. For example, a manual by Cassiodorus (c. 490–c. 585), a medieval scholar, included 15 pages on geometry, and Boethius wrote a small corrupted geometry about 500 A.D. The above mentiond printed translations, plus others, later led to the introduction of Euclid in geometry in most higher schools of Western Europe, and later in America, including many secondary schools.

One of the greatest revisions of Euclidian geometry appeared in a French geometry textbook written by A. M. Legendre in 1794. Translations of this book greatly influenced American geometry textbooks during the 19th century. More specific references about this will be made in the treatment of American published textbooks.

### A. *Geometry in Omnibus Textbooks*

As was true of the earliest teaching of algebra in American schools, apparently some of the earliest teaching of geometry was from omnibus mathematics textbooks. One of the earliest of these was John Ward's *The Young Mathematician's Guide* published in London in 1719 and brought here. Parts III and IV of this book consisting of 150 pages dealt with geometry. The last part dealt with practical gauging or surveying.

Some of the larger arithmetics contained either a section entitled geometry, or dealt extensively with mensuration which really was applied geometry. Also, many contained material dealing with conic sections.

Likewise some of the earliest algebras contained geometrical material. For example, a Philadelphia reprint of John Bonnycastle's *Introduction to Algebra* (1806) contained nine pages of geometrical proportion, and 26 pages of algebra applied to geometry. This was also true of Thomas Simpson's *Treatise of*

*Algebra* reprinted here in 1809. In addition to geometrical proportion it devoted 47 pages to geometrical problems.

Still another type of mathematics books in which considerable geometry was presented was those on surveying. The writer's collection contains a book entitled, *Geodaesia; or, The Art of Surveying and Measuring Land Made Easy.* This was printed in New York in 1796, and was the 13th edition. Pages 16 through 43 dealt with geometry. The book also dealt with trigonometry and logarithms. Another was a book compiled from various authors by Abel Flint entitled *A System of Geometry and Trigonometry, Together with a Treatise on Surveying* in 1804. An American edition of Robert Gibson's *A Treatise of Practical Surveying* appeared in 1806. Geometry received 44 pages of treatment in this book. Trigonometry and logarithms likewise received treatment.

It is evident from the foregoing discussion that much of the earliest teaching of geometry in America apparently was from general mathematics books, arithmetics, algebras, and books on surveying. In all of them the geometry content was limited in amount. In fact, regardless of their titles, many of these books really constituted correlated mathematics. These facts point to the fact that early Americans were not so much interested in pure mathematics and science as in their application to the problems with which they were confronted. For example, they were more interested in surveying their new lands than in studying all of Euclidian geometry. Thus the geometry with which they were concerned was merely enough to provide the bases for gauging and surveying. In the arithmetics geometry was related to mensuration and conic sections. In fact, before about 1810 more textbooks appeared dealing primarily with surveying and trigonometry than with geometry.

### B. *Early Geometry Textbooks; European*

THE author's collection contains a number of very old leather bound geometry textbooks written by European authors. Some of these were reprinted here, but some of the oldest apparently were not. Since the writer obtained these copies in this country it may be that they were imported and studied here. These were all rather good sized Euclidian geometries.

*Isaac Barrow and Thomas Haselden.* Very early Isaac Barrow, Master of Trinity College in Cambridge, wrote *Euclide's Elements: the Whole Fifteen Books.* Later Haselden revised it and added a "Brief Treatise of Regular Solids." The writer's copy was printed in London in 1732, and contained more than 500 pages. Whether this book was studied here, and if so, at the secondary level, may be questioned. It certainly was a thorough and technical treatment of geometry.

*Thomas Simpson.* Another old book was Simpson's *Elements of Geometry* printed in England in 1760. He was a member of the Royal Academy of Sciences. This was more than 200 pages briefer than Barrow's text. In purpose he stated:

> "My design in writing upon the subject of Geometry, was to open an easy way for young beginners to arrive at a proficiency in that useful science; without either being obliged to go thro' a number of unnecessary propositions, or having recourse to the ungeometrical methods of demonstration, that abound in most modern compositions of this nature."

It was much less complicated and technical than Barrow's treatise.

*Joseph Fenn.* Another old text was Fenn's *Euclid's Elements of Geometry* printed in Dublin (no date given). This was a very attractively printed volume of 344 rather large pages. At the bottom of most pages there appeared decorative designs or figures, many of them floral in nature. The geometrical figures appeared in frames and the demonstrations were briefer and less technical than in some books.

*Robert Simson.* He was a professor of mathematics in the University of Glasgow. In 1803 his *Elements of Euclid* was reprinted in Philadelphia. It contained the first six books together with the eleventh and twelfth. It contained 518 rather large pages, but 37 pages dealt with plane and spherical trigonometry. Neither the figures nor the demonstrations were attractively presented. In fact, the demonstrations were very long and detailed. Nevertheless it apparently was the first Euclidian geometry to become at all popular in America, for it appeared here in at least eleven reprintings until even as late as 1838.

*John Playfair.* Playfair, who had been a professor of mathematics in the University of Edinburgh, also wrote a text entitled, *Elements of Geometry*. It contained the first six books of Euclid with a supplement on the "Quadrature of the Circle, and the Geometry of Solids," together with a few elements of plane and spherical trigonometry. A reprint first appeared in New York in 1806. Soon thereafter it gradually began to replace Simson's *Elements* as a popular text. It later appeared in more than thirty editions until past 1850. Although the book contained 311 pages, only a few more than 200 pages dealt directly with geometry. Evidently this brevity contributed to its popularity, together with the fact that 37 pages in the back dealt with explanatory notes on the Six Books.

*John Bonnycastle.* Bonnycastle, who was a member of the Royal Military

Academy, wrote *An Introduction to Mensuration and Practical Geometry* in England. In 1812 a reprint from the tenth London edition appeared in Philadelphia. Ultimately it appeared in about 20 editions in America. Thus it vied in popularity with the texts by Simson and Playfair. It was smaller, more attractively printed, and contained more practical problems than the other texts. Only a few more than 100 pages dealt with plane geometry. Then nearly 50 pages were devoted to mensuration of solids. The figures of the solids were attractively shaded. Then such matters as gauging, mason's work, carpenter's rule, timber measure, mechanical powers, and so on, together with a long list of practical miscellaneous questions, were given attention. It can easily be seen why this book became popular in America, where practical applications have always received attention. It was one of the few imported books to contain exercises and many practical applications.

*A. M. Legendre.* One of the most marked departures from pure Euclidian geometry was made by Legendre, a French mathematician, in his *Elements of Geometry* in 1794. This was translated into English by John Farrar of Harvard and published here in 1819. Legendre abandoned the sequence of Euclid, simplified the subject matter, and arranged the material logically. This book appeared in about ten editions until the 1840's.

In 1828 another translation of Legendre's book was made by David Brewster and published in New York. It was revised and altered for use in the U.S. Military Academy at West Point. This translation, together with further revisions of Legendre made by Charles Davies, continued to appear throughout the middle of the centuury. Davies' revision claimed that in the other translations the propositions had not been "enunciated in general terms, but with reference to, and by aid of, the particular diagrams used for the demostrations." He favored the teaching of general truths in order to increase "intellectual labour." It is clear that Legendre greatly influenced the geometry teaching in America, as had two other French mathematicians in the field of algebra, Bourdon and La Croix.

*Comments.* The foregoing discussions indicate rather clearly that the teaching of geometry in American schools before about 1825 took two more or less extreme and opposite forms. On the one hand, the simple elements of geometry, generally of a rather practical nature, were taught from books on arithmetic, algebra, trigonometry, or surveying. Commonly fewer than 30 or 40 pages would be devoted to geometry in these books.

On the other hand, textbooks had been written in England and France

# *EUCLIDE's* ELEMENTS;

The whole FIFTEEN BOOKS
compendiously Demonstrated:

WITH

ARCHIMEDES's Theorems of
the Sphere and Cylinder Investigated
by the *Method of Indivisibles.*

By ISAAC BARROW, D.D. *late Master*
*of* Trinity *College in* Cambridge.

To which is Annex'd,

EUCLIDE's *Data*, and a brief
*Treatise of Regular Solids.*

The Whole revis'd with great Care,
and some Hundreds of Errors of the
former Impression corrected.

By THOMAS HASELDEN, *Teacher*
*of the Mathematicks.*

Καθαρμοὶ ψυχῆς λογικῆς εἰσιν αἱ μαθηματικαὶ ἐπιστῆμαι.

*LONDON*: Printed for *Daniel Midwinter* and *Aaron*
*Ward* in *Little-Britain*; *Arthur Bettesworth* and *Charles*
*Hitch* in *Pater-noster-row*; and *Thomas Page* and *William*
*Mount* on *Tower-Hill*, 1732.

7  Euclid's *Elements* became the basis for
American geometry textbooks

A

# SYSTEM

OF

## GEOMETRY AND TRIGONOMETRY:

TOGETHER WITH A

### Treatise on Surveying;

TEACHING VARIOUS WAYS OF TAKING THE SURVEY
OF A FIELD; ALSO TO PROTRACT THE SAME
AND FIND THE AREA.

*LIKEWISE,*

## *Rectangular Surveying;*

OR,

AN ACCURATE METHOD OF CALCULATING THE AREA OF
ANY FIELD ARITHMETICALLY, WITHOUT THE
NECESSITY OF PLOTTING IT.

To the whole are added several Mathematical Tables, necessary
for solving Questions in Trigonometry and Surveying; with
a particular explanation of those Tables, and the manner of
using them.

*SECOND EDITION.*

COMPILED FROM VARIOUS AUTHORS,

## *BY ABEL FLINT, A. M.*

### HARTFORD:
PRINTED FOR OLIVER D. COOKE,
BY LINCOLN & GLEASON.

1808.

*Copyright 1804*

8  This became a popular book in American academies for
teaching geometry, trigonometry, and surveying

which viewed geometry as an abstract science largely based on Euclid. Most of these were books of good size. Among the authors whose geometries were reprinted in America, and which gained wide circulation during the first half of the 19th century, were Robert Simson, John Playfair, John Bonnycastle, and A. M. Legendre.

Furthermore, it is not entirely certain now in what kinds of schools these various geometries were used. The Euclidian geometries likely were most commonly taught in most American colleges. It was not until 1844 that credit in geometry was required for college admission, when this was done by Harvard. However, according to Brown[3] some grammar schools and academies, even in the colonial period, taught geometry. Northampton Academy under Doddridge taught it in his school which opened in 1729. Gloucester Academy taught it very early, and Phillips Exeter was teaching it in 1818. The first American high school (Boston) taught it from its beginning in 1821. A Massachusetts Law of 1827 required it to be taught in all towns having over 500 families. It is evident that geometry was taught in some secondary schools rather early, but not too commonly. Too, it is not certain which of the above mentioned geometries were most frequently used in these secondary schools.

## C. *American Geometry Textbooks Before 1850*

LIKE in the field of algebra, the earliest American written geometries were either very small or were closely patterned on European books. Good American written geometries were even slower to appear than in most other fields.

*Abel Flint.* One of the first American written mathematics books bearing the title of geometry was Flint's *A System of Geometry and Trigonometry: Together with a Treatise on Surveying* published in 1804. This, like other books dealing with surveying or trigonometry, also dealt with geometry. Although geometry is first mentioned in its title, only 12 pages were devoted to it. Then 15 pages dealt with trigonometry, and 42 pages with surveying proper. The last 88 pages were devoted to mathematical tables. In the back there were four plates of geometrical drawings. The book apparently met a need in early America, for it appeared in about 15 editions even as late as 1847. This book, like other similar ones, apparently was used in many academies, for many of them taught surveying, and navigation, as well as geometry. So dealing with these subjects in one text was an economy of time and money. Knowledge of surveying was very imporrtant during the early development of United States.

*Charles Davies* (1798–1861). Davies was graduated from the U.S. Military

E

Academy, after which he taught there over twenty years. After teaching in several colleges, he ended his carreer at Columbia University. His prolific writing of mathematics books has been mentioned in the previous chapter.

In 1826 he published the *Elements of Descriptive Geometry*. These elements included their application to spherical trigonometry, spherical projections and warped surfaces. It included 34 plates. More than a dozen editions eventually were published even as late as 1870. In 1834 he published a revision of Dr. Brewster's translation of Legendre's *Elements*. Editions of this continued to appear even long after Davies' decease. Apparently this was the most widely used geometry in America until about 1870.

In 1836 he published the *Elements of Analytical Geometry*. It was primarily prepared for use at the U.S. Military Academy. He acknowledged his use of similar works by Biot and Bourdon in its preparation. Since this was a very technical book, it is doubtful whether it was widely used in secondary schools. It appeared again as late as 1849.

In 1839 Davies published the *First Lessons in Geometry*, with their "practical applications in mensuration and artificer's work and mechanics." He aimed to "present all the important truths of Geometry in such a way as to render them accessible to the general reader, without departing from the exactness of the geometrical methods." However, to make these truths less complicated he omitted the demonstrations. The truths were presented as rules to be applied. It was a very attractive book of 252 pages. He claimed the book to be "adapted to the wants of academies and the higher grade of schools." It appeared in a number of editions, with some of them bearing the title of *Practical Geometry*.

In 1841 Davies' *Elements of Geometry* appeared. It stressed applications to mensuration. This was the smallest of his geometry books, containing only 216 pages. It appeared frequently for at least a decade. The recital of the appearance of these geometries written by Davies attests to his prolific writing, and also to the evident wide usage of his books.

*Francis J. Grund.* In 1830 he published the *First Lessons in Plane Geometry*. This was a very attractive book of 254 pages, and was one of the earliest geometries to be bound in paper board cover rather than in leather. It was immediately adopted for use in the Boston English Classical School (America's first high school), the Young Ladies' High School of Boston, and in the Monitorial School of Boston. At least eight editions of it appeared. In 1831 Grund published *An Elementary Treatise of Geometry*, which contained only 195 pages. It was not as popular as the *First Lessons*.

*Benjamin Peirce*. Peirce, a professor at Harvard, in 1837 published *An Elementary Treatise on Plane and Solid Geometry*. Although this was a rather small book of 150 pages plus six plates, yet it must have been rather difficult for the students in that it contained no geometrical figures except the plates in the back. The presentation was very different from most other geometry textbooks. For example on page 25 one finds:

> 91. *Theorem*. Every chord is less than the diameter. *Proof.* Thus BE (fig. 43) is less than DB. For, joining AE, we have BD=BA+AE, but BE<BA+AE, therefore BE<BD.

In this brief manner all of the theorems, corollaries, problems, solutions, and proofs were presented. It appeared in a number of editions without change as late as 1871. In the back of the 1853 edition twelve pages were devoted to advertising other textbooks for sale by the publisher.

*George Perkins*. Perkins, like a number of authors of mathematics books, also wrote arithmetics and algebras. In 1847 he published his *Elements of Geometry*, "with practical applications." This was a well organized book of 320 pages. Basically he followed Euclid, but added two features. First, he brought to aid the principles of algebra, which had not been done by the ancients. Next, to make geometry more useful and appealing he added in smaller type, suggestions for practical applications. It included eight books and an appendix. It continued to be published into the 1870's. In 1854 he published a more advanced book for colleges.

*Elias Loomis*. Also in 1847 Loomis' *Elements of Geometry and Conic Sections* appeared. This text presented six books of plane geometry, four books of solid geometry, and 46 pages dealing with conic sections. Loomis attempted to combine the "peculiar excellencies of Euclid and Legendre." Euclid's *Elements* were accepted for their finished logic, but were inadequate for an adequate treatment of solids. So Euclid was followed considerably in plane geometry, but Legendre in the treatment of solid geometry and in dealing with conic sections. This book was recopyrighted in 1858, but without change, and continued to appear into the 1870's. Then in 1876 it was considerably revised and enlarged to include plane trigonometry and logarithms. The book was enlarged from 222 pages to 443. The question arises regarding the extent to which these books were used in secondary schools, particularly the 1876 revised edition.

*Other geometry textbooks*. Some of the earliest geometries written by American authors apparently felt that Euclidian geometry was too difficult and abstract for American students. One of the earliest of these was Josiah Holbrook's *Easy Lessons in Geometry* (1828), consisting of 36 pages. Other small books were written by L. Gaultier (1829, 54 pages), T. Walker (1829, 104 pages), N. I. Larkin (1830, 64 pages), Nicholas Tillinghast (1841, 96 pages,) and Dennis M'Curdy (1845, 60 pages). These likely found little use in secondary schools.

Other geometries appearing before 1850, but which failed to gain wide usage, were written by the following authors:[4] John D. Craig (1818), Rev. John Allen (1822), Rev. Joseph Caldwell (1822), Ferdinand R. Hassler (1828), Michael O'Shannessy (1828), James Hale (1829), James Hayward (1829), Martin Roche (1829), B. F. Callender (1836), W. E. Dean (1836), Eugenius Nulty (1836), William Smyth (1836), J. B. Biot (1840), Dennis McCurdy (1840), Mrs. Anna Cabot Lowell (1843), Nathan Scofield (1845), William Vodges (1846, several editions), Alpheus Crosby and Stephen Chase (1847), Charles W. Hackley (1847), A. D. Stanley (1848), George Whitlock (1848), Daniel Wilder (1848), and Almon Ticknor (1849). It can be noted that a goodly number of geometries were written during the 1840's.

*Comments.* Most of the geometry textbooks written by Americans before 1850 either were revised editions of the traditional geometry of Euclid or Legendre or were marked departures from them by presenting concrete and practical applications of the elements of geometry. These applications commonly applied to mensuration, surveying, and navigation. In a rather new and developing country like United States, the practical rather than the abstract often received prime attention. However, in 1847 in Perkin's *Elements of Geometry* an attempt was made to combine the most common aspects of traditional geometry with suggestions for practical applications.

### D. *Geometries, 1850–1900*

A number of the geometries first written in the previous period continued in circulation long after 1850, particularly the books by Davies and by Loomis. As a result few of the geometries first written after 1850 really gained wide circulation before 1900, except those written by Wentworth. However, attention will be given to a number of authors whose books did appear in several of editions.

*Thomas Hill.* Hill believed that children should be introduced to non-technical geometry rather early, particularly addressing the imagination rather than the reason. So in 1855 he wrote a text of 144 pages entitled, *First Lessons in Geometry*. This was a very interesting and attractive book. He claimed that it should appeal both to children and "to pupils of adult age." The paragraphs were numbered, and at the bottom of each page there were questions on the text. It appeared in several editions. Its use in secondary schools was likely limited.

*Benjamin Greenleaf.* Having had experience in teaching in an academy and a teacher's seminary, he was conscious of the learning process. After having written very popular arithmetics, and also an algebra, Greenleaf decided to write a geometry. So in 1858 his *Elements of Geometry*, with "Practical Applications to Mensuration" was published. On the fly leaf of a copy there is a statement that it was used in the New Jersey State Normal School and in "upwards of 60 seminaries in the Eastern States." Among the ads of the 1859 edition mention was made that it was also used in some Massachusetts high schools. In arrangement he claimed to follow the "elegant order" of Legendre, but in the methods of demonstrations there were departures. In the eleventh and twelfth books he added applications to mensuration, in order to show how the theoretical principles were connected with "manifold practical results." Miscellaneous geometrical exercises were also included.

*Horatio Robinson.* In 1860 he published his *Elements of Geometry.* He also wrote a *New Geometry and Trigonometry.* These appeared in several editions. In 1862 he published a *Key to Robinson's New Geometry and Trigonometry.* He claimed that keys to geometry were not common. Regarding its value he said that it depended on its use. It should not "supersede investigation and labor," but should lessen the "mechanical" labor of teaching by showing how to study and how to teach. He also wrote popular arithmetics and algebras.

*Edward Brooks.* As professor and later as the principal of Pennsylvania's first state normal school at Millersville, Brooks was very conscious of students' ability to learn. Thus in the writing of his arithmetics, algebras, and later geometries, he wrote them to be teachable. In 1865 he published *The Normal Elementary Geometry* of 179 pages. It presented eight books of geometry and a section on mensuration. He claimed four particular features: brevity, simplification, concrete examples and problems, and undemonstrated theorems to "cultivate the power of original thought." The title page stated it to be for "Academies, Seminaries, High Schools, Normal Schools, and Advanced Classes in Common Schools." It appeared as late as the 1880's.

*William Chauvenet.* In 1870 he published a *Treatise on Elementary Geometry.* It was a rather large book and contained nine of the traditional books of geometry. Although the title used the word *Elementary*, it was a very technical book. An ad in the 1888 edition stated that it was used at Harvard, Yale, West Point, and Annapolis. In 1887 it was revised and abridged by W. E. Byerly. This simpler edition may well have been used in some secondary schools.

*Edward Olney.* Olney, a Professor of Mathematics at the University of Michigan, published *A General Geometry and Calculus* in 1871. This was intended for college use. Then in 1872 his *A Treatise on Special or Elementary Geometry* was published. This was published in two editions. The one consisted of two parts of 239 pages, and the other known as the *University Edition* included four parts. The one of two parts evidently was intended for use in secondary schools. Olney abandoned the use of the traditional classification by *Books*, but divided it into parts and sections. It was well organized. In 1883 Olney revised and slightly enlarged the *Elementary* book. It was made unusually attractive with the geometrical figures drawn in white lines on a black background. In the preface he stated that the earlier *Elementary* edition had "gone into use in every State of the Union," in all grades of schools.

*William F. Bradbury.* In 1872 Bradbury wrote *An Elementary Geometry and Trigonometry.* This consisted of five books and 110 pages of geometry, 66 pages of plane trigonometry, and 62 pages of logarithmic tables. He claimed to have omitted every unimportant theorem, so as to make the presentation more meaningful. Only 81 propositions were used. Practical questions and applications appeared at the close of each book. In 1877 this book was revised and enlarged to include nine books, followed by exercises in relation to each book. It apparently was well adapted for use in secondary schools.

*George A. Wentworth* (1835–1906). After his graduation from Harvard, Wentworth taught at Phillips Exeter Academy for thirty years. Then he discontinued teaching to spend full time at textbook writing. He wrote arithmetics, algebras, trigonometries, as well as geometries. He was the most prolific mathematics textbook writer during the latter part of the 19th century. In fact, his were by far the most popular geometries written between 1850 and 1900.

In 1877 Wentworth's *Elements of Geometry* appeared. In organization he reverted to the Euclidian organization of books, using eight. However, he greatly revised the traditional ways of presentation. All unnecessary "discussions and scholia" were avoided. Fewer abstract symbols were used. He made the pages attractive by placing rather large and distinct figures in the middle of the page. The given lines were full lines, those used as aids short-dotted, and the resulting lines long-dotted. The statement of the proposition, what was required, and the demonstration, each was printed in different kind of type. Thus the appearance of the work was not forbidding to the student, and the steps were differentiated. It was sold both as plane geometry only or as plane and solid. In 1883 and in 1887 the identical book appeared under the title of *Elements of Plane and Solid Geometry*. In 1888 separate revised editions of plane and solid geometry appeared.

Wentworth's *Elements of Analytic Geometry* was published in 1886, and like his other books appeared in a number of editions. Then in 1890 *A Text-book of Geometry* was published. This was apparently a revision of the *Elements*. It, too, covered both plane and solid geometry in eight books, but was considerably revised and larger.

From this recital of Wentworth's *Geometries* it is evident that not all of these editions were new and separate books. In some cases titles were changed without marked change in content, and then some editions were only plane geometry, others only solid, and others plane and solid.

After 1900 other authors joined Wentworth in writing and revising these books. In 1901 *First Steps in Geometry* appeared under the names of Wentworth and George A. Hill. Then after Wentworth's decease David E. Smith revised some of these books in 1913, which continued in circulation for some time. Certainly Wentworth's influence on the teaching of mathematics in American schools just before and at the turn of the century was strong.

*Webster Wells*. In 1887 Wells wrote a *Plane and Solid Geometry*. Then in 1894 *The Elements of Geometry* was published, which also appeared in a reprint in 1899. However, his geometries never became as popular as his algebras.

*Other geometries, 1850–1900*. Other authors who wrote geometries during this period, but whose books failed to gain wide circulation, were: Albert E. Church (1851), B. Sestini (1856), Gerardus B. Docharty (1857), E. W. Evans (1862), Charles H. Haswell (1866), Eli T. Tappan (1868), Thomas Hunter (1871), William G. Peck (1873), Robert Wallace (1873), W. G. Peoli (1873), Charles S. Venable (1875), William G. S. Spencer (1876), A. Schuyler (1876), G. M. Searle (1877), Alfred Welsh (1883), Simon Newcomb (1885), Linus Faunce (1888), H. S. Hall and F. Stevens (1888), J. W. McDonald (1889), Edward A. Bowser (1892), Arthur Baker (1893), W. W. Beman and David E. Smith (1895), George Edward (1895), John Macnie (1895), J. A. Gillet (1896), Andrew W. Phillips and Irving Fisher (1896), George W. Null (1897), James H. Gore (1898), William J. Milne (1899), and H. S. MacLean (1899).

*Comments*. A number of the geometries written during this period were less abstract and technical than the books of the earlier period, which had been largely patterned on Euclid or Legendre or partly on both. Particularly, more exercises and applications were included. It may be that some became so simple that they failed to include all of the basic geometrical principles. Possibly one reason why the Wentworth books became so popular was because he tried to present all the basic principles, but to present them attractively and plainly. Too, fewer geometry books included trigonometry in them than was true before 1850. More keys and manuals made their appearance after 1850. This was true because fewer proofs of the theorems were fully presented, and so some poorly prepared teachers needed help in the proofs.

### E. *Characteristics of Geometry Textbooks*

THUS far our treatment has been to discuss some of the more popular geometries that were used in American schools before 1900. Details of their content were mentioned only in a few instances. Now a more detailed treatment of the actual nature of more books needs to be made. For this treatment the writer will depend heavily on the findings of a study made by Wilson.[5] His study involved an analysis of 61 geometries. Other than the English and French geometries that were reprinted here, all were written and published in America. It is assumed that the imported books that were reprinted in America also were used here. So the findings should reflect what geometric principles and content were studied by American students before 1900.

*Authors.* A dominant number of the authors were professors in some institution of higher learning. Furthermore, nearly all of the authors whose geometries became more or less popular also wrote other books of mathematics, such as texts on arithmetic, algebra, trigonometry, surveying, or navigation. Many of them wrote texts in three or four mathematics fields.

*Aims.* The aims of geometry teaching were definitely stated in 27 of the 61 texts, and implied in 23 others. The general types of aims most often stated were: (1) The disciplinary aim, and (2) acquisition and application of geometric knowledge.

Only three of those who stated aims failed to mention the disciplinary value. Such expressions as "discipline of the mind," "to make good reasoners," "to develop the power of independent thought," "invigorate the mind," and "to train habits of consecutive reasoning," were used in various texts. Thirteen authors were concerned with the acquisition of geometric knowledge, and its application to concrete problems.

Furthermore, 40 authors stated particular purposes for the writing of their books. Some wanted to present Euclid's *Elements* more accurately, while others purposely tried to deviate from Euclid for stated reasons. Others mentioned omitting matters that were already evident, and stressing others. Some wanted to simplify geometry by omitting the more technical matters. The later authors in general favored including more exercises and applications.

*Content.* Many of the geometries written during the first half of the 19th century were rather omnibus in nature. A number even included treatment of surveying and navigation. Wilson's findings in Table IV show the percentage of texts having dealt with the various aspects of geometry by subperiods. An examination of the table reveals that a large percentage of the earlier books included treatment of trigonometry, while only one book did after 1882. On the other hand, practically no attention was given to mensuration, conic sections, and modern geometry before 1838. It was not until the end of last century that separate textbooks appeared in plane geometry. Only four of the 61 texts used the title *Plane Geometry,* and only one of these was published before 1870. On the other hand 37 books used the term "Elements" in the title, which of course usually referred to the *Elements* of Euclid, and thus involved more than plane geometry.

Next, reference should be made to certain details of the geometric content, such as the inclusion of axioms, postulates, theorems, and exercises. Wilson found that more than half of the 61 texts included the following eight axioms:

1 Things which are equal to the same thing are equal to each other.
2 The whole is greater than any of its parts.
3 If equals are subtracted from equals, the remainders are equal.
4 If equals are added to equals, the sums are equal.
5 The whole is equal to the sum of its parts.
6 If equals are added to unequals, the sums are unequal.
7 If equals are subtracted from unequals, the remainders are unequal.
8 Things which are doubles of the same thing, are equal to one another.

Five other axioms were found in more than twenty books.

Only half of the texts before 1864 included postulates, but 29 of the later 36 texts dealt with them. Postulates were defined in several ways, such as, "a postulate is a problem, the method of solving which is obvious," "a postulate is a indemonstrable, practical proposition," or it is "anything that must be taken for granted without proof." The mean number of postulates per book was 2.5.

## TABLE IV: *Percentage of Geometry Textbooks Containing Each of the Divisions of Subject Matter in Given Time Periods*

| PERIOD | NUMBER OF TEXTBOOKS | PLANE GEOMETRY | SOLID GEOMETRY | PLANE TRIGONO-METRY | SPHERICAL TRIGONO-METRY | TRIGONO-METRIC TABLES | MENSURA-TION | CONIC SECTIONS | MODERN GEOMETRY | EUCLID'S DATA |
|---|---|---|---|---|---|---|---|---|---|---|
| 1811–1837 | 12 | 100. | 83.3 | 58.3 | 41.7 | 8.3 | 8.3 | 0.0 | 0.0 | 8.3 |
| 1838–1863 | 13 | 100. | 84.6 | 38.5 | 30.8 | 30.8 | 46.1 | 7.7 | 0.0 | 0.0 |
| 1864–1881 | 18 | 100. | 94.4 | 33.3 | 16.7 | 33.3 | 22.2 | 16.7 | 11.1 | 0.0 |
| 1882–1899 | 18 | 100. | 83.3 | 5.6 | 0.0 | 5.6 | 5.6 | 5.6 | 5.6 | 0.0 |
| 1811–1899 | 61 | 100. | 86.9 | 31.1 | 19.6 | 19.6 | 19.6 | 8.2 | 4.9 | 1.6 |

Wilson found that all 61 books contained theorems, problems, and corollaries. Theorems averaged 105 per book, problems 37.7, and corollaries 69.8 Six of the geometries included 140 or more demonstrated theorems in plane geometry. On the other hand, five presented fewer than 60. Four texts included more than 53 demonstrated problems, while five contained fewer than 20. Five texts included more than 110 corollaries, while six contained fewer than 27. The common belief has been that geometry had been so rigidly standardized that the textbooks varied little through the years. These findings show, however, that this has been far from true about American textbooks before 1900.

The earliest texts, which were often Euclidian in pattern, contained few, if any, exercises. Only three of the texts before 1838 contained any. After 1881 all texts contained some. In order of frequency the following types of exercises were most commonly used: Geometric construction, geometric demonstrations required, numerical exercises in mathematical terminology, and numerical exercises in nonmathematical terminology. Since neither Euclid's nor Legendre's *Elements* contained exercises, it is evident that the inclusion of exercises was an American development. It has been an American trait to apply truths and principles to concrete situations. This has been true of American textbooks both in algebra and geometry.

*Answers.* Twenty-three of the 41 texts containing numerical exercises included some answers, of these, 14 included answers for all numerical exercises. Most of the later books did not include answers for all exercises. However, a number of authors published separate manuals for teacher use only. These would deal both with the process of solution and the answer.

*Final comments.* Through the years certain changes in the nature of geometry texts were made. Among these changes were the increase of student exercises, a decrease in the fully demonstrated propositions, and an improvement in the teachability of the books. Later books more commonly contained tables of contents, suggestions to teachers, indexes, reviews, and summaries. Although the earlier books were bound in leather, their contents and figures were not as attractive and appealing as in the later ones. The earlier authors were very conscious of including the traditional Euclidian content, the later authors were more conscious of the learning processes of the students.

[1]  Lao Genevra Simons, *Bibliography of Early American Textbooks on Algebra*. New York: Yeshiva College, 1936.

[2]  Angie Turner King, "An Analysis of Early Algebra Textbooks Used in American Schools Before 1900." (Unpublished Ph.D. dissertation, University of Pittsburgh, 1955.)

[3]  Elmer Ellsworth Brown, *The Making of Our Middle Schools*. N.Y.: Longmans, Green & Co., 1914.

[4]  The writer consulted Louis C. Karpinski's *Bibliography of Mathematical Works Printed in America Through 1850* for the listing of some of these books.

[5]  John D. Wilson, "An Analysis of Plane Geometry Content of Geometry Textbooks Published in the United States Before 1900." (Unpublished Doctor of Education thesis, University of Pittsburgh, 1959).

CHAPTER THREE

# The Sciences

ALTHOUGH many aspects of science were discovered and developed in early times, the teaching of science in secondary schools was very tardy in its appearance. It is true that astronomy was included in the *quadrivium* of the Seven Liberal Arts, its teaching was mainly only in the universities. The Latin Grammar school, the earliest type of secondary school in America, did not include science in its curriculum.

The earliest teaching of science in American secondary schools was in the early academies. When high schools made their appearance they also taught the sciences. The science subjects that gradually found their place in these secondary schools were natural philosophy (physics), chemistry, astronomy, natural history (zoology), botany, geology, and physiology. Eventually astronomy and geology ceased to be popular in secondary schools. The old physiology textbooks have been rather fully discussed in my other volume, *Old Textbooks* (Chapter 9). So only the old textbooks in the fields of chemistry, physics, zoology, and botany will receive treatment in this volume. Soon after 1900 the content of zoology, botany, and often some physiology was absorbed in biology textbooks.

SECTION ONE

## NATURAL HISTORY (ZOOLOGY)

### Introduction

*Evolution of natural history.* From time immemorial man must have been conscious of the presence of various forms of animal life. However, there is little evidence that any systematic study of it was made before Aristotle (384–322

B.C.) began doing so. By keen observation and generalization he arrived at a system of classification, which he presented in his *History of Animals*. This continued to be a source of reference for many centuries. Although some of his generalizations have been proven false, others have withstood the test of time. He has been referred to as the "Father of Zoology."

The only Roman to have done much in this field was Pliny (A.D. 23–79). He wrote a *Natural History*, which dealt with some elements of physics, astronomy, geography, and meteorology, as well as natural history. His work was chiefly one of compilation from other sources, rather than making any marked original contribution to the field.

Claudius Galen (A.D. 131–201), a leading Greek physician, examined the bodies of monkeys, so that he could gain a better understanding of the human anatomy. His writings were studied for centuries in the medieval universities. Little original work in the field of natural history was done during the Dark Ages.

Discoveries made during the Renaissance, particularly geographical discoveries, began to exert an impulse for the study of natural history. One of the first to rebel against the science of the Dark Ages was Andreas Vesalius, when he was only 28, in publishing his *Structure of the Human Body* in 1542. Soon thereafter Konrad von Gesner, a Swiss, made extensive collections of animals and plants and published his great *History of Animals*, in which he attempted to describe all the animals then known.

Later John Ray (1627?–1705) began his great work. He was a famous English naturalist, and has been even referred to as the "Father of English Natural History." He established some of the foundations of modern zoology. In his *Synopsis* (1693) he attempted to classify animals according to structure. He was the first to define the use of the word "species."

Carolus Linnaeus (1707–1778), a Swedish botanist and naturalist, attempted to end the confusion among naturalists regarding the names of plants and animals. Recognizing the need for classifying groups higher than species, he defined six classes of animals: (1) Mammalia, (2) Aves, (3) Amphibia, (4) Pisces, (5) Insecta, and (6) Vermes.

Another contributor to the field was G. L. Buffon (1707–1788), a French naturalist. His particular contribution lay in description. His *Natural History* was a popular and interesting account of the animal kingdom. He was one of the pioneers in the study of modern evolution. Georges Cuvier (1769–1832) was another French naturalist to contribute to the development of this field.

Although zoological data had been accumulated, and more or less systematized before his time, yet they had not been arranged according to law. His study led him to generalize that the most comprehensive groups of animals were based on different designs of structure. He then classified the animal kingdom into four groups: Vertebrata, Mullusca, Articula, and Radiata. Among his works were: *An Elementary Table of Animals, Lessons in Anatomy,* and *the Animal Kingdom.*

Others who have made contributions to the field were C. Lamarck (1744–1829), who formulated his "transmutations of species through accumulated and inherited use"; Louis Agassiz (1807–1873), whose researches were extensive, particularly relating to fossil fish; Charles Darwin (1809–1882), whose *The Origin of Species by Means of Natural Selection* (1859) worked a virtual revolution in biological science; Herbert Spencer (1820–1902), philosopher and scientist, whose writings helped support and clarify the principles of evolution; and Thomas Huxley (1825–1895), who travelled widely to gather additional data in this field. Thus it can be seen that it took many centuries and scientific investigators to establish natural history (zoology) as a systematic field of science.

*Zoology in American secondary schools.* Science was not taught in the early American Latin Grammar schools. However, when Benjamin Franklin was instrumental in the founding of America's first academy, in 1851 in Philadelphia, he proposed a program of studies to be followed, among which were to be readings in natural history, agriculture, and horticulture. It is not certain now how many other academies introduced the study of natural history before 1800, but many did soon thereafter. Wesleyan Academy, Massachusetts, definitely did so in 1818. Even some girls' schools followed suit. Abbot Academy, at Andover, Massachusetts, a school for girls, introduced Smellie's *Philosophy of Natural History* as a text in 1829. Mount Holyoke Seminary for girls introduced natural history in 1837. Other academies and seminaries followed.

When America's first high school was opened in Boston in 1821, natural history was listed among the subjects that were offered. Although natural history did not become as popular in the high schools as natural philosophy (physics) and physiology, nevertheless, according to Stout's study of midwestern high schools during the latter half of the 19th century, about half of the high schools taught either natural history or zoology.

Ultimately after 1900 the separate fields of zoology, botany, and physiology began to be combined into the single field of biology, at least in the high schools of the U.S. The change took place very rapidly between 1915 and 1925. E.R. Downing found that out of 128 schools studied in 1915, not one offered biology. On the other hand, G. W. Hunter found that out of 357 schools studied in 1923 only 1.8 per cent offered zoology. Very few high schools today offer zoology.

## A. *European Written Natural History (Zoology) Textbooks*

As was true of the textbooks in other fields of science, the earliest texts in natural history were also first written in Europe and later republished here, often with certain revisions by an American editor. Just which ones were used in the early academies is now uncertain, except in certain instances.

*William Smellie.* One of the first natural history textbooks to be reprinted here was written by Smellie, member of Antiquarian and Royal Societies of Edinburgh. It was *The Philosophy of Natural Science* republished in Philadelphia in 1791. Its 490 pages meant that it was larger than most early secondary school texts, so it may not have been used in academies, unless possibly in the so-called Franklin Academy in Philadelphia. It was again reprinted here in 1808.

In 1824 John Ware, M.D. edited, revised, reduced, and republished the Smellie textbook. It was reduced to slightly over 300 pages. More than 80 pages were devoted to such introductory matters as the nature of living bodies and their structure. The remainder of the book dealt with such characteristics of animals as their respiration, motions, instinct, senses, food, growth, habitation, hostilities, artifices, society, docility, torpidity, and longevity. No pictures were included. In the back there appeared an analytical table of contents of nine pages, and five pages of explanations of scientific terms. The 1834 edition was the fifth. In 1835 it was recopyrighted without any changes of content, but the size of the pages reduced, 30 pages of questions were added in the back, and was bound in leather. It was reprinted many times even through the 1850's. It is known that some of these editions were used in academies and female seminaries.

In 1860 Ware rather radically revised and enlarged Smellie's text. It was enlarged by more than a hundred pages, and many pictures added. Chapters particularly dealing with the classification of animals, mollusca, articulata, and radiata were added. It also appeared in later editions. Smellie's texts apparently were among the more widely used reprinted natural histories.

*Dr. I. G. Burkhard.* In 1804 there was published in New York Burkhard's

## ORDER 3.  BIVALVA.

*Soft animals, having shells with two valves.*

Mya, (pearl-muscle, gaper,) animal an ascidia; shell bivalve, generally gaping at one end ; hinge with broad thick strong teeth, seldom more than one, and not inserted into the opposite valve.

Solen, (razor sheath,) animal an ascidia; shell bivalve, oblong, open at both ends ; hinge with a subulate reflected tooth, often double, and not inserted in the opposite valve.

Tellina, animal a tethys ; shell bivalve, generally sloping on one side ; in the forepart of one valve a convex, of the other a concave, fold ; hinge usually three teeth, the lateral ones smooth in one shell.

Cardium, (cockle,) animal a tethys ; shell bivalve, nearly equilateral, equivalve, generally convex ; longitudinally ribbed, striate or grooved, with a toothed margin ; hinge with two alternate teeth near the beak in the middle, and a larger remote lateral one each side, each locking into the opposite.

Mactra, animal a tethys ; shell bivalve, unequal sided, equivalve ; middle tooth of the hinge complicated, with a small hollow each side, lateral ones remote and inserted into each other.

Donax, animal a tethys ; shell bivalve, with generally a crenulate margin, the frontal or anterior margin very obtuse ; hinge with two teeth, and a single marginal one placed a little behind, which is rarely double, triple or none.

Venus, (common clam,) animal a tethys ; shell bivalve, the frontal margin flattened with incum-

9  A page from Amos Eaton's *Zoological Text-Book*, 1826

*Elementary or Fundamental Principles of the Philosophy of Natural History*, translated from the German by Charles Smith. This was a small leather bound book of 251 pages of text. Its contents were similar to Smellie's, but more briefly treated. In fact, acknowledgment was made of its debt to Smellie. The president of the Society of Associated Teachers of New York highly recommended it for "the instruction of Youth."

*Goldsmith.* Also in 1804 Goldsmith's *Natural History* was reprinted in Philadelphia. This book must have appeared in numerous editions here, for Mrs. Pilkington's *Goldsmith's Natural History* published here in 1823, abridged for "use in schools," was the tenth American edition. The contents were presented in 18 brief chapters dealing with animals, nine with birds, and 15 with fishes, in all covering 331 pages. The 1835 reprint, which was 15th edition, contained identical content but had 80 additional pages. This enlargement was largely due to the addition of many pictures. Each chapter descriptively dealt with a particular type of animal, fish, or bird. For example, Chapter III dealt with ruminating animals—the cow, urus, bison, buffalo, and zebu. The fact that this book appeared in so many editions is evidence that it attained considerable circulation.

*Amos Eaton.* In 1826 Eaton published a *Zoological Text-Book*, "comprising Cuvier's Four Grand Divisinos of Animals; also, Shaw's Improved Linnean Genera, Arranged According to the Classes and Orders of Cuvier and Latreille, for "students exercises." This book was primarily prepared for Rensselaer School and the "popular class-room." It was a beautifully bound book of 282 pages of text. The text began with the following definition: "Zoology is the science which treats of material organized beings, which are endowed with sentient principle." It was organized in entirely different manner than the texts by Smellie and Burkhard. It really catalogued and briefly described hundreds of animals in alphabetical order with an identification of each by Class and Order. The four grand divisions were: Radiated, molluscuous, articulated, and vertebral animals. In turn, the vertebral animals were distributed into the four following classes: Mammalia, aves, amphibia, and pisces; the articulated into annelida, crustacea, arachnida, and insecta; the molluscuous into mollusca; and the radiated into echinoderma, intestina, acalepha, polypi, and infusoria. Then the classes were further divided into from two to twelve orders. While the outside of the book looked attractive, its contents looked very forbidding and overly technical.

*J. Frost* (Editor). In 1836 *The Class Book of Nature*, "comprising Lessons on the Universe, the Three Kingdoms of Nature, and the Form and Structure of the Human Body," was published. Originally it was published as one of a series of school books by the Committee of General Literature and Education. Later it was revised and enlarged for use in schools in this country. About two-thirds of the content dealt with animals and man. It contained many pictures and questions at the end of each chapter.

*W. S. W. Ruschenberger, M.D.* In the 1840's a series of eight books was published by Ruschenberger entitled, *First Books of Natural History*, for "Schools and Colleges." Five of these dealt with subjects commonly covered in natural history textbooks; namely, *Elements of Mammalogy, Elements of Ornithology, Elements of Herpetology and Ichthyology, Elements of Conchology*, and *Elements of Entomology*. One of these contained ten pages in very fine print of "Recommendatory Notices." These consisted mainly of recommendations by doctors, reviewers of journals, and four U.S. senators. One statement mentioned that one of the books was used in the public schools of Pennyslvania.

These were well organized and attractive books varying in size from 120 to 150 pages. The paragraphs were numbered, questions appeared at the bottom of the pages, numerous pictures were included, and good glossaries presented in the back. These features indicate that they were meant for classroom use. Mention should be made that the contents were largely borrowed from a text written by Milne Edwards and Achille Comte, Professors in the Colleges of Henri IV and Charlemagne.

*D. M. Reese, M.D.* (Editor). In 1849 Reese, a former Superintendent of Schools of New York City, published the *Elements of Zoology, or Natural History of Animals*. This book apparently was a revision of a book written by Professor Grant of London, who in turn had borrowed heavily from Cuvier of France. This was a book of more than 500 pages, which dealt with mammalia, birds, reptiles, amphibia, fishes, insects, mollusca, radiata, and some lesser classes. Reese stated that explanations and analytical questions have been added to "facilitate the use of the book in schools." It appeared in several editions.

*Comments.* The discussion of the above mentioned books indicates clearly that in the field of natural history (zoology) American schools depended heavily upon republished European texts until about 1850. This was a more extended dependence than in most fields. It was noted that originally the texts were written by authors of England, France, and Germany. However, American editors usually made certain revisions to make them more suitable for school use. Likely there were other texts reprinted here not known to the writer.

### B. *American Written Zoology Textbooks Before 1870*

ONE likely reason why American authors did not write zoology textbooks as early as was true in the fields of chemistry and natural philosophy was because zoology did not become as popular as a school subject. It did not have the *practical* appeal of the other two.

*A. Ackerman.* One of the first zoology texts written here was the *First Book of Natural History* by Ackerman in 1846. He regretted that a study of this field had been neglected. A reason given was that the "works on this subject for schools. . . are either so childish as to be disgusting to the *child,* or so abstrusely metaphysical as to be beyond the comprehension of the pupil." These extremes he attempted to avoid. The book consisted of 286 pages. The material was presented in 81 brief chapters, each dealing with a particular creature or topic. Interesting pictures and questions enliven the book. Likely to increase its sale at lower cost, it was mechanically rather cheaply printed. It appeared in at least seven editions.

*Louis Agassiz (1807–1873) and A. A. Gould.* Agassiz was born in Switzerland, and studied in Zurich, Heidelberg, Erlangen, and Munich. He often visited Paris and England to meet other scientists. From 1832 to 1846 he taught at Neuchatel. While there he carried on researches and published about fossil fishes. He also studied and wrote about glaciers. In 1846 he came to America to lecture at Lowell Institute, Boston. Then in 1848 he became Professor of Natural History in the Lawrence Scientific School of Harvard, where he remained until his death, except when he was away doing research elsewhere.

In 1848 Agassiz and Gould published their *Principles of Zoology,* "touching the structure, development, distribution, and natural arrangement of the races of animals, living and extinct." Since the book was intended for American students, the illustrations were drawn mostly from American objects. Most of these were portraits from original drawings. The book aimed to furnish "an epitome of the leading principles of the science of zoology, as deduced from the present state of knowledge, so illustrated as to be intelligible to the beginner." They claimed that no such treatise existed in the country. New stress was given to embryology and metamorphosis. The chapters dealt with the general properties of organized bodies, functions and organs of animal life, intelligence and instinct, nutrition, blood and circulation, respiration, secretions, embryology, peculiar modes of reproduction, metamorphoses of animals, and geological succession of animals. It is clear that this book was not a copy of other zoology textbooks. However, it contained fewer than 250 pages. It was slightly revised in 1851, and reprinted often thereafter. In 1863 Agassiz published the *Methods of Study of Natural History*. He was also the author of two series of published lectures on natural history.

*Worthington Hooker, M.D.* Hooker, who was a professor at Yale, wrote textbooks in chemistry, natural philosophy, geology, natural history, and a *Child's Book of Nature*. In 1860 he published his *Natural History*, for use of "schools and families." He bemoaned the fact that zoology was not more commonly taught in schools. He acknowledged that there were some good books an zoology, but "none are properly adapted to instruction in schools. Some were too popular in character, others too scientific." Thus with this book Hooker attempted to avoid these objections. He even argued for the practical value of zoology, as relating to the "extensive occupations of man, agriculture, horticulture, etc." The book contained more than 300 engravings and 374 pages. The book dealt with quadrupeds, birds, reptiles, fishes, insects, arachnida, crustaceans, mollusks, and radiates. It continued to appear without change even into the 1880's.

*Sanborn Tenney*, Tenney, who was a professor at Williams College, in 1865 published *A Manual of Zoology*, for "schools, colleges, and the general reader." This was a rather large book of more than 500 pages, illustrated with over 500 engravings. Since it was rather large it is not now certain whether it was more commonly used in secondary schools or colleges. It evidently became rather popular, for in 1869 the 8th edition was printed. Later editions appeared in the 1870's. The body of the text dealt with vertebrates, articulates, mollusks, and radiates.

Tenney apparently believed that zoology should be taught for more than one year in the schools, so in 1866 he together with Abby A. Tenney published a *Natural History of Animals*, which contained only half as many pages as the *Manual*, and which was intended for grammar schools. It largely contained the same engravings as the larger work. Since such a large fraction of the space was taken up by the 500 engravings, it evidently appealed to the younger youth. It continued to appear at least to 1875.

In 1875 Sanborn Tenney alone published the *Elements of Zoology*. This was a revision and refinement of the *Manual*. It contained 503 pages and was illustrated with 750 engravings. Tenney was very professional in acknowledging free use of the writings of other zoologists, and listed the source of each engraving. It is evident that Tenney's textbooks must have influenced the teaching of zoology in American schools during the 1860's and 1870's.

*Other zoologies before 1870.* A number of other texts in natural history or zoology were published before 1870. Some of these were very large and evidently intended chiefly for colleges, and others were very small and likely intended for grammar schools. Among the larger texts was J. G. Wood's *The Illustrated Natural History* (1854). Other books were: Charles Brooks' *Natural History*, (1846), Philip H. Gosse's *The Romance of Natural History* (1860), Chambers' *Elements of Zoology*, W. B. Carpenter's *Zoology*, and *The Reason Why Natural History*, which was a book of 372 pages written in catechetical form. Likely there were others.

*Comments.* Apparently the writers of the earlier American natural histories lacked the confidence to write fully on their own, for nearly all of them listed many European writers to whom acknowledgments were made. However, most of the American authors tended to make their books more attractive and teachable. There was a gradual shift in titles from natural history to zoology.

## C. *Zoology Textbooks, 1870–1900*

APPARENTLY zoology became a little more popular after 1870, for many more books were written during this period. However, only a few apparently attained wide acceptance.

*J. Dorman Steele* (1836–1886). The most popular zoology textbook written during this period was Steele's *Fourteen Weeks of Zoology* in 1872. This was merely one book of the Fourteen Weeks' Courses in Natural Science by Steele. The Series consisted of science textbooks in the fields of natural philosophy, chemistry, astronomy, geology, physiology, botany, and zoology. Most of these had wide circulation. He had mastered the technique of writing attractive and teachable textbooks. Among the mentioned features of this book were: "Brevity; directness of statement; . . .frequent footnotes, containing anecdotes, curious facts, explanations, etc.; a uniform system of analysis in bold paragraph titles; and a gradual introduction of scientific terms and language." The book consisted of 277 pages of text, 20 pages of a Systematic Arrangement of the Representative Forms, and eleven pages in very fine print of a Glossarial, Explanative, and Referential Index. The book was amply illustrated with 470 pictures.

The contents consisted of 14 pages of introduction; then 188 pages were devoted to the vertebrate animals, which were the mammals, birds, reptiles, amphibians, and fishes; and lastly, the treatment of the invertebrates in 75 pages, which included the articulates, molluscans, echinoderms, coelenter-ates, and protozoans. Each animal was briefly but clearly described, and most of them illustrated with a picture. Many interesting anecdotes were told in footnotes.

In 1876 the book was recopyrighted, but without change. In 1887, after Steele's decease, the book was revised by J. W. P. Jenks. It was printed in types, and on larger pages. The order of treatment was reversed by dealing first with the invertebrates and next with the vertebrates. Otherwise most of the features originally used by Steele were retained, but its title was changed to *A Popular Zoology*. This book in turn was recopyrighted and enlarged to 355 pages in 1895. The body of the text was not changed, but a new section "Helps to Laboratory Work," of 38 pages was added. Thus laboratory work was introduced in zoology, althought the earlier editions provided directions for collecting and preserving specimens. These books constituted further evidence of Steele's success as a textbook wirter.

*Edward S. Morse.* In 1875 Morse published a *First Book of Zoology*. This was a small book of less than 200 pages, but apparently designed for secondary schools, for it placed great stress on collecting and studying specimens. Strangely Morse paid particular attention to the lower animals "more often neglected in textbooks." The figures were largely drawn from nature by the author. While most zoology textbooks dealt extensively with the vertebrates, Morse used only two of his 24 chapters for them. Sixteen pages in the back of the book advertised other textbooks by the publishing house.

*James Orton.* In 1876 Orton's *Comparative Zoology, Structural and Systematic* was published. This was a well planned and organized book. Some of its fea-tures were to treat the whole animal kingdom as a unit, to make a "com-parative study of the development and variations of organs and their func-tions," and to withhold the systematic treatment of zoology until after a study of the structural affiinities. More than two-thirds of the book dealt with struc-tural zoology, which was followed in Part II with Systematic Zoology. In the back there appeared a Systematic Arrangement of Representative Forms; Notes, which were amplifications to matters referred to in the text; the Naturalist's Library; and the Index. In all the book contained more than 400 pages. The author claimed that it was fitted for high schools and mixed schools. After Orton's decease it was slightly revised by Edward A. Birge. It appeared in a number of editions.

*A. S. Packard.* Packard was Professor of Zoology at Brown University, and

Editor of the *American Naturalist*. He wrote numerous books in this field. In 1883 he produced his *Zoology*. This was intended for grammar and high schools. Its 338 pages were less than half the size of his *Advanced Zoology*. He suggested that no study of zoology "should depend on a book alone, but specimens should be in constant use." The textbook was rather to be a reference book. In fact, he favored that each member of the class examine and dissect a fish according to given directions before studying the book. Laboratory lessons were to be held once or twice a week. The book began with protozoa, and then continued by treating porifera, coelenterata, echinodermata, vermes, mollusca, arthropoda, and finally in the last half of the book vertebrata. The book contained 334 figures and a glossary. In 1886 the third revised edition was published.

In 1886 Packard produced an even smaller text of 290 pages entitled, *First Lessons in Zoology*. Apparently some users of the previous book considered it a little too technical, so in this book he dealt with fewer examples or types, used fewer technical terms and names, and aimed to provide an elementary guide to the "principles of Biology." It was well organized and attractively printed. Its fifth edition appeared in 1892.

*C. F. Holder* and *J. B. Holder*. In 1883 the *Elements of Zoology* by these authors was published. This was a book of nearly 400 pages, containing 383 figures. The arrangement of the topics was similar to Packard's *Zoology*, by beginning with protozoa and ending with the vertebrata. They attempted to avoid being highly technical, in saying, "technical terms have only been employed where there was no simple equivalent." Long tables of classification, so commonly used in some other texts, were omitted. It was a well-bound book, and appeared in a number of editions.

*Buel P. Colton*. Colton, who taught in the Illinois State Normal University, stated that in the "absence of any handbook of zoology adapted to the grade of work in which he was engaged," he began to prepare "simple guides" to the study of a few common animals. After repeated tests in the class-room he decided to put these guides into book form. So in 1886 *An Elementary Course in Practical Zoology* was published. This was a small book containing fewer than 200 pages and no pictures. It dealt mainly with what we commonly call bugs, worms, snakes, fish, and other forms of sea life. No treatment was given to the larger vertebrates. One edition appeared as late as 1898.

In 1903 Colton wrote a *Zoology, Descriptive and Practical Part I, Descriptive*. This was twice as large as his earlier book and contained 201 figures. It covered the full array of animal life generally dealt with in other zoology books. It was well bound and attractively printed.

*Margaretta Burnet*. She was a teacher of zoology in Woodward High School, Cincinnati. Her experience convinced her that in the average high school little was being done in providing proper laboratory facilities for zoology as suggested in most books. So she proceeded to write a book suitable for such schools and academies. In 1895 her *Zoology* was produced by a mid-west publishing house. This was an attractive book of over 200 pages illustrated with 197 figures. The topics and their order were similar to those in Packard's text, but more briefly and simply treated.

*J. S. Kingsley*. In 1897 Kingsley's *Elements of Comparative Zoology* was published. Although the book contained only 344 pages of text, which was the size of many secondary school zoology textbooks, yet it is not certain whether it was primarily for high schools or colleges. He merely stated it to be an introduction to the "serious study of zoology." Its treatment was rather technical. Considerable space of the book was used to explain the laboratory work. So if it was used in high schools likely it would have been only in those with well equipped laboratories. Directions were given for dissecting many forms of lower animal life. A later edition appeared in 1899.

*Other zoology textbooks, 1870–1900.* Many other zoology textbooks were written during this period, but these were not all suitable for secondary school use. Some were too elementary and others too advanced. However, it may be well to list some additional texts. Among them were: Adrian J. Ebell's *Natural History* (1870), Robert Patterson's *Introduction to Zoology* (1872), W. H. G. Kingston's *Stories of Animal Sagacity* (1874), David Starr Jordan's *Manual of the Vertebrates of Northern U.S.* (1876), Selim H. Peabody's *Cecil's Books of Natural History* (1879), Henry Nicholson's *Textbook of Zoology* (1885), and *A Manual of Zoology* (1893), C. De Montmabou and H. Beauregard's *A Course on Zoology* (1893), James G. Needham's *Elementary Lessons in Zoology* (1895), and J. Arthur Thomson's *Outlines of Zoology* (1899). Likely there were many others.

### D. *Characteristics of Zoology Textbooks*

*Some general characteristics*. One interesting feature of these books was their evolutionary change of titles. The earlier texts all bore the title of natural history. Of the books here discussed only Agassiz's (1848) used the title of zoology before 1870. However, Eaton used the term zoology in the textual definitions in 1826. After 1870 most texts used the title of zoology. Then in the

1890's a few books bearing the title of biology appeared. In 1890 T. J. Parker, New Zealand, published *Lessons in Elementary Biology*, which later was reprinted here. Also in the 1890's W. T. Sedgwick and E. B. Wilson published their *General Biology* of 231 pages. However, many texts in this field continued to appear as zoologies until the 1920's. Thereafter the term biology became common for texts in secondary schools.

Texts in natural history fully authored by American writers were later in appearing than in natural philosophy and chemistry. Most zoology texts until 1850 were reprints of European books. Since the study of natural history was not considered as practical as the other two fields, it did not become as popular as a school subject. Even after 1850 only about half of the high schools taught zoology. Even when American authors began to write zoology books, they commonly listed foreign texts from which they borrowed heavily. Likely this was done not so much to be honestly professional, but rather to lend authority to the contents of their books.

Since the schools of all levels were not standardized as is true of schools today, due to the lack accrediting agencies, authors rarely recommended definitely for what level or type of school for which the text was written. Likewise courses such as zoology would not be given the same way in all seocndary schools. One school may give it in one of the lower years, another in the upper years. One may give it only for a semester, another for a year. One may give it only two or three days per week, another every day. Hence authors in order to sell more books would say for "schools and academies," for "schools and colleges," etc. These conditions made it difficult for the writer to determine accurately just which books were used in secondary schools.

*Aims.* According to an analysis of 57 zoology texts made by Casile[1] 161 statements of aims were found in these books. In some of the earliest books the religious aims was dominant. Even Agassiz aimed "to produce more enlarged ideas of man's relation to Nature and more exalted conceptions of the Plan of Creation and its Great Author." However, many other aims were given attention. In summary, it was found that the religious aim was mentioned by nine authors; the acquisition of knowledge, 30; arousal of interest in animal life and nature, 16; cultural and intellectual development, five; scientific thinking and observing, three and so on with fewer mentioned aims.

*Content.* Table V shows the categories that were treated in the books, the number of books that dealt with each category, and the average percentage of space devoted to them by periods. It will be seen that six of the categories

TABLE V: *Number of Zoology Books Treating and Percentage of Space Devoted to the Various Categories by Periods*

| | PERIODS | | | | | | | | | |
|---|---|---|---|---|---|---|---|---|---|---|
| | 1812–1869 | | 1870–1885 | | 1886–1899 | | 1900–1920 | | | |
| TOPICS | 1 | | 2 | | 3 | | 4 | | | |
| | * | ** | * | ** | * | ** | * | ** | * | ** |
| 1 Nature of Living Things | 3 | 1 | 2 | 1 | 0 | 0 | 4 | 1 | 9 | 1 |
| 2 General Animal Classification | 6 | 1 | 4 | 1 | 1 | 1 | 5 | 1 | 16 | 1 |
| 3 Geographical Distribution and Succession of Animals | 3 | 1 | 1 | 1 | 2 | 1 | 8 | 1 | 14 | 2 |
| 4 Animal Functions & Structure | 5 | 7 | 2 | 7 | 4 | 6 | 8 | 4 | 19 | 4 |
| 5 Animal Habits & Characteristics | 3 | 8 | 1 | 1 | 2 | 1 | 7 | 4 | 13 | 3 |
| 6 Protozoa | 4 | 1 | 9 | 4 | 11 | 4 | 19 | 4 | 43 | 3 |
| 7 Porifera | 2 | 1 | 6 | 1 | 8 | 4 | 16 | 2 | 32 | 1 |
| 8 Coelenterata | 6 | 2 | 9 | 9 | 10 | 5 | 17 | 3 | 42 | 4 |
| 9 Echinodermata | 9 | 1 | 8 | 4 | 11 | 6 | 17 | 4 | 45 | 3 |
| 10 Vermes | 9 | 1 | 9 | 7 | 9 | 4 | 17 | 7 | 44 | 6 |
| 11 Mollusca | 10 | 6 | 11 | 11 | 11 | 7 | 18 | 6 | 50 | 6 |
| 12 Anthropoda | 11 | 15 | 11 | 21 | 11 | 18 | 19 | 27 | 52 | 21 |
| 13 Tunicata | 2 | 1 | 6 | 1 | 4 | 1 | 9 | 1 | 21 | 1 |
| 14 Vertebrata | 14 | 52 | 11 | 31 | 11 | 45 | 19 | 36 | 55 | 44 |
| Number of Books Analyzed | 51 | | 11 | | 11 | | 20 | | 57 | |

*Number of books treating the categories
**Percentage of space devoted to the categories

received attention in fewer than half of the books. On the other hand, seven categories were covered in three-fourths of the texts, but no topic was treated by all. Vertebrata was treated by 55 books, anthropoda by 52, and mollusca by 50. The percentage of space devoted to the habits and characteristics of animals declined after the first period, while that of vermes increased greatly. The number of books dealing with protozoa, porifera, tunicata, greatly increased. However, it can be seen that the books became more or less standardized in dealing with protozoa, porifera, coelenterata, echinodermata, vermes, mollusca, anthorpoda, and vertebrata.

*Illustrations or pictures.* Casile found that five of the oldest six books he analyzed contained no pictures. However, only two of the next 51 books contained none. In all, the books averaged 233 pictures per book. The fifty books containing pictures averaged 265 per book. Two books included 590 each. The nature of the placement and size of the pictures in the books varied greatly. The average size of the pictures ranged from. 85 × . 98 to 4.40 × 4.56 in. No books published before 1900 contained colored pictures. These data show that the authors of zoology textbooks saw the need of using visual aids amply.

*Laboratory work.* Attention to laboratory work was much slower to appear than was true in physics and chemistry. One of the first authors to approach it was Morse in 1875, when he placed stress on collecting and studying specimens. In 1883 Packard mentioned that the textbook should be mainly a reference book, while specimens should be in constant use. The 1895 edition of Steele's text included a section entitled, "Helps to Laboratory Work." However, even some of the late books largely ignored the need for laboratory work.

*Concluding comment.* An analysis of old zoology textbooks has shown that many evolutionary changes took place between the earliest texts and those of 1900. These changes were in the titles of the books, the content, the nature of the learning aids, the clearness of organization and presentation, and the ultimate attention to laboratory work.

## SECTION TWO

# BOTANY

### Introduction

MAN has always been interested in plants. However, in primitive times man's chief interest in the value of plants was for food and medicine. One of Aristotle's pupils, Theophrastus, about 300 B.C., made a serious attempt to describe and classify plants in The *Enquiry into Plants.* He had accompanied the army of Alexander the Great to increase his knowledge of plants. About 50 A.D. Dioscorides, a Greek botanist and a physician for a Roman army, described some 400 medicinal plants in his *Materia Medica.* His contemporary, Pliny the Elder, a Roman, described about 1000 plants, many of which were of reputed medicinal value. Subsequently numerous *Herbals* appeared, large books containing descriptions of plants, often particularly stressing the medicinal virtue of certain plants. Most of these *Herbals* contributed very little scientific knowledge to the field. Only the writings of Theopharastus, Dioscorides, and Pliny were really acceptable botanical works before the 16th century.

Andreas Cesalpino (1519–1603), an Italian botanist and physician, in his

*De Plantis* (1583), attempted a classification of plants based on their similarities and dissimilarities of form. He claimed that the medicinal qualities of certain plants were merely accidents. He divided plants into trees, shrubs, and herbs. Similarities of fructification were given attention. The 1520 then-known plants were divided into 15 classes.

In 1698 John Ray in England published his *Historia Generalis Plantarum*, in which a more natural classification was made. He divided the lower groups into algae, fungi, mosses, ferns, and equisetums, and the higher or seed-bearing plants into dicotyledons and monocotyledons based on the number of leaves in the embryo. In 1698 Tournefort described about 8000 species of plants, dividing them into 22 classes largely based on their corolla (colored parts of flowers). In 1694 sex in plants was proven experimentally by R. J. Camerarias in Germany. In 1719 a description of an experimentally produced hybrid was made by Bradley. It was the result of crossing a carnation and a sweet william. Since then hybridization has been highly developed.

One of the greatest contributions to scientific botany was made by Linnaeus (1707–1778), a Swedish botanist, who was the first to make extensive use of the binomial nomenclature of plants. In this system the first name refers to the genus and the second to the species. Two of his famous works were: *Systema Naturae* (1737), and the *Species Plantarum* (1753). He has been referred to as the founder of modern taxonomy (plant classification). This system is still considerably followed.

Several French botanists, however, refused to follow the system of Linnaeus. Among them were Laurent de Jussieu, who sought a more natural system; and Pyramus de Candolle, who held that morphology (form and structure) should be the basis for the classification of plants. Revised systems were proposed by George Bentham and Joseph Hooker in their *Genera Plantarum* (1862–1883); and by Adolf Engler in *Die Natürlichen Pflanzenfamilien* (1892). The Englerian system has been considerably followed in many countries. Most of the more recent contributions to scientific botany have been in relation to the more specialized divisions of botany.

*Botanic Gardens.* It seems that before botany became a regular school subject, except in certain medical schools, where they studied plants for their medicinal value, the most extensive cultivation and study of plants was in botanic gardens. Pliny (23–79 A.D.) mentioned one existing in Rome. Some early apothecaries cultivated "physick gardens." Later such gardens took on a more public nature. One of these was the Jardin des Plants, Paris (1610), where public lectures were given on Sunday afternoons on botanical subjects. In 1638 one was founded in Tokyo, which later became the garden of the Imperial University. Many were founded in Germany. Others were in Chelsea, England (1673), Philadelphia 1728, Edinburgh (1763), Harvard (1805), Buitenzorg, Java (1817), and St. Louis, Missouri (1859). Eventually there were hundreds.

The programs and purposes naturally varied, but their educational work often consisted of: (1) Providing information of well labeled specimens; (2) offering popular lectures about plants; (3) carrying on research; (4) publishing periodicals; and (5) offering organized courses and lectures.

## A. *Early Books on Botany*

APPARENTLY more books on botany were written before 1800 than was true in the fields of natural philosophy, chemistry, and zoology. However, these were not all used in schools as textbooks. In fact, the schools in which botany was most commonly taught at first were the medical colleges, due to the attention given to the medicinal values of certain plants. Many of the earlier books merely dealt with the flora of particular areas. In nearly every European country books were published dealing with the flora of their various geographical regions. Evidently the work done in the many botanical gardens greatly stimulated the study of plants. Some of these books were of a highly technical nature, while others were popular in treatment, evidently partly due to the developed interests in the various forms of plant life. Apparently very few of these books before 1800 were republished in America, but some were brought here. The writer's collection contains a number of them obtained here.

*D. C. Willdenow.* One of the enlightening books of this group was *The Principles of Botany and of Vegetable Physiology* by D. C. Willdenow, a Professor of Botany at Berlin, which book was translated into English and published in Edinburgh in 1811. Forty five pages of the book dealt with the "History of the Science." He divided the history into eight epochs. The Eighth Epoch covered the years 1782 to 1805. In it he discussed the botanical contributions of 30 writers from Germany, Sweden, France, Spain, Switzerland, England, Portugal, Denmark, Russia, and Austria. In addition to the specifically discussed 30 writers, Willdenow at the end listed more than 90 other botanists who had made contributions to the field.

Willdenow also devoted a chapter to the various types of classification of plants. He held that no system was complete. The three most common systems mentioned were: The Natural System, which arranged plants by their external characteristics; the Artificial System, which was based on the "number, proportion and agreement of minute and not obvious parts"; and the Sexual System, which was based on the number and variety of the sexual parts of plants. He then proceeded to discuss the contributions made by fifteen botanists in the development of these systems. In the back of the book there were presented 292 rather fine pictures of plants.

*Priscella Wakefield.* One example of the popular type of botany book was Wakefield's *An Introduction to Botany.* The writer's copy was the fifth edition published in London in 1807. The contents were presented in the form of 27 letters from Celicia to Constance. The book was beautifully bound in leather and trimmed with gold. It contained 180 pages and many pictures of flora. Apparently its objective was to encourage the study of botany by girls. Many of the pictures were of flowers and fruits.

*Robert J. Thornton, M.D.* One of the botany books written in England and republished here was Thornton's *A Grammar of Botany* (1818), "Containing an explanation of the System of Linnaeus." He was connected both with the University of Cambridge and the Royal London College of Physicians. It was one of the first botany books to state on the title page, "For the Use of Schools and Students." Its contents consisted of 133 pages of regular textual material, 21 pages of questions, a brief glossary, 40 pages of plates with explanations, 23 pages of Index of the Botanical Terms, in all 225 pages. Then bound in the back of the book there was a reprint of *A Dictionary of Botanical Terms* (1813) by James Lee, which consisted of 88 pages, and three pages listing the "Names of All the Classes and Orders of the Linnaeus System." It is likely that this book was used in some American schools.

*Sir James E. Smith, M.D. F.R.S.* One other botany written in England may be mentioned. It was Smith's *A Grammar of Botany* (1820). It claimed to be "Illustrative of Artificial, as well as Natural, Classification, with an explanation of Jussieu's System." It was a book of 240 rather large pages. Its 264 pictures were largely of flowers. Chapter IX dealt with a detailed comparison of the "Natural Orders of Linnaeus with those of Jussieu." Its contents looked less forbidding than of most early botany books.

### B. *American Botany Books**

*Amos Eaton.* Eaton was Professor of Botany and Chemistry in the Vermont

Medical Institution, connected with Middlebury College, and he also lectured at Troy Lyceum. His *Manual of Botany for the Northern and Middle States of America* (1817) apparently was one of the earliest botany texts written in America. The third edition appeared in 1822. This was a large book of 534 pages bound in leather. In the back appeared a notice addressed to "Teachers of Academies and Popular Lecturers." In it he called attention to booksellers in twelve cities where the book may be purchased. The book began by listing 58 of the Natural Orders of Linnaeus, followed by 98 Orders of Jussieu. Then 96 pages were devoted to "A System of Genera, for the Northern and Middle States." Part II of 368 pages listed and described the "Species of Plants growing in the Northern and Middle States," alphabetically arranged. In footnotes of the preface he acknowledged other botanical works from which he borrowed data about plants in different areas and names of other persons who gathered data for him.

In 1829 the so-called fifth edition appeared, but which bore the title of *Manual of Botany, for North America*, claiming to deal with the "Indigenous Plants and Common Cultivated Exotics, growing North of the Gulf of Mexico." It began by listing the generic classes and orders of plants. Then 363 pages were devoted to the species alphabetically arranged. Again he acknowledged the help of many other botanists. In the back of the book 63 pages dealt with the Grammar of Botany, and 71 pages with a Botanical Dictionary.

In 1833 Eaton's *Manual* was again considerably revised. Part First dealt with North American Plants arranged according to the "Linnean Artificial Method," improved by Parsoon, Pursh, Nuthall, and others. The arrangement of this part was similar to that in the fifth edition. However, Part Second dealt with the plants arranged according to "Jussieu's Natural Method," improved by Lindley, Brown, DeCandolle, and others. The number of Genera described was 1228, and Species 5267. At this time Eaton was connected with Rensselaer Institute, Troy. A 7th edition appeared in 1836.

All these editions appeared to be carefully prepared and exhaustive in nature. However, the encyclopedic nature of the detailed content made these books rather forbidding to study. Although they apparently were used as textbooks, today we would think them to be better as reference books. Nevertheless, they apparently exerted considerable influence on the study of botany in American schools for several decades. None of the editions included any pictures.

In 1820 Eaton published his *Botanical Exercises*, which included "directions, rules, and descriptions, calculated to aid pupils in the analysis of plants; with a labelling catalogue for the assistance of teachers." This was a rather small book of 165 pages of text, which was designed to accompany the *Manual*. It contained six pages of detailed instructions to teachers on how to teach botany effectively. Eaton also published a *Botanical Dictionary*, which appeared in several editions.

*William Mavor*. In contrast to Eaton's voluminous *Manual* Mavor published a small *Catechism of Botany* in 1814. This book, intended for "schools and families," contained only 67 pages written in catechetical form. Just in what type of school this book was used is not now certain, but in addition to its use in families, it may have been used in such seminaries as the one opened in Keene, N.H., in 1814 by Catherine Fiske, in which botany and chemistry were taught. She taught there 23 years. A later Mavor edition was printed in 1820.

*Locke*. About 1820 (title pages missing) Locke's *Botany* was published. This was an attractive and well organized book of about 170 pages in all. It began with introductory definitions and then presented the contents in five parts, as follows: I, Root; II, Herbage; III, Fructification; IV, System of Linnaeus of Classes and Orders, and Genera and Species; and V, Anatomy and Physiology of Vegetables. The main text of 122 pages was followed with questions, directions for preparing and maintaining a herbarium, and 16 plates each containing from 10 to 25 fine pictures each of plants and flowers. This book appears to have been a teachable one.

*George Sumner*. In 1820 his *A Compendium of Physiological and Systematic Botany* was published. In the preface Sumner acknowledged the merits of such European written books as Smith's and Willdenow's, heretofore discussed, and Keith's, but since these were not republished here, and since they dealt with many plants not known here, he thought it would be well to prepare a botany modeled after them but better adapted to American use. It was organized into 18 chapters dealing with such subjects as germination, vegetation, sap, roots, trunks, leaves, flower, fruits, and so on. It consisted of 292 pages of text and VIII plates showing 130 fine pictures of flora, and an index.

*Thomas Nuttall*. In 1827 Nuttall, whose help had already been mentioned by the authors of several earlier botanies, published *An Introduction to Systematic and Physiological Botany*, which was dedicated to the Hon. John Lowell, President of the Massachusetts Society for Promoting Agriculture. In the preface he acknowledged that most botany books were derived from the Linnaean system, but which made them very technical. So he attempted to make his

# MANUAL

OF

# BOTANY,

FOR THE

## NORTHERN AND MIDDLE STATES
## OF AMERICA.

CONTAINING GENERIC AND SPECIFIC DESCRIPTIONS
OF THE INDIGENOUS PLANTS AND COMMON
CULTIVATED EXOTICS, GROWING
NORTH OF VIRGINIA.

*TO WHICH ARE PREFIXED,*

THE NATURAL AND ARTIFICIAL CLASSES AND ORDERS OF LINNEUS;
AND THE NATURAL ORDERS OF JUSSIEU, WITH THE
MEDICINAL PROPERTIES OF EACH ORDER.

---

## BY AMOS EATON, A. M.

Professor of Botany and Chemistry in the Vermont Medical Institution, which is con-
nected with Middlebury College, and Lecturer in the Troy Lyceum;
Member of the American Geological Society; Corresponding
Member of the New-York Lyceum of Natural
History, and Honorary Member of
the Hudson Lyceum.

---

" THAT EXISTENCE IS SURELY CONTEMPTIBLE, WHICH REGARDS ON-
" LY THE GRATIFICATION OF INSTINCTIVE WANTS, AND THE PRESER-
" VATION OF A BODY, MADE TO PERISH." *Linneus.*

---

## THIRD EDITION, REVISED AND CORRECTED.

---

*ALBANY:*
PRINTED AND PUBLISHED BY WEBSTERS AND SKINNERS.

1822.

10  One of the earliest popular textbooks of botany

work more appealing by making certain adaptations. Since most people love flowers, he began by devoting more than 200 pages to the study of flowers according to the Linnaean method. Then a chapter was given to the study of the class Cryptogama. Part II followed dealing with the Physiology of Plants. This part he said was an abridgment of a much larger work by Anthony Todd Thompson of England. In it he first dealt with the general characteristics and structure of plants, and then devoted chapters to the treatment of stems, branches, and leaves. Seventeen pages were devoted to a glossary, followed by a section presenting 12 fine plates with ample explanations. It was a very attractively bound and printed book.

*Mrs. Almira Hart Lincoln Phelps.* (1793–1884). She became known for her many science textbooks. She studied the sciences under Amos Eaton, heretofore discussed, and then taught science in the Troy Female Seminary, of which her sister, Mrs. Emma Willard, was the head. Later she became the principal of a school in West Chester, Pennsylvania, and lastly principal of the Patapasco Institute in Maryland. Many of her pupils later became distinguished teachers.

In 1828, when she was Mrs. Lincoln and Vice-Principal at Troy Female Seminary, she published the *Familiar Lectures on Botany*. It was intended for high schools and academies. After acknowledging her debt to numerous authors for most of the botanical facts she claimed certain features for her book, such as a clear and methodical arrangement of the topics, perspicuity of language, and a pleasing style with interesting illustrations. In 1831 it was recopyrighted as a second edition. The main text consisted of four parts, 48 lectures, and 309 pages. These were followed by 118 pages dealing with lists of genera of plants, species of plants, vocabulary of botanical terms, language of flowers (a woman's touch), and an index.

Part I was mostly devoted to the analysis of plants or practical botany. In Part II consideration was given to the various organs of plants, "beginning with the root and ascending to the flower." In Part III the different systems of botany were given attention, particularly the Linnaean System. Part IV dealt with the progressive appearance of flowers by seasons, regions, and climate.

Even though still appearing under a 1831 copyright, the 1838 edition (the 7th) was considerably revised. The main text was increased to 246 pages, and was followed by a Part V, which was an Appendix of Lectures on Botany consisting of 186 pages. The 1841 reprint was the 13th edition. In 1845 it was again revised and recopyrighted. The main text of the 48 lectures remained

G

the same, but Part V was enlarged to 220 pages. The increase was due to presenting a greater number of generic and specific descriptions of plants, particularly those of the southern and western states. All of these editions were bound in leather.

In 1833 she published a *Botany for Beginners,* which was to serve as an introduction to *Lectures on Botany* and was intended for the "use of common schools and the younger pupils of higher schools and academies." This was a small book bound in cloth of a few more than 200 pages. The 10th edition appeared in 1842 under her new name of Mrs. Phelps. The same book appeared again as a stereotyped edition as late as 1855. It is evident that these books must have had a rather wide usage in secondary schools for a considerable period.

*John L. Comstock* (1789–1858). Comstock was a prolific writer of science textbooks. His texts in natural philosophy and chemistry were particularly popular. In 1832 he published *An Introduction to the Study of Botany*. He attempted to make this a popular book, but without sacrificing its scientific value. The 2nd edition appeared in 1833. It began by dealing with the roots, stems, leaves, armatures, flowers, fruits, and seeds of plants. Then he discussed the systems of classification of plants. He leaned toward the Linnaean System. Comstock divided the vegetable kingdom into 24 classes, and these in turn into orders. Then he devoted 120 pages to a discussion and description of these classes and orders. The last 38 pages dealt with a Natural System of Botany and a glossary. In all the book contained 260 pages.

In 1837 a revised edition was published as the fifth. About 30 pages were added to the earlier edition on "The language of Plants." Then in 1854 it was recopyrighted and greatly enlarged, but mentioned as the 31st edition. The first 250 pages were similar in structure to the 1832 edition, except somewhat expended. Then 24 pages dealt with Vegetable Physiology, 12 pages with the Language of Flowers, 68 pages with Practical Botany, and 26 pages with a glossary and an index. In all the book contained 485 pages. The numerous editions constitute evidence that Comstock's books were widely used. A number of old actual fern leaves were found pressed in 1854 copy.

*Other early botany books.* Reference has been made to the fact that a number of the authors acknowledged their debts to other botanists, most of whom had also written one or more botany books. The following were among the most frequently mentioned, in the order of the date of their earlier writings: John Bartram (1807), Henry Muhlenburg (1813), Jacob Bigelow (1814), Frederick Pursh (1814), W. P. C. Barton (1815), F. A. Michaux (1819), E. P. James (1820)

S. Elliot (1821), L. De Schweinitz (1821), William Darlington (1826), John Torrey (1826), Lewis Beck (1828), and Chester Dewey (1840). However, only a few of these botanists wrote general botany textbooks. Most of their writings were either studies of the flora of particular regions or a mere catalogue of plants. However, a few of their books may well have been used as general texts. Among them were Beck's *Geographical Botany of the U.S.*, Michaux's *American Sylva*, Pursh's *Plants of North America*, and Torrey's *A Compendium of the Flora of North America*. A number of these wrote more than one book. Likely there were many other botanies of one kind or another written in America before 1840. Due to the fact that European botanies written largely about European flora would not be very appealing for study in America, so only a few botanies written across were republished here, at least not without considerable revision. So more botanies were written here rather early than in the fields of natural, philosophy, chemistry, and natural history.

### C. *American botanies, 1840–1869*

VERY few newly written botanies appeared between 1833 and 1842. The books written by Eaton, Mrs. Lincoln Phelps, and Comstock apparently largely met the botany textbook needs during that period.

*Asa Gray* (1810–1888). One of the authors whose botanies became very popular during this period was Asa Gray. Most of his schooling and early experiences were in the State of New York. He early bought a copy of Eaton's *Manual of Botany*, which aroused his interest in botany. Then he attended a medical school from which he received a M.D. degree before he became of age. Then he had varied experiences of lecturing on botany in a medical school, teaching in Utica H.S., making summer field studies, and working some with Torrey, another famous botanist. His most fruitful years were spent as a professor at Harvard. He helped in founding several scientific societies, and contributed many articles to the *American Journal of Science*.

In 1842 he published *The Botanical Text-Book*, "for Colleges, Schools, and Private Students." The first edition contained a few over 400 pages. Then in 1845 a second edition appeared, without a change in the copyright date, but enlarged to 509 pages. Part I dealt with "An Introduction to Structural and Physiological Botany" and Part II with "The Principles of Systematic Botany." He maintained that systematic botany can adequately be studied only when grounded upon the principles of "Vegetable Organography and Physiology." That is why in Part I he dealt with structural and physiological botany. It was this part that he enlarged over the first edition. On the other hand he condensed the treatment of the natural orders in the 2nd edition. Chapters dealing with the root, stem, leaves, plant food, the flower, fruit, and seed of plants were certainly more appealing to students than the sole approach by orders and classes. In 1850 it was again rewritten, somewhat reorganized, and enlarged, but appeared as the third edition. The 1857 edition appeared as the fifth. However, he stated each edition was in good part rewritten. In 1879 it was again largely rewritten to serve for "higher and completer instruction." It was more technical than the earlier editions, dealing largely with structural botany. Some of the titles of chapters were: General Morphology of Phaenogamous Plants. Phyllotaxy, and Taxonomy. Its last 50 pages constituted a very detailed glossary.

Gray later evidently realized that there was a demand for a smaller book. So in 1857 he published his *First Lessons in Botany and Vegetable Physiology*. This soon appeared in a number of reprints without revision. This book was intended for use in "common and higher schools." Its contents were largely similar but simpler than Part I of his earlier text. It began with eight pages entitled "Analysis of the Lessons," which somewhat detailed the contents of the 34 lessons. It contained more than 360 wood engravings from original drawings by Isaac Sprague. The text proper contained only a few over 200 pages, but in the back there appeared 34 pages of glossary and dictionary. It was an attractive and well organized book.

In 1868 the 236 pages of *Lessons in Botany* were incorporated into a double volume with 374 pages of the *Field, Forest, and Garden Botany*. The latter was a simple introduction to the common plants of the U.S. east of the Mississippi. It was to be used for flower and plant analysis. Then in 1869 it was recopyrighted and again appeared as a double volume. The first 236 pages again were an exact reprint of the earlier editions of *Lessons*, but a second volume was bound with it, entitled, *Manual of the Botany of the Northern United States*, which the writer thinks first appeared as a separate book in 1848. The latter was to be used by students to identify and analyze the flora of northern U.S. It consisted of 606 pages of detailed descriptions of flora by orders and classes, plus 14 plates each including many illustrations of flora.

In 1858 Gray published an even more appealing book entitled, *How Plants Grow*, illustrated by 500 wood engravings. It began with a biblical quotation from Mathew vi: 28–29, about lilies together with pictures of them. Part I dealt with how plants grow, and what their parts and organs are: Part II with how plants are propagated and multiplied; Part III with why plants grow; and Part IV with how plants are classified, named, and studied. Its approach was appealing and functional. Its chapters were divided into meaningful sections, and the paragraphs were numbered and introduced with key words in larger and darker type. Thus the student was carefully guided in his study. The illustrations were very appealing. The writer's collection contains seven copies of different dates between 1858 and 1880, but without any change.

In 1887 Gray published *The Elements of Botany*, which was to take the place of the *Lessons in Botany*. The first 226 pages constituted a slightly rewritten and condensed version of the *Lessons*, followed by 374 of the *Field, Forest, and Garden Botany*, which was a reprint of the latter half of the 1868 edition. It may be added that the titles printed on the outside covers of some of these later books were not always the same as those found on the title page. This practice was more or less common with popular textbooks. Apparently either the author or the publishers did this to stretch the use of popular texts.

Gray wrote a number of other books dealing with botany. These dealt either with highly technical aspects of botany or only with particular regions. It is evident from the foregoing discussions that Gray was the first American botanist whose books had real wide and extended use. He seemed to be less concerned with the conflict between the natural and artificial systems of classification, thus making his books less confusing.

*Alphonso Wood.* Wood, who for a time was the principal of a female academy in Brooklyn, was dissatisfied with the botany texts available for his students. To meet his students' needs he prepared *A Class-Book of Botany* in 1845. Soon a wider use for it opened. Under the copyright date of 1846 it appeared in many editions. The 1851 edition was the 33rd. It was designed for "Colleges, Academies, and other Seminaries." On the title page in fine print there appeared these quotations: "He spoke of trees, from the Cedar of Lebanon even unto the Hyssop that springeth out of the wall. I Kings, iv. 33; "and "Consider the Lilies of the Field—. . .even Solomon, in all his Glory, was not arrayed like one of These." Matthew, vi, 28, 29." Part I dealt with the Elements of Botanical Science, covering more than 100 pages. Part II dealt with the Natural Orders, which were illustrated by flora of the northern, middle, and western states. In the 1851 edition this Part was given over 500 pages. This book differed from most other current botanies in at least two respects. He strongly followed the natural method rather than the artificial of Linnaeus, and secondly he suggested doing away with the "former drudgery of botanic analysis, necessary in every other School Botany," by obviating this work by a "new system of Analytical Tables, near 200 in number." This was done in Part II by beginning with a detailed synopsis of the natural system, followed by descriptions of the flora of the northern part of our country. Four pages were devoted to the language of flowers, such as: Alyssum, Merit before beauty; Bachelor's Button, Single blessedness; Goldenrod, Encouragement; Mistletoe, Meanness, Indolence; and Sweet-pea, Must you go? In the back of this edition there appeared four pages of testimonials for the book, mostly by principals of academies and college professors.

In 1860 the *Class-Book* was radically revised and enlarged. It now attempted to cover the flora of all U.S. and Canada. Its contents were presented in four parts, dealing with structural botany, physiological botany, systematic botany, and lastly and extensively descriptive botany. In Part III he also explained the artificial system as well as the natural system of classification. In 1869 it was again revised in "accordance with recent discoveries." The *Class-Books* which bore the copyright dates of 1846, 1860, and 1869 all appeared in later reprints.

In 1848 Wood published his *First Lessons in Botany*. This was an attractive and well illustrated small book of more than 250 pages. Although it was designed for the "common schools" it may well have been used in some academies.

In 1860 Wood published one of his most attractive books; namely, *Leaves and Flowers: or Object Lessons in Botany*, prepared for "Beginners in Academies and Public Schools" with 665 illustrations. The contents were presented in 34 interesting lessons, which constituted less than half the book. These lessons were brief, were well illustrated, and included questions at the bottom of the pages. The latter half began with nine pages in fine print of the anaylsis of the natural orders. Then followed 180 pages describing the more common flora of 152 orders, the last one dealing with the spider wort. The last 21 pages were devoted to a brief glossary and an extensive index of the names of plants, with page references to the illustrations in the book.

In 1870 Wood published *The American Botanist and Florist*. He aimed to present a "complete manual within the compass of a duodecimo volume." In other words, he aimed to present most of what was in the voluminous *Class-Book*, but occupying only about two-thirds the space. The text proper consisted of Part I, Structural Botany; Part II, Physiological Botany; and Part III, Systematic Botany; in all 172 pages. Then bound in the same volume appeared Part Fourth, Descriptive Botany of 392 pages. In it 159 orders of flora were described. Thus the *Botanist* contained 566 pages compared with the 832 pages in the 1870 edition of the *Class-Book*. Part Fourth was also published as a separate book, entitled, *Descriptive Botany*. Many chapters were considerably rewritten and enlarged by 100 pages, but the organization of the book was retained. Also in 1889 the first three parts of the *Botanist* were published separately, as *Lessons in the Structure, Life, and Growth of Plants* "for schools and academies," under the names of Wood and Willis. This was an attractively bound and printed text.

It is very evident that Alphonso Wood, like Asa Gray, was a prolific writer of botany books. These books together with the revisions covered more than 40 years of publication. The fact that the writer has been able to collect 16 of Wood's texts of different dates and titles is some evidence of their wide circulation between 1845 and 1889.

*Frances H. Green.* In 1854 she published the *Primary Class-Book of Botany*, which was intended for "Common Schools and Families." On the title page she quoted Cowper, as follows:

"For they whom truth and science lead,
May gather honey from a weed."

This book had the proportions of a geography rather than a botany. Its pages were 8 × 9 1/2 inches and were divided into two columns. The print was rather small. Thus its 100 pages would have been equivalent to about 250 pages of an average sized book. So it may well have been used in some seminaries. The contents were presented in 33 chapters and 29 large illustrative plates, each of which presented from 11 to 21 clear reproductions of flora. The paragraphs were numbered and many pages had questions at the bottom. The emphasis was on flowers and garden plants. It appeared as a reprint in 1855.

*Worthington Hooker M.D.* In 1857 Hooker's *Child's Book of Nature* was published in three parts. Part I—Plants was printed as a separate volume. This was a small book of 120 pages. It was mainly intended for families and schools. The contents were presented in 33 brief chapters in a very non-technical manner. The three parts may have constituted a course in some seminaries.

*Other botanies, 1840–1869.* In 1848 Mrs. Sarah J. Hale published the *Flora's Interpreter and Fortuna Flora*, which was really a book of poems written about flora. It appeared in several editions. In 1851 Theodore Thinker published his *First Lessons in Botany*, which was very elementary. In 1854 Harland Coultas published the *Principles of Botany*. Likely there were many others published during this period, particularly botanies dealing with the plants of specific geographical areas or regions.

## D. *Botany Textbooks, 1870–1900*

THE botany books of no author became as popular during this period as those of Gray and of Wood during the previous period. A good number of authors wrote botanies, but the competition for circulation had become much keener. An attempt willl be made to discuss those books that appeared in at least several editions.

*Eliza A. Youmans.* In 1870 Miss Youmans published *The First Book of Botany* designed to "cultivate the observing powers of children." It soon appeared in numerous editions. The 1880 and 1882 editions contained a few more than 200 pages. About half of the space of these pages was used to present 300 fine illustrations. It was an attractive book. In the back 15 pages of blank forms for leaf, stem, and inflorescence schedules appeared to be filled out by the students. These referred back to the pages and exercises in the text. Six pages in back presented testimonials for this book. These were chiefly written by super-intendents of schools, principals of female seminaries, and editors.

In 1873, partly due to many requests for a second book, Miss Youmans published the *Second Book of Botany*, which was to be a "practical guide to ob-servation and study of plants." It was a book of over 300 pages. She strongly believed that, like in arithmetic, the rudiments must first be mastered. Then this understanding must be applied to objects. This book then was to be ac-companied by Henslow's *Botanical Charts*, of which she was the editor. The text proper consisted of Course First, composed of chapters of descriptive botany dealing with such matters as the flower, stamens, pistil, fruit and seed, floral symmetry (a woman's touch), and a number of specific classes of flora. Course Second dealt with vegetable anatomy and physiology. Its chapters dealt with such matters as the internal structure of plants, stems, the root, the leaf, the plant in action, and collecting and preserving plants.

Although the book had 420 figures or drawings, she still favored the use of the Botanical Charts by Professor J. S. Henslow, an eminent English botanist. It consisted of large colored diagrams. The plant was first represented in natural size and color, and then magnified sections of the flowers given. She substituted American specimens for some English species. Throughout the book careful directions were given for the work to be done. In addition to a glossary an appendix appeared in the back. The latter was a 25 page essay

"On the Education Claims of Botany." First she discussed the development and growth of the child, both physically and mentally, together with existing methods. Then she suggested what was needed for improvement, and argued how the study of botany could help in the process. The book appeared in several editions.

In 1886 Miss Youmans also published a *Physiological Botany*, which was an abridgment and revision of a book written in England by Robert Bentley. It appeared under the joint authorship of Bentley and Youmans. It was an attractive book of 292 pages.

*Charles E. Bessey.* Bessey, who had taught botany in several midwestern universities, published his *Botany* in 1880. It was intended for "high schools and colleges." Very minor revisions were made in the 1881 edition, in 1883, and in the fourth edition in 1885. Bessey's *Botany* was a great contrast to Miss Youman's texts. These texts contained more than 500 pages, to which were added four pages of double column for an index to the 573 illustrations and 37 pages of a general index. Bessey confessed that this book was an expansion and modification of several courses of lectures given to college students. He aimed to guide the student to become himself an observer and investigator.

Part I—General Anatomy and Physiology dealt with protoplasm, plant-cell, cell walls, new cells, tissues, intercellular spaces, and various matters about plants. Part II—Special Anatomy and Physiology dealt briefly with classification, and then with protophyta, zygosporeae, oosporeae, carposporeae, bryophyta, pteridophyta, and phanerogamia, ending with certain concluding observations. Although he claimed it to be for high schools as well as colleges, its size and technical nature likely did not recommend itself invitingly as a high school text, at least not in the smaller high schools. Nevertheless it apparently had considerable circulation.

*Volney M. Spalding.* Spalding, who was Professor of Botany at the University of Michigan, published the *Guide to the Study of Common Plants* in 1893, which was primarily intended for high schools. In the beginning of the book he used 17 pages for instructions to the student and to the teacher, for works of reference, and for listing what was needed for the laboratory and permanent outfit. The body of the 1894 text contained 246 pages. The main parts dealt with the organs of flowering plants, natural groups of plants, gymnosperms, monocotyledons, and dicotyledons. The directions in the book were specific and clear. The sections commonly ended with specific exercises or with a review or summary. Peculiarly, it contained no pictures. Spalding expected the students to bring in specimens for study in the laboratory, even with a microscope if necessary. Then they were to make the proper drawings. The smallness of the book did not fully indicate the amount of work required of the student. His work would include what was done in the laboratory. The book was less technical and very different from Bessey's.

*J. Y. Bergen.* Bergen, who was an instructor in biology in the English High School, Boston, in 1896 published the *Elements of Botany*. He used it in a half-year course in botany in his school. It was a well organized and attractively printed book of 245 pages of regular text. Then 29 pages were given to five appendices and an index. The use of microscopes, apparatus, and reagents were given particular attention. Bound in the back of the book Part II of 57 pages appeared, dealing with a catalogue and key to flora.

In 1901 Bergen published his *Foundations of Botany*. Part I was written on the same plan as his *Elements*, but was greatly enlarged. However, Part II dealt with "Ecology, or Relations of Plants to the World about Them." Then what was Part II in the *Elements* became an added book of over 250 pages in the back, entitled, Bergen's *Botany, Key and Flora*. In it were classified and described 98 of the most important families of flora of the northern and central states.

In 1906 there was published the *Principles of Botany* by Bergen and B. M. Davis. It was from this book that the writer first studied botany. Its three parts dealt with "The Structure and Physiology of Seed Plants," "The Morphology, Evolution, and Classification of Plants," and "Ecology and Economic Botany." Although our aim has been to discuss only books before 1900, yet since Bergen's *Elements* appeared in 1896, mention has been made of these later editions also.

*L. H. Bailey.* Bailey had published a number of books relating to botany and gardening after which in 1900 his *Botany* appeared. This was a well organized and profusely illustrated beginner's text of a total of 355 pages. Most of the 500 illustrations apparently were photographs rather than drawings, which had been true in most other texts. The paragraphs were numbered and the statements he considered most important were in italics. Review questions were asked at the end of chapters. In the back descriptions and illustrations of 25 families of plants were presented. Its make-up and procedure, as well as its topics, must have been appealing to students. It soon appeared in reprints.

*Other botany textbooks, 1870–1900.* More different botany textbooks apparently were written during this period than in either of the two earlier periods, yet none appeared in as many editions as those written by Gray and Wood in the previous period. In addition to books already discussed for this period a number of others may be mentioned. Among them were: John H. Balfour's *First Book of Botany* (1872), August Koehler's *Practical Botany, Structural and Systematic* (1876), Goodale's *Physiological Botany* (1888), Sydney H. Vines' *Lectures on the Physiology of Plants* (1886), Abbie G. Hall's *Botany* (1887), George G. Groff's *The Book of Plant Descriptions* (1889), W. A. Kellerman's *A Textbook of Elementary Botany* (1898), Charles Reid Barnes' *Outlines of Plant Life* (1900), Douglas H. Campbell's *The Evolution of Plants,* William F. Ganong's *The Teaching Botanist,* D. T. MacDougal's *The Nature and Work of Plants,* and a number of late books written in Europe and reprinted here. There is evidence that many other books were written on botany during this period, but most of them dealt either only with certain special aspects of botany or with the botany of particular regions.

## E. *Characteristics of Old Botany Textbooks*

*Earliest developments.* The study of botany received only meager attention in ancient times. The plants that were studied were largely those thought to possess medicinal values. Little scientific study of plants was made until nearly 1600, after which date many scientists turned their attention to a scientific study and classification of plants. Also soon after 1600 botanic gardens were opened in many cities, especially in western Europe. These not only facilitated and encouraged the scientific study of plants, but helped to popularize the study and appreciation of them. The study of flowers, with their beauty, aided in the popularization of the study of botany, particularly by women.

It naturally followed that publications would appear reporting findings of studies. Since plants varied from region to region, many publications appeared enumerating and explaining these variations, often with varying theories concerning their classification. The result was that seemingly more books dealing with botany appeared during the 18th and the early 19th centuries than was true in other fields of science, such as natural philosophy, chemistry, and natural history. However, only a fraction of these were written primarily as textbooks for use in schools.

*Systems of plant classification.* Many systems of classification of plants have been advocated by various botanists. Among them were Cesalpino's approach based on similarities and dissimilarities of the form of plants; Ray's more natural classification; Tournefort's system based on the corolla of flowers; the system by Linnaeus; another by de Jussieu and his followers, and many others. Of these the most frequently followed systems were by Linnaeus and by de Jussieu. The Linnaean or commonly known as the artificial system became the most popular in botany textbooks in America. He made use of the binomial nomenclature of plants. In it the first name referred to the genus and the second to the species. DeJussieu, de Candolle, and some others held that the morphology (form and structure) of plants should be the basis for classification. This was known as the natural system. Many other botanists held that no one system explained all the classes of plants.

Most of the early American botany texts explained both systems, and some listed plants under both the artificial and the natural systems. However, more attention was commonly given the Linnaean than the de Jussieu system. Of the texts of the two most popular botany authors, Gray followed nearly exclusively the Linnaen artificial system, while Wood favored more fully the natural system of de Jussieu. Most botany textbooks written after 1870 paid little or no attention to the conflict between these two systems.

*Few early European reprints here.* In the other science fields many European written textbooks were reprinted and popularized in America before any American written book became very popular. In the field of botany this was different. This was due largely to the fact that America had many plants that were different than those in Europe. So European written books were not fully adapted to American needs. However, American authors borrowed the theories of plant classification and other ideas from European written botany books. This was not only true of the earlier American textbook authors, but even to the end of the 19th century.

*Nature of content treatment.* The earlier textbooks tended to be very technical and encyclopedic in nature. For example, Eaton's 1822 edition listed 58 orders of Linnaeus, 98 orders of de Jussieu, and devoted 96 pages to the genera and 368 pages to the species of plants of the Northern and Middle States. Similar lists appeared (usually in the back) in many early texts. With time more interesting approaches were followed.

On the other hand, some authors like Sumner (1820) had chapters dealing with such functional topics as germination, vegetation, sap, roots, trunks, leaves, flowers, fruit, and so on. This approach gradually became more and more common. The popularity of Gray's *How Plants Grow* was evidence of the acceptance of such approach.

Mrs. Lincoln Phelps' books even devoted a section to the Language of Flowers and another part to the progressive appearance of flowers by seasons, regions, and climate. Later a number of others included similar matters.

*Use of pictures.* The use of pictures and illustrations by the different authors varied greatly. For example, Eaton's books (first one in 1817) and Spalding's (1893) included no pictures. However, Spalding expected the students to draw their own from specimens. Most other Ameican texts used illustrations of the more common classes of plants. The illustrations in most early books were on plates in the back. In most later books the illustrations would appear with the treatment of topics in the text. One of Wood's books (1860) included 665 illustrations, and one of Bessey's texts contained 573. In the earlier books these were drawings, while in some later ones they were photographs.

*Herbarium and laboratory exercises.* Most botany texts implied or directed work to be done by students either in identifying or analyzing specimens of plants. As early as 1820 Eaton's *Botanical Exercises* included "directions, rules, and descriptions, calculated to aid pupils in the analysis of plants; with a labelling catalogue for the assistance of teachers." Locke's text (about 1820) included directions for preparing and maintaining a herbarium. Some of Miss Youman's texts had blank forms for leaf, stem, and inflorescence schedules to be filled in by students. She also suggested the use of Henslow's *Botanical Charts.* Spalding's text (1893) suggested that students bring specimens to the laboratory and even make drawings of them. Bergen (1896) provided instructions for the use of a microscope and other apparatus. In summary, it can be said that botany books were earlier in providing student activities than the texts in the other science fields.

*Contributions of women authors.* The field of botany attracted more women authors than the other science fields. Among the women authors were Priscella Wakefield, Mrs. Lincoln Phelps, Frances Green, Sarah Hole, and Eliza Youmans. They emphasized the study of flowers, which approach evidently helped to popularize the study of botany, especially by girls. Too, they seemed to possess fine pedagogical sense in writing texts that were appealing. After Mrs. Lincoln Phelps attractive books appeared many later male authors imitated some of her features, for example, the inclusion of a section entitled, "Language of Flowers." Pedagogically these contributions should not be overlooked.

# NATURAL PHILOSOPHY (PHYSICS)

## Introduction

*Early natural science.* Natural science has been referred to as that branch of knowledge dealing with the natural world and its pehenomena. In the beginning it embraced elements of knowledge relating to astronomy, chemistry, geology, zoology, and physics. With time these elements began to be treated as separate subject fields, and natural philosophy (physics) was considered to deal only with inanimate objects not involving chemical change.

*Evolution of natural philosophy.* Even though the history of science ought to be more interesting than the history of wars and empires, yet relatively little has been written on the history of physics. This was partly true because little scientific work was done in this field until the 16th century. Although the ancient Greeks did much early creditable work in several other fields of science, they did little in this field. Their emphasis on logic and philosophy virtually stood as a barrier to the development of experimental science. However, Archimedes (287–212 B.C.), a Greek who did considerable experimental work in Alexandria, dealt with several mechanical devices, such as the lever and screw, and the cogwheel, and he also worked on the determination of the density of substances. Several other also did some experimenting at the Alexandrian Museum and Library.

Unfortunately, this great library was partly burned by the Romans under Julius Caesar, and the remainder was destroyed by Christian monks about 390. The supernatural and metaphysical ideas of the early Christians conflicted with the scientific studies. Thus much of the best knowledge of the past was virtually lost or neglected during the middle ages, and little new was discovered. However, the work of Roger Bacon (1214–1294) and Galileo Galilei (1564–1642) helped keep the spark of experimentation alive. Bacon worked on optics and mechanically driven machines, and Galileo discovered the law regulating falling bodies and also discovered Jupiter's satellites. In a sense, Galileo's experiments on motion date the beginning of modern science.

By the end of the 17th century a sufficient number of persons became interested in science to form scientific societies. The Royal Society of London was formed in 1662, and the Academie des Sciences in Paris in 1666. A similar one was formed in Germany. These societies provided a great stimulus to scientific experimentation on the part of its members and then to make known their findings.

One of the Royal Society's members, and for some years its president, was Isaac Newton (1642–1727). Interestingly, he was born the year Galileo died. He made great contributions to astronomy, mathematics, and physics. He discovered the law of gravitation, invented a refracting telescope, and contributed to a better understanding of color and light. His outstanding works were: *Optics*, and the *Principia*. The latter laid the foundation for modern physics. Others who contributed to a broader understanding and application of mechanics were Hooke, Halley, and Cavendish.

The period from 1800 to 1895 has been referred to as the age seeking scientific certainty. The experiments of Volta, Ampere, Maxwell, Ohm, Faraday, and others, contributed much to a better understanding of electricity and magnetism. The discovery of electromagnetic induction made possible the invention of the dynamo. Helmholtz, Mayer, Rumford, and Joule explained the idea of the conservation of energy. Lord Kelvin and Carnot worked on thermodynamics. The ideas involved in all of these findings were soon applied to the telegraph, telephone, electric lights, electric traction, and many forms of electrical engineering.

After 1895 many further developments took place. The X-ray was invented by Roentgen in 1895. The Curies carried on significant experiments with radium. The later great experimental findings that have contributed to a fuller understanding of the various aspects of physics are too numerous to enumerate, such as nuclear physics.

*Natural philosophy in secondary schools.* Natural philosophy rather than physics was commonly used as the title of American textbooks in this field until about 1880. It is not certain now just which secondary school first taught this subject. Apparently it was not taught in any of the early Latin grammar schools. Its first acceptance as a secondary school subject was in the academies. It is a matter of record that Phillips Exeter in 1818 included natural philosophy in the third year of the English Department. Evidently other academies soon followed, for numerous textbooks in the field were soon published.

Boston High School, America's first, from its beginning in 1821 taught natural philosophy, including astronomy, in its third year offering. The New York High School in 1826 listed philosophy, likely physics, as one of the subjects taught. The fact that these two important early high schools taught natural philosophy evidently helped make it an acceptable secondary school subject. According to Stout's study of the curriculum offering of midwestern high schools between 1860 and 1900 nearly all of them either listed natural philosophy or physics.

Apparently little laboratory work was provided until after 1865. In 1878 Frank W. Clark made a survey of the teaching of physics and chemistry in secondary schools. His findings were published in a U.S. Bureau of Education *Bulletin* in 1880. According to this report 81% of 609 secondary schools offered courses in physics with class experiments, but no laboratory work. Four schools offered laboratory work in physics. About two-thirds of the schools reported apparatus of some value. Of these schools 53 were providing experiments by the teacher, while 153 were giving mere textbook instruction. Later evidence has shown that after 1880 more and more secondary schools began to offer laboratory work in connection with the teaching of physics.

## A. *Earliest Natural Philosophy Textbooks*

As was true of most early American used secondary school textbooks, the earliest natural philosophy textbooks used here were reprints of books first written in England. Apparently about all the textbooks in this field printed here before 1830 were reprints or revisions of those published abroad. Thus in this section attention will be given to a number of these reprinted textbooks that apparently were used in some American academies and early high schools.

*William Enfield.* Certainly one of the first of the natural philosophy textbooks to be reprinted here was by Enfield, who was an instructor in Warrington Academy in England. It was entitled, *Institutes of Natural Philosophy.* In the preface he stated that the reason for writing this book was because no suitable text was available for his classes. He dedicated the book to Joseph Priestly. The first American edition, which appeared in 1802, was a revised reprint of the second London edition of 1799. It was edited by Samuel Webber of Harvard. Although Enfield wrote it for use in an academy, Webber prepared the revision to be used in American colleges. Whether or not it may also have been used here in academies is not now certain.

The 1802 American edition was a large leather bound book, 8 by 10 inches in size, containing 448 pages plus numerous folded plates in the back. The contents were: Book I, Of Matter; II, Of Mechanics, or the Doctrine of Motion; III, Of Hydrostatics and Pneumatics; IV, Of Magnetism; V, Of Electricity; VI, Of Optics, or the Laws of Light and Vision; VII, Of Astronomy; followed

# A
# GRAMMAR

OF

## Natural and Experimental

# PHILOSOPHY;

INCLUDING

| | |
|---|---|
| PHYSICS, | ACOUSTICS, |
| DYNAMICS, | OPTICS, |
| MECHANICS, | ASTRONOMY, |
| HYDROSTATICS, | ELECTRICITY, |
| HYDRAULICS, | GALVANISM, |
| PNEUMATICS, | MAGNETISM, |

ACCORDING TO THE LATEST DISCOVERIES.

## WITH ONE HUNDRED ENGRAVINGS ON WOOD.

BY THE

## REV. DAVID BLAIR, *Pseud*

*Author of the Class Book, Universal Preceptor, English Grammar, Reading Exercises, Models of Letters, &c.*

*Sir Richard Phillips*

### TWENTIETH EDITION,

*From the Twelfth London Edition, Improved and Enlarged.*

### HARTFORD,

OLIVER D. COOKE AND SONS.

1824.

11  A rather popular early physics textbook used in America

by an Appendix to the Astronomy, and an Appendix of the Fictitious Airs, and the First Principles of Chemistry. It, like many other early textbooks, really was an omnibus science book. The first 244 pages were devoted to physics, 149 pages to descriptive astronomy, 35 pages to solar and lunar tables, and 20 pages to chemistry. The plates were to be used in connection with treatment of astronomy. The book was highly organized into books, the books in parts, the parts into chapters, and the chapters into propositions. No pictures were included.

*Sir Richard Phillips*, (Pseudo *David Blair*) (1767–1840). The preface of *An Easy Grammar of Natural and Experimental Philosophy* was signed by David Blair, Islington, (England), August 1807. This book was actually written by Sir Richard Phillips. He attained fame as an author, editor, bookseller, and publisher. While an editor he got into trouble by publishing statements unfavorable to the English government, for which he served some time in prison. He wrote several books which were reprinted in America, France, and Italy under pseudonyms. Thus this book was written by Sir Richard Phillips, not by Reverend David Blair.

In 1809 it was copyrighted in U.S. It soon became rather popular, for a fifth edition was printed in Philadelphia in 1821. This was a small leather bound book of 160 pages. Sixteen of the pages dealt with astronomy. Thirty pages in the back were devoted to detailed questions on matters of the text, and ten pages in fine print constituted a glossary "of terms used in the volume." Throughout the paragraphs were numbered. Thus the book lent itself to careful and directed instruction.

In 1824 an eighth American edition from the London twelfth appeared in Hartford. It was enlarged by 50 pages and an index added. More pictures were included, and the questions appeared at the end of each section rather than in the back of the book as in the fifth edition. The topics treated in the Hartford edition were: physics, dynamics, mechanics, hydrostatics, hydraulics, pneumatics, acoustics, optics, astronomy, electricity, galvanism, and magnetism," "according to the latest discoveries, with one hundred engravings on wood." When one compares this book with Enfield's text it can readily be seen why the Blair books became popular.

*D. and G. Bruce* (printers). In 1808 a book entitled *Elements of Natural Philosophy* was printed in New York. No authors name was mentioned. Its title should have been *Philosophy (or Science) of Nature,* for it dealt with matters of physics, astronomy, fossils, plants, animals, and the "Human Frame." It really

H

was a general science book of 272 pages. It was not organized in very teachable form, and likely was not widely used as a text.

*John Webster.* In 1808 Webster's *Elements of Natural Philosophy* was reprinted in Philadelphia under the editorship of Robert Patterson. This was a book of 709 pages dealing with mechanics, sound, heat, magnetism and electricity, optics, and astronomy. More than half of the book dealt with mechanics. In 1824 Amos Eaton, Professor of Natural Philosophy and Chemistry in the Vermont Academy of Medicine, revised and republished Webster's text, because the Patterson edition was out of print. It was called the *Philosophical Instructor; or, Webster's Elements of Natural Philosophy,* intended for "Academies, Medical Schools, and the Popular Class-Room." Eaton claimed that Webster's *Elements* "was written in the true character of a well proportioned abridgment" of natural philosophy. This edition was an attractive book, and contained many pictorial illustrations. It was pedagogically well written. The principles were printed in italics, which were then followed by more lengthy illustrations and explanations.

*J. Joyce* (1763–1816). Reverend Joyce published his *Lectures on Natural Philosophy* in England in 1810. Later he prepared his *Scientific Dialogues,* "intended for the Instruction and Entertainment of Young People: in which the First Principles of Natural and Experimental Philosophy are fully explained." These *Dialogues* appeared in three volumes. Volume III, "Of Optics, Magnetism, Electricity, and Galvanism," was reprinted in Philadelphia in 1819, and again by a different printer in 1829. The *Dialogues* on these topics took place between a tutor and two boys, James and Charles. Whether or not Joyce got the idea of trying to teach by conversation from Mrs. Marcet, who in 1806 had published her *Conversations in Chemistry,* cannot now be stated. Such dialogues were a much improved modification of the old catechetical (memoritor) method in which numerous elementary school textbooks were written. It is doubtful whether all three volumes were used in many secondary schools here.

*Mrs. Jane Marcet* (1769–1858). Of the natural philosophy textbooks written in England, the one to attain widest usage in America was written by Mrs. Marcet. She was the daughter of a wealthy Swiss merchant, who had an establishment in London. In England she married Dr. Alexander Marcet. She developed a flair for writing, particularly in terms to be understood by young people. She wrote a text of *Conversations on Chemistry* in 1806, which became very popular. Later she wrote her *Conversations on Political Economy* in 1816. This won praise from Lord Macaulay and others. Other writings followed.

In 1819 she published her *Conversations on Natural Philosophy*, "in which the Elements of that science are familiarly explained, and adapted to the comprehension of young pupils." Soon it began to be reprinted here. In 1821 it was reprinted in Hartford without any acknowledgment of the true authorship. It contained 311 pages. Also 1821 it was published by a different printer in Philadelphia in 256 pages. However, the material in the two books was identical, the latter merely had more lines per page. Both books had an index. The content of each consisted of XVII "Conversations." These related to such topics as, properties of bodies, gravity, motion, mechanical powers, planets, the earth, the moon, hydrostatics, pneumatics, sound, and optics. Both books presented illustrative plates. The conversations took place mainly between Emily and Mrs. B., and sometimes Caroline. The Hartford reprint appeared in several editions.

In 1824 Reverend J. L. Blake improved the *Conversations* by including detailed questions about the content at the bottom of the pages, adding illustrative notes, and presenting twelve pages in double column of fine print as "Dictionary of Philosophical Terms." The illustrative plates were all in the back of the book. The Blake texts appeared in many editions at least as late as 1839. A statement in one of the editions mentioned its use in the "Female Department of the Publick Schools in Boston."

In 1826 Dr. Thomas P. Jones, Professor of Mechanics in Franklin Institute, published an edition, which like Blake's, added questions and a glossary, but also, in his own words, he "determined to revise the whole work, and with the most perfect freedom, to make such alterations in the body of it, as should, in his opinion, best adapt it to the purpose for which it was designed." However, a comparative examination of a considerable number of pages revealed few changes. So his claims were exaggerated. The Jones book also appeared in several editions.

A quotation of a few lines indicated the nature of the conversations, as follows:

"*Emily*. If you throw a stone perpendicularly upwards, is it not the same length of time ascending that it is descending?

*Mrs. B.* Exactly; in ascending, the velocity is diminished by the force of gravity; in descending, it is accelerated by it.

*Caroline*. I should then have imagined that it would have fallen quicker than it rose?

*Mrs. B.* You must recollect that the force with which it is projected must be taken into the account; and that this force is overcome and destroyed by gravity before the body falls."

*Comments.* It is apparent that the earliest natural philosophy textbooks to be used in American schools were those first published in England and then reprinted here. A number of these writers were ministers, such as Priestly, pseudonym Blair, Joyce, and Blake. Both in England and in early America, as a professional group, ministers were generally the most highly educated, and were more accustomed to writing than others. Hence many textbooks were written by them.

Most of these books did suggest demonstrations to be performed, but evidently they were generally done by the teacher, if at all, rather than the students. Laboratories were not yet common. More than half of the suggested demonstrations related to mechanics. Most of the remainder related to optics and to magnetism and electricity.

Very few formulas were presented. All the texts contained problems as examples, but virtually no problems for pupil solution appeared. Mathematics played only a small part in these early books.

### B. *Early American Natural Philosophy Textbooks, 1830–1850*

*John Lee Comstock, M.D.* (1789–1858). The first well recognized natural philosophy textbook written in America was prepared by Comstock. After receiving a common school education in Connecticut he studied medicine. Soon after his certification as a doctor he served as a surgeon in the U.S. Army during the War of 1812. Following the War he practiced medicine in Hartford until the 1820's. Then he turned his labors to the writing of textbooks, mostly in various fields of science, and became a professional textbook writer.

In 1822 he published his *Conversations on Chemistry*. Following this he wrote textbooks in the fields of natural history (biology), botany, mineralogy, physiology, astronomy, physical geography, and zoology. In several of these fields he wrote more than one textbook. However, the field in which his books were most successful was natural philosophy.

It was in 1830 that Comstock first published his *System of Natural Philosophy*. This book was not only widely used here, but was translated into German, Greek, and other languages. It was revised and enlarged in 1838, 1844, 1848, and 1852. It is stated on the title page of the 1855 reprint that it was the 188th edition. It has been estimated that over 600,000 copies were sold by 1860. The writer has twelve copies of different dates of his *System*, and two smaller texts of different titles. The latter two apparently never were very widely used.

In the preface of the first edition of his *System of Natural Philosophy* Comstock mentioned that greatly improved textbooks had appeared in geography, arithmetic, grammar, reading, and spelling, but that none had been offered in this field. He then referred to the rather extensive use of (Mrs. Marcet's) *Conversations on Natural Philosophy*, which "though beautifully written," was by most instructors considered deficient, particularly in its explanations. Too, conversations were questioned as the best form of book instruction. Thus he followed a more standard form of presentation. The 1831 edition contained eight testimonials written by leading educators for the book.

This edition devoted 63 pages to the properties of bodies, 29 to mechanics, 16 to hydraulics, 7 to pneumatics, 10 to acoustics, 58 to optics, 75 to astronomy 13 to electricity, and 5 to magnetism. More than 200 engravings were included to help explain and illustrate the matters of the text. Searching questions on the text appeared at the bottom of each page. Some asked for demonstrations.

In 1831 his *System* was recopyrighted, but no changes were made except the format of the title page. In 1838 Comstock revised the book by adding 45 pages. Twenty new cuts were added, chiefly dealing with the steam engine and electromagnetism. In 1844 it was again revised and enlarged to 360 pages. The new matter covered such subjects as, *"Water Wheels, Gunnery, Electrotype,* showing the manner of gilding, silvering, and making copper casts, Photography, Daguerreotype," etc. In 1848 it was again revised and enlarged to 393 pages. The publishers announced in this edition that Comstock's text had been reprinted both in Scotland and in London, with a few corrections. This 1848 edition contained some of these corrections. The last revision of which the writer knows was made in 1852. The book was enlarged to 408 pages.

A few peculiarities may be mentioned. The 1830 and 1831 copyrighted editions contained a table of contents, but no index. The 1838, 1844, and 1848 editions contained no table of contents, but had indexes, but which appeared in the beginning of the book. The 1852 had its index in the back. While the title of the books remained the same, the format of the title pages changed several times. All of these volumes were bound with leather. In order to keep his books in line with new scientific discoveries, he revised them frequently. Frequent revisions were not common in textbooks in those days.

In 1834 Comstock published the *Youth's Book of Natural Philosophy*. It consisted of 244 pages 4 1/4 by 5 1/2 inches in size. Its purpose was "to afford a facility to the introduction of Natural Philosophy into common schools, which has not heretofore existed in our country." The topics were briefly and simply treated, and many were illustrated with cuts. Its success must have been limited. Then in 1839 he published a *Common School Philosophy*. Its preface was the same as in the *Youth's Book*. It was slightly larger and bound in leather. Some minor topics were omitted, but nearly 50 pages dealing with gravity were added. Apparently the common schools of America were not yet ready to teach this subject.

*Mary Swift*. Miss Swift was the Principal of the Litchfield Female Seminary. She felt that the children of her school ought to learn something about natural philosophy. So she began preparing simple lessons for them. Then in 1833 she published the *First Lessons on Natural Philosophy*. It may be noted that this was a year before Comstock published his book for youth. Miss Swift published her *Lessons* in two parts or books. Part First contained 107 small pages, and Part Second 176. The type was rather large. Both books contained some simple cuts, and both were written in catechetical form. This form logically led to memoriter learning. These books were likely mostly used in private seminaries.

*Denison Olmsted* (1791–1859). Much of Olmsted's life was connected with Yale, as a student, tutor, and professor from 1825–1859. As early as 1831–1832 he published a work on *Natural Philosophy* in two volumes for college students. This appeared in several revisions and editions. In 1844 the fifth edition was entitled, *An Introduction to Natural Philosophy*, which was a large book of 592 pages, and was reprinted several times later. Likely it was not used in secondary schools.

In 1837 Olmsted published *A Compendium of Natural Philosophy*, which was "adapted to the use of the General Reader and of Schools and Academies." It was bound in leather and contained 359 pages. He stated that the object was to present "the most important Practical Results of Natural Philosophy, (without demonstrations) in as condensed and intelligible form as possible." He favored leaving demonstrations "to such as are professionally devoted to science." The contents dealt with preliminary principles, motion, gravity, gunnery and machinery, hydrostatics, hydraulics, pneumatics, atmosphere, air and steam, acoustics, electricity, magnetism, and optics. The topics were pedagogically well presented. The principles appeared in italics, which were followed by explanations and applications. Questions appeared at the bottom of the pages. All principles were numbered and many illustrated with cuts. Its popularity is evidenced by the fact that by 1844 it reached the 20th edition.

In 1844 it was revised and enlarged by 60 pages. In addition to its use in secondary schools, he suggested its use to two other classes: *educated men* for refreshment, and *practical men* for consultation for applied use. Most of the additional pages were in the Supplement, which dealt with instructions to young experimenters; and with select experiments, with directions for performing them. Apparently he was influenced to change his mind about the use of demonstrations and experiments in secondary schools since writing the 1837 text.

In 1851 Olmsted rather fully revised his *Compendium* to 456 pages. In this preface he mentioned that 70,000 copies had been sold of the earlier editions. Its organization was considerably changed. It was divided into parts, then into chapters, and lastly topics. The parts were: Part I, Mechanics; Part II, Hydrostatics; Part III, Pneumatics, Meteorology, and Acoustics; Part IV, Electricity; Part V, Magnetism and Electro-Magnetism; and Part VI, Optics. The Supplement was similar to the one in the 1844 edition. Later editions of this revision appeared.

*Mrs. Lincoln Phelps.* She, like Mrs. Swift a few years earlier, attempted to write books in science in very simple terms. She wrote in the fields of botany, chemistry, and natural philosophy. In 1838 she published a *Natural Philosophy for Beginners.* No doubt, it was mostly used in grammar schools, but a few academies may well have used it. It was a very attractive and well organized book. The five parts dealt with: Mechanical Properties of Solids; Mechanics; Hydrostatics, or the Subject of Liquids; Pneumatics, or the Subject of Air; Acoustics, or the Subject of Sound; Optics, or the Subject of Light; and Animal Mechanics. To the writers knowledge, her book was the first to use the terms, air, sound, and light, instead of only the more technical terms. Her use of the more simple terms set a pattern for what became common practice later in the century. Many cuts were used, the paragraphs were numbered, and many questions were included. It appeared in a number of editions.

*John Johnston.* In 1845 Johnston published a *Manual of Natural Philosophy.* He did not claim any particular originality for this work, and frankly mentioned other natural philosophy textbooks which he consulted in his writing. He did claim to "condense more within the limits of the work, and to preserve a greater uniformity of style." Its content was rather standard. It was well illustrated, but its print small. Hence, it did not look too appealing. It contained 302 pages. It was revised several times. The 1858 edition was much more attractively printed in larger type, and contained 379 pages.

*John W. Draper.* In 1847 Draper published his *Text-Book on Natural Philosophy.* The popularity of his earlier written *Text-Book on Chemistry* led him to believe that he could also write a popular book in this field. He acknowledged consultation of other works, particularly texts written by foreign authors. In approach he said that the "proper course is to teach physical science experimentally first." The technical and mathematical aspects may be taught later. He included many wood cuts "with a view of supplying, in some measure, the want of apparatus or other means of illustration." Questions appeared at the bottom of the pages. The content was presented in 73 lectures. Practical applications were made throughout. However, apparently it did not become popular, possibly because it was in lecture form.

*Golding Bird.* His *Elements of Natural Philosophy* was first written in England. Then in 1848 a reprint of the third London edition was published in Philadelphia. The reason he gave for writing this text was because of the "absence of any system of physics, sufficiently extended to include all those subjects with which men of education, . . . ought, and are required, to be familiar." However, the topics covered were little different from those that had appeared in books heretofore discussed, but more extensive and detailed treatment was given to light and electricity than in most texts. The sub-title was "Being an Experimental Introduction to the Study of the Physical Sciences." The contents were presented in thirty chapters, and included 372 illustrations. The book was printed in rather small type.

*Other textbooks, 1830–1850.* Other natural philosophy textbooks written during this period, but apparently gained only meager circulation, were: Frederick C. Bakewell's *Philosophical Conversations* (1834); Francis J. Grund's *Elements of Natural Philosophy* (1835); James Renwick's *Familiar Illustrations of Natural Philosophy* (1840), and his *First Principles of Natural Philosophy* (1842); Robert A. Coffin's *A Compendium of Natural Philosophy* (1844); Walter R. Johnson's *A System of Natural Philosophy* (Basis of the Book of Science by John M. Moffat, 1845); Reynell Coates' *First Lines of Natural Philosophy* (1846); Horatio N. Robinson's *Elements of Natural Philosophy* (1848); and Alonzo Gray's *Elements of Natural Philosophy* (1850).

*Comments.* After 1825 the number of academies in America greatly increased, reaching 6085 by 1850. Also a number of high schools were established before 1850. In both types of schools the teaching of natural philosophy became common practice. Thus it is clear why certain textbooks reached wide circulation. The *Conversations of Natural Philosophy* written by Mrs. Marcet, and republished

OF

# NATURAL PHILOSOPHY;

IN WHICH

## THE PRINCIPLES

OF

| MECHANICS, | ACOUSTICS, |
|---|---|
| HYDROSTATICS, | OPTICS, |
| HYDRAULICS, | ASTRONOMY, |
| PNEUMATICS, | ELECTRICITY, |

AND

## MAGNETISM,

ARE FAMILIARLY EXPLAINED, AND

ILLUSTRATED BY MORE THAN TWO HUNDRED

### Engravings.

TO WHICH ARE ADDED QUESTIONS FOR THE EXAMINATION OF THE PUPILS.

**DESIGNED FOR THE USE OF SCHOOLS AND ACADEMIES.**

SECOND EDITION.

---

### BY J. L. COMSTOCK, M. D.

Mem. Con. M. S.; Hon. Mem. R. I. M. S.; Author of Notes to Conv. on Chemistry ;
Auth. of Gram. Chem.; of Elem. Mineralogy; of Nat. Hist.
of Quadr. and Birds, &c.

---

### Hartford :

**PUBLISHED BY D. F. ROBINSON & CO.**

SOLD BY COLLINS & HANNAY, J. LEAVITT, AND R. LOCKWOOD, NEW-YORK;
TOWAR, J. & D. M. HOGAN, PHILADELPHIA; J. JEWETT, AND J. J. HAR-
ROD, BALTIMORE; LUKE LOOMIS & CO., PITTSBURGH; C. D. BRADFORD
& CO., CINCINNATI; RICHARDSON, LORD & HOLBROOK, AND CARTER &
HENDEE, BOSTON; A. S. BECKWITH, PROVIDENCE; J. & J. W. PRENTISS,
KEENE; GLAZIER & CO., HALLOWELL; P. A. BRINSMADE, AUGUSTA, J. I.
CUTLER & CO. BELLOWS FALLS; and Booksellers generally.

1831.

12  A very widely used physics textbook

here by Blake and by Jones, first published in the earlier period, evidently continued in use in many schools for some time after 1830. However, the texts which attained unusually wide usage were written in America by Comstock and by Olmsted. Apparently little attention was given experiments until just before 1850 by Draper and by Bird. All but the very smallest books were still bound with leather. Only one author, Mrs. Phelps, began to use the simple terms of air, sound, and light rather than the Greek technical terms only for these topics.

## C. *Natural Philosophies, 1850–1870*

EVEN though many of the more popular texts first written during the previous period continued in use in some secondary schools during this period, in this section treatment will be given only to those first published after 1850. It can be expected that certain changes will be evident in these later texts. Again, only the more commonly used texts will be discussed.

*Richard G. Parker* (1798–1869). Parker, who had written a popular *English Composition* and also readers, eventually became interested in the field of natural philosophy. In 1837, while Parker was principal of a Boston grammar school, the Boston School committee ordered a few pieces of philosophical apparatus to be used in the grammar schools. Directing the use of the apparatus led Parker to write a simple book in the field in 1848. Since this book was intended for elementary school use, it was not discussed in the previous period. Then in 1853 he published *A School Compendium of Natural and Experimental Philosophy,* which apparently was primarily intended for secondary schools.

This book consisted of 400 pages of text and 45 pages in the back of pictures of pieces of apparatus. These pictures were in addition to the many cuts appearing throughout the book. The book was carefully organized. It presented the most important principles in larger type. The questions, instead of appearing at the bottom of the page, as was most usual, appeared in indented spaces in italic type beside the topics, which were numbered. Thus the pupil's study was virtually directed. In the beginning of the book were listed the pieces of apparatus used in the Boston schools in 1847 classified under the various topics. The *Compendium* continued to appear in reprints until Parker's decease. This book indicated the coming of a change of name for the field. The first sentence of context of the book defined the field, as follows:

"Natural Philosophy, or Physics, is the science which treats of the powers, properties and mutual action of natural bodies, and the laws and operations of the material world."

After Parker's death the book was theoretically revised and recopyrighted by George W. Plympton in 1871. However, virtually no changes were made in the body of the book. However, the Appendix of 42 pages was new. Instead of consisting merely of pictures of apparatus, it consisted of summary statements on various topics, problems for solution, further discussion on certain topics, and pictorial illustrations.

*David A. Wells* (1828–1898). Before Wells turned to textbook writing he was an economist, and had served as a consultant for several industries. Apparently it was when he was a business consultant for a publishing house that he became interested in attempting to write textbooks. So in 1857 he published two books: *The Science of Common Things*, and a *Natural Philosophy*. It is the writer's opinion that he wrote the first mentioned book first. Its subtitle was "First Principles of Physical Science." It contained only 312 pages of text, and was intended for "Schools, Families, and Young Students." Likely it was mostly used in grammar schools. Its topics were those commonly found in natural philosophy books. He used the simpler terms of sound, light, and heat, rather than the more technical terms.

The *Natural Philosophy* (1857) contained 441 pages of content, and a good index. It included the topics commonly found in such texts, except he omitted the treatment of astronomy. He expanded the treatment of heat and meteorology. Under heat he dealt with warming and ventilation, and under meteorology he discussed dew, clouds, rain, hail, snow, winds, and weather. In this book he still used the technical terms of pneumatics, acoustics, and so on. It was organized so that both the teacher and pupils were well guided in the learning process. The paragraphs dealing with the sub-topics were numbered. Following the statement of a principle there appeared in fine type the explanation or illustration together with a cut. On the margin of most paragraphs were printed questions in fine type. Altogether it included 375 engravings. By 1860 the 15th edition appeared.

In 1879 Well's text was revised, enlarged, and somewhat rearranged by Worthington Ford. Many new engravings were added. Among the reasons given for the revision was the "recent and extensive progress in scientific discovery, especially in the departments of heat, light, electricity, and magnetism." The frontispiece was the Table of Spectra in color. Colored illustrations were few before that date. The Well's text appeared in numerous reprints.

*G. P. Quackenbos* (1826–1881). He was a principal of the Collegiate School in New York. Before writing in this field he had written texts in English composition and American history. In 1859 he published *A Natural Philosophy*, "embracing the most recent discoveries in the various branches of physics, and exhibiting the application of scientific principles in every-day life." It was adapted to be used with or without apparatus, and included full descriptions of experiments. It may be noted that the term "physics" was used, and that experiments were explained. These two features were not common in texts before 1840. The description of experiments were printed in fine print following the statement and discussion of the topics. Questions appeared at the bottom of pages, and examples for practice at the end of the chapters. It is evident that this book was not written for memoritor learning. The last 33 pages were used to present cuts of apparatus which had been referred to in the body of the text. These were in addition to many cuts in the body of the text. It was frequently reprinted in the 1860's, and in 1871 was recopyrighted, but with little apparent change.

*William G. Peck*. Peck taught natural philosophy and mechanics at Columbia College. In 1859 he published the *Elements of Mechanics*, which he suggested for use in colleges, academies, and high schools. It contained 344 pages of text. It dealt with motion, forces, gravity, machines, fluids, gas and vapors, and pumps. It appeared in several editions. It is doubtful whether it was used in many secondary schools. Advertisements appeared on the last 18 pages.

In 1860 he published an *Introductory Course of Natural Philosophy*, which really was a translation and slightly revised edition of M. Ganot's popular *Physique*. *Fac-simile* copies of Ganot's engravings were used, which were very attractive, but Peck added a chapter on the application of machines. It contained both a table of contents and an index, but the index was merely an expanded table of contents in outline form. Its 500 pages of content constituted a somewhat larger book than most American texts of that period. After many reprinted editions, it was recopyrighted in 1875, but without any changes.

In 1881 this book was rather thoroughly revised by Levi Burbank and James Hanson. After each major section there now appeared an outline summary, and in the back of the book a list of 85 experimental problems and 591 review questions. Apparently an attempt was made to improve it pedagogically, as well as to bring it up-to-date scientifically. The copyright was renewed in 1888. It is evident that Peck's *Ganot* was well received in American schools.

*Le Roy C. Cooley*. Cooley was teaching natural science at the State Normal

School, Albany, when he published *A Text Book of Natural Philosophy* in 1868. It was intended for "High Schools and Academies." All earlier texts mentioned academies before high schools. Apparently he viewed the future of high schools more promising than of academies. This was a book of 315 pages, without an index. In the beginning of the book there was a list of "Topics for Review," which really was like a detailed table of contents, but without reference to pages. The chapters dealt with properties of matter, motion, sound, light, heat, and electricity. He omitted astronomy and meteorology. He claimed to have omitted that what was "merely novel or amusing," and dropped the use of such classical terms, as acoustics, pneumatics, and hydraulics as the titles of chapters. At the end of each major section there was a list of problems illustrating the principles involved. Most of these involved mathematics, including the answers. From these comments it is evident that this book was a forerunner of what later physics textbooks were like.

This book was thoroughly revised in 1880, and the title was changed to *The New Text-Book of Physics*. It contained both a good table of contents and a good index. The content was more attractively presented and more engravings included. Each chapter concluded with a summary and a list of problems. In all, it appeared much more teachable.

In 1871 Cooley also wrote a simpler book, entitled, *Natural Philosophy for Common and High Schools*. The textual matter consisted only of 192 pages. It was an attractive and a well illustrated book. In 1881 it was revised and enlarged to 242 pages. The last 18 pages consisted of a "Summary of Principles." While it was claimed to be intended also for high schools, it likely was used in few, unless only for a semester or for several days per week.

*W. J. Rolfe and J. A. Gillet.* Both of these men were teachers in the high school of Cambridge, Massachusetts. Gillet for some years had been trying out certain of these materials in his classes. Then with the aid of Rolfe they published their *Natural Philosophy* in 1868. Soon it appeared in several editions. This was a book of more than 500 pages of well presented material. The main body of the book dealt only with what they considered the basic aspects of the subject; namely, mechanics, sound, light, heat, and electricity. Then an appendix of 80 pages dealt with physics of the atmosphere, sources and conversion of energy, a list of tables and problems, and questions for review and examination. The book was well illustrated, and each section ended with a summary. In the back of the 1870 edition 18 pages of testimonials and advertisements appeared.

In 1869 these authors published a *Handbook of Natural Philosophy*. This book was primarily written for the upper grammar grades, but they added 94 pages of more advanced material in an appendix so that it could also be used in high schools not having time for a larger work. It soon appeared in a number of editions. It was a simple and attractive book. These authors also wrote texts in chemistry and astronomy.

*Joel Dorman Steele* (1836–1886). Steele attended several academies in New York state and later Genesee College (now Syracuse), after which he taught in several academies. While principal at Elmira Academy he began to teach several sciences from his own prepared outlines, rather than from textbooks. With some additions he began to publish these outlines as textbooks. They became known as "Fourteen Weeks Series in the Sciences." He ultimately published texts in natural philosophy, chemistry, geology, physiology, and astronomy, as well as in American history jointly with his wife. In 1872 he resigned his position at Elmira to devote full time to textbook writing.

In 1869 Steele published the *Fourteen Weeks Course in Natural Philosophy*. This was an attractive and well illustrated book of 340 pages. He stated that as "physics is generally the first branch of Natural Science pursued in schools, it is important that the beginner should not be disgusted with the abstractions of the subject." Thus he attempted to make his presentation clear and interesting. The contents dealt with matter, attraction (gravity), motion, mechanical powers, liquids and gases, sound, and light. Each section ended with a long list of practical questions. In the back 20 pages were devoted to "Notes," which dealt with apparatus and experiments. Each suggested experiment referred to the page in the context which presented the corresponding principle of physics. This book appeared in reprinted editions nearly every year until 1878, when it was rather radically revised. The body of the text was reduced in volume, new cuts appeared, and in the back 26 pages of blackboard drawings with dark background were introduced. Each section began with an analytical outline, and ended with an historical sketch of that phase of science.

After Steele's decease the publishers employed W. Le C. Stevens, Professor of Physics of Packer Collegiate Institute, Brooklyn, to revise Steele's text, under the title of *Popular Physics*. Its organization was similar to the 1878 edition, but its content was brought up-to-date and somewhat increased. This book was again revised and slightly enlarged in 1896.

In 1889 *The Chautauqua Course in Physics* was published with Steele's name, even though he had died several years before. This was one of the required books of the Chautauqua Literary and Scientific Circle for the enrolled readers for that year. It was printed in very attractive form by the Chautauqua Press.

*Other texts, 1850 to 1870.* In addition to the texts heretofore discussed the following were also published during this period: Leonard D. Gale's *Elements of Natural Philosophy* (1851); A. W. Sprague's *Elements of Natural Philosophy* (1856); Elias Loomis' *Elements of Natural Philosophy* (1858); and J. D. Everett's *Deschanel's Elementary Treatise on Natural Philosophy* (1863).

*Comments on the 1850 to 1870 texts.* A number of marked changes took place in the natural philosophy textbooks during this period. Very few were bound in leather, while nearly all before this period were. Secondly, the authors paid more attention to the form of presentation of the material. Pedagogical considerations in the arrangement became more marked, such as questions on the margin of pages, different type for the statement of the principles than for the illustrations, together with more attractive cuts. Thirdly, authors began the use of the term "physics" in the context, although not in the titles, except in the later revised editions. Too, several dropped the classical terms for sound, light, and heat. Fourthly, a number of the texts included lists of experiments in the back of the book. It is rather clear that the texts of this period represented a transition from the older more classical texts to the more modern texts which were to appear in the next period.

## D. *Physics Textbooks, 1870–1900*

A number of the texts first published in the previous period continued in circulation into this period. This was particularly true of the texts written by Peck, Cooley, and Steele. In fact, some of the revised editions of these authors appeared even in the 1890's. Apparently no texts first written in this period became as popular as earlier books written by Comstock, Olmsted, Parker, and Steele. Again only the books appearing in a number of editions will be discussed in this section.

*Sidney A. Norton.* In 1870 Norton's *Elements of Natural Philosophy* was published. The main text consisted of 444 pages, with 18 pages of problems added in the back. The pictures numbered 350. A recapitulation appeared at the end of each section. In the discussion of the topics he used both the older more technical terms and the newer simpler ones.

In 1875 Norton published *The Elements of Physics*. This was one of the first texts to use the term "Physics" in the main title. He claimed to have prepared this much simplified text "at the request of many teachers, for the use of pupils in academies and common schools." The object was to give a "systematic and symmetrical epitome of the Science." Problems appeared at the end of the chapters. It was an attractive and well illustrated book.

*Elroy M. Avery.* In 1878 Avery published his *Elements of Natural Philosophy* of 456 pages for high schools and academies. Although the title page still bore the term, "Natural Philosophy," the first section was entitled, "The Domain of Physics." Likewise the chapter titles used the newer terms of liquids, heat, light, and sound. This book contained more exercises and experiments than any book thus far discussed. However, he stated that it was not intended that "each member of each class shall work all of the problems." In notes "To the Teacher" he suggested where the apparatus mentioned in the book may be obtained. The book contained nearly 400 engravings. In addition to the exercises and review questions at the end of sections and chapters, 14 pages in the back provided further exercises. The principles were printed in italics and explanations in different type. The engravings were well placed in relation to the explanations. This book appeared in frequent reprints. Then in 1885 it was revised and enlarged by nearly 150 pages. The make-up of the book remained the same.

In 1884 Avery published his *First Principles of Natural Philosophy* of 402 pages. It was intended for schools not wanting to give the time required for his larger book. Simple experiments not requiring expensive apparatus were provided. In 1897 this book was thoroughly revised and appeared under the title of *Elementary Physics*. It was even a little smaller that the *First Principles*. Apparently Avery attempted to meet varied textbook requirements in the science textbook field. Not only did he publish these different sized natural philosophy books, he also wrote two different sized books in chemistry.

*Alfred P. Gage.* Gage was an instructor of physics in the Boston English High School. Thus he had very definite ideas as to what could or could not be well taught in high school. In 1882 he published *A Textbook on the Elements of Physics.* He, like Avery, greatly stressed experimentation and laboratory work. He argued that in most schools where chemistry was taught laboratory work was included, but not so in physics. Suggested experiments appeared throughout the book. In the back of the book there was a Syllabus of 30 pages, which really was a recapitulation of the various physical principles that had been dealt with in the text.

In 1887 Gage published an *Introduction to Physical Science,* which really was a physics treatise. Even though somewhat smaller than his *Elements*, it even more fully provided for experimentation. In the preface he expressed satisfaction of the "successful adoption of laboratory practice in all parts of the U.S.; likewise its adaption by some leading universities as a requirement for admission." Both of these books appeared in several editions.

In 1890 he published a *Physical Laboratory Manual and Note Book*. Two quotations were printed on the cover. The first one by Thomson was: "One's knowledge of science begins when he can measure what he is speaking about and express it in numbers." Blank pages were interspersed between the pages on which the results of the experiments were to be written. In all, 206 experiments were included. A note in the back mentioned where a price-list catalogue of apparatus could be obtained.

In 1895 Gage's *Principles of Physics* was published. This was a larger book than his earlier ones. It was intended to replace the two-course feature of his previous books. It was suggested that it be taught through formal lectures illustrated experimentally, together with informal recitations and conferences. Experimentation was not so fully stressed. In 1907 an edition revised by Arthur W. Goodspeed was published. It was planned for secondary schools and some colleges.

*Isaac Sharpless and George M. Philips.* In 1883 these authors published a very attractively printed *Natural Philosophy of* 350 pages. More than 300 attractive figures illustrated the various topics. Suggested exercises and experiments were interspersed throughout the book after each topic and chapter. In 1892 this book was revised and enlarged by C. C. Balderston. The chapter on electricity was entirely rewritten, and the chapters on matter, motion, force, and light largely rewritten. The body of the text contained 368 pages. Then *A Laboratory Manual of Physics* of 89 pages was incorporated in the back of the book. It provided detailed instructions for 117 experiments. These were in addition to the 182 suggested experiments which appeared throughout the body of the text. A good summary ended each chapter.

*Henry S. Carhart and Horatio N. Chute.* In 1892 these authors published their *Elements of Physics*. This was a well illustrated book of 400 pages. The chapter titles were: Matter, mechanics of solids, mechanics of fluids, heat, magnetism and electricity, sound, and light. The principles were printed in italics, the discussion in regular type, and the suggested experiments in smaller type. A list of exercises followed each section. In the preface it was mentioned that the experiments described, for the most part, were designed to illustrate principles.

This evidently meant that the teachers should conduct the experiments as demonstrations. However, they further recommended that "teachers supplement the classwork in this book with practical work in the laboratory." This text was soon followed by later editions. An appendix, consisting mainly of tables, was added to the 1897 edition. In 1901 the authors published their *Physics for High School Students*, which was a revision of the *Elements*. More problems were added at the end of sections. These were to be studied in the classroom. If laboratory work was to be done, it should be based on a separate manual. Evidently the Carhart and Chute texts were among the leaders at the turn of the century.

*George A. Hoadley.* It has been the writer's intention to deal only with textbooks published in America before 1900, but since Hoadley's *A Brief Course in General Physics* was published in 1900, a brief treatment of it will be included. He stated in the preface that an effective study of physics should include the use of a good text, class demonstrations, practical problems and questions, and experimentation in the laboratory. Description of experiments appeared throughout the book, which apparently were meant to be demonstrated in the classroom. Then at the end of each section were problems for solution and experiments for the laboratory. In the back there were the answers to numerical problems, a list 407 formulas, and a number of tables. Later Hoadley published the *Essentials of Physics*, and a *Physical Laboratory Handbook*.

*Other physics textbooks, 1870–1900.* In addition to the books discussed a few others were published. Among them were: Edwin J. Houston's *Elements of Natural Philosophy* (1879); and D. E. Jones' *Examples in Physics* (1888). Most of the other texts in this field were either meant for the elementary school, for college, or were reprints of texts first published in the earlier period.

### E. *Characteristics of Natural Philosophy Textbooks*

*Some general characteristics.* The earliest textbooks used in America in this field were reprints of texts written in England. The editors of the American reprints commonly made some changes, such as adding questions, providing summaries or outlines, and so on. No American written text gained attention until Comstock's *System of Natural Philosophy* was published in 1830. After that date few foreign written texts were reprinted here. Until 1850 nearly all of these texts, both foreign and American, were bound in leather. After that date very few were.

The term "natural philosophy" was commonly used in the titles until the

I

1890's. Of the 160 texts in the writer's collection fewer than a dozen used the term "physics." The first one to do so was Norton's in 1875. However, several authors much earlier used the term "physics" in the context but not in the title. For example, in 1853 Parker defined "Natural Philosophy, or Physics, . . ." in his *Compendium of Natural and Experimental Philosophy*. Soon others did the same.

All the early texts used the classical scientific terms of dynamics, hydrostatics, hydraulics, pneumatics, acoustics, and optics, instead of the more common terms of power, liquids, air, sound, and light. The first text to modernize in this respect was Mrs. Phelps book for *Beginners* in 1838. She used both types of terms, as follows: "Hydrostatics, or the Subject of Liquids," etc. One of the first secondary school texts to use the simpler terms was a text by Wells in 1857. Shortly after that most authors did so.

*Aims.* Shank[1] found that all but three of the 45 texts analyzed mentioned one or more aims, usually in the prefaces. Altogether he found 24 different aims presented. In general, however, the books did not present very many clear-cut aims for the teaching of natural philosophy, as is true in most modern physics texts. Roughly the mentioned aims can be classified into two general types: (1) Those that gave purposes for the teaching of natural philosophy in the schools, and (2) those that mentioned reasons or justification for the writing of the texts.

The aims for the teaching of natural philosophy were: To present useful scientific knowledge (in 10 books), to create an interest in scientific matters (6), to teach the meaning of the scientific method (5), to provide mental training (4), to present scientific applications, (4) and to provide directions for the use of apparatus. It may be seen that the authors were not very conscious of the values of the teaching of natural philosophy. However, it should be added that many texts accomplished a number of these purposes even though they were not specifically mentioned as aims.

Authors were more particularly concerned with the reasons or justification for the writing of the books than they were for the value of teaching the subject. The most frequently given reasons were: Include new developments in the field (11 books), suggest better teaching method (7), use better book organization (7), add more illustrations (5), minimize use of mathematics (5), revise old editions (5), correct errors (4), and add more cuts and pictures. On the basis of these findings, the authors were more interested in creating a sale for the books than in showing the value of studying natural philosophy.

*Consistency of topics.* Except that many of the early texts included a treatment of astronomy, and a few meteorology, there was more consistency in the use of particular topics of subject matter than was true in the textbooks of most fields. Shank found that nine of the fourteen published before 1845 dealt with astronomy, several devoting more than half of the book to it, while only eight of the 31 of the later ones dealt with it, and only one after 1860. Of the 45 texts all except five dealt with matter, all with mechanics, 43 with sound, 38 with heat, 43 with and/or magnetism and electricity, and all with optics.

*Content.* It was found that very nearly all of the content of these 45 physics books could be classified under the eight following categories with the average percentage of space devoted to each: Nature and structure of matter, 3.9%; mechanics, 40.3%; sound, 5.9%; heat, 7.9%; magnetism and electricity, 16.7%; optics or light, 18%; astronomy, 6.5%; and mathematics, 0.2%.

Table VI shows how the percentages varied during the four 18-year periods. It can be seen that two-fifths of the space was related to the various aspects of mechanics. The next topics given most space were light and electricity. In fact, three-fourths of all space was devoted to mechanics, light, and electricity.

Some marked changes in space allotment occurred during the four periods. The two most marked changes were in the treatment of heat, increasing from 1.4% during the first period to 12.3% in the last; and the space devoted to astronomy, decreasing from 20.5% to 1.4%. In fact, most of the later books omitted astronomy entirely. The treatment of sound increased from 3.6% to 9.2%, and of structure of matter from 2.7% to 4.9%. The treatment of the other topics did not vary much during the periods. Of course, the nature of the treatment given a number of these topics was very different in the earlier books than in the later, particularly in the fields of electricity and light. For example, photography was unknown when the earliest books were written.

*Demonstrations and experiments.* Reference has already been made to a national study reported by Clark in 1880 concerning experiments and laboratory work. He reported that 81% of the secondary schools offered physics courses with class experiments, but no laboratory work. Only four out of 609 schools offered laboratory work. This meant that likely most experiments were conducted by the instructor as demonstrations.

Shank found that all of the books analyzed contained some suggested demonstrations or experiments. The average number per book of suggested demonstrations by topics were: Matter, 7.7; mechanics, 73.6; heat, 13.2; sound, 9.8; electricity and magnetism. 42.8; optics, 23.4; and astronomy, 0.9.

However, the topic of mechanics was the only one for which all books suggested demonstrations. The total average number of suggested demonstrations per text were 116 in the first period, 117 in the second, 182 in the third, and 205 in the last. To what extent most instructors actually conducted the suggested demonstrations is not now known.

*Pictures.* Everyone of the 45 texts contained pictures. Commonly these were pictures of apparatus related to the suggested demonstrations. The average number of cuts or pictures per book was 246. On the average 2.4 related to matter, 115 to mechanics, 11 to sound, 13 to heat, 40 to magnetism and electricity, 52 to optics, and 10 to astronomy. Of the 115 related to mechanics, on the average 64.5 pertained to solids, 27.1 to liquids, and 23.7 to gases. Some books contained no pictures related to electricity, while one contained 107. It is evident from these data that old natural philosophy books freely used visual aids.

*Improvement in teachability.* The books first written in England were very formal, technical, and unattractive. Few or no student helps were given in them. Several of the editors who republished these books in America added some teching aids. The American written texts were better pedagogically. Among the improvements were: (1) Inclusion of questions. Some placed them at bottom of page, some at end of sections or of the book, and later a number placed them at the side of the topics. (2) Use of different sizes of type. Beginning with Eaton's text in 1824, more and more of the books would have the principles either printed in larger type or in italics, the context in regular type, and the explanations of the demonstrations and experiments in small type. (3) Books later numbered the paragraphs or sub-sections for easy reference. (4) A few of the books were in conversational or dialogue form (Joyce and Marcet).

*Anecdotes and oddities.* Most early natural philosophy textbooks contained anecdotes about certain scientists of the past and/or about certain principles and applications of physics. For example, an anecdote about the indestructibility of matter, follows:

> "Sir Walter Raleigh, while smoking in the presence of Queen Elizabeth, offered to bet her majesty that he could tell her the weight of the smoke that curles upward from his pipe. The bet was accepted. Raleigh quietly finished, and then weighing the ashes, subtracted this amount from the weight of the tobacco he had placed in the pipe; he thus found the exact weight of the smoke."

TABLE VI: *Date Showing the Percent of Space of Printed Subject Matter Devoted to the Topic Divisions of the Natural Philosophy Textbooks for Each of Four Eighteen–Year Periods during 1808–1879, and the Averages Devoted to Each Topic—1808–1879*

| PERIOD | STRUCTURE OF MATTER | MECHANICS | SOUND | HEAT | MAGNETISM AND ELECTRICITY | OPTICS | ASTRONOMY | MATHEMATICS | MISCELLANEOUS | TOTAL |
|---|---|---|---|---|---|---|---|---|---|---|
| | 1 | 2 | 3 | 4 | 5 | 6 | 7 | 8 | 9 | 10 |
| 1808–1825 | 2.7 | 42.5 | 3.6 | 1.4 | 13.7 | 15.1 | 20.5 | 0.5 | 0.0 | 100.0 |
| 1826–1843 | 4.5 | 37.9 | 2.6 | 9.3 | 14.4 | 19.3 | 11.7 | 0.0 | 0.3 | 100.0 |
| 1844–1861 | 3.1 | 43.7 | 5.1 | 5.2 | 16.8 | 18.7 | 6.4 | 0.3 | 0.7 | 100.0 |
| 1862–1879 | 4.9 | 36.0 | 9.2 | 12.3 | 18.4 | 16.9 | 1.4 | 0.0 | 0.9 | 100.0 |
| 1808–1879 | 3.9 | 40.3 | 5.9 | 7.9 | 16.7 | 18.0 | 6.5 | 0.2 | 0.6 | 100.0 |

Interesting anecdotes involving Archimedes, Sir John Herschel, Benjamin Franklin, and Guericke were mentioned. These anecdotes related how some of the early scientists applied various principles of physics to unusual situations. For example, Parker's text mentioned:

"It is related of Archimedes that he employed burning-mirrors, two hundred years before the Christian era, to destroy the besieging navy of Marcellus, the Roman consul."

Other similar stories were told about use of mirrors.

Numerous incidents involving superstitions about comets were related. One was that a great comet in 1556 led to the abdication of Emperor Charles V. Also one telling how in 1066 William the Conqueror was aided in conquering England due to the superstitious effect a comet had on the English people.

SECTION FOUR

# CHEMISTRY

## Introduction

*Evolution of chemistry.* The science of chemistry owes its existence to a long and slow development and to many persons. Through experience and observation the ancient Egyptians learned to apply certain principles of chemistry to fermentation, dyeing, metal working, and to making such things as glass and pottery. On the other hand, the ancient Greeks were not so much concerned with the practice of chemistry as with speculating about the kinds of matter and their properties. They paid little attention to chemical processes.

During early Christian times the art of alchemy arose. Alchemy was based on a theory, such as held by some Greeks, that color, luster, malleability, and other qualities of precious metals, could be imparted or transmuted to baser metals in a laboratory. The chief aim apparently was to produce the "Philosopher's Stone"; namely, to produce such precious metals as gold and silver. Alchemy often was a mysterious mixture of science, religion, superstition, and black magic. Many laboratories arose and existed for many centuries practicing its theories. Many of its practitioners wrote about its theories and claims. Apparently the Roman Emperor, Diocletian, feared the Egyptian writings bearing on alchemy, so he ordered them burned lest the Egyptians would succeed in enriching themselves by producing large amounts of silver and gold. The practices in alchemical transmutations roughly continued for about 1500 years. Ultimately the failures of the alchemists in their primary purposes resulted in alchemy falling into disrepute. However, their experiments did lead to the discovery of three important acids; sulphuric, nitric, and hydrocloric.

Such discoveries and others led to the transition from alchemy to iatrochemistry or chemistry applied to medicine. In this regard a great contribution was made by Paracelsus (1493–1541), when a number of his discoveries were applied to pharmacy. Findings by J. B. van Helmont (1577–1644) made further applications to medicine.

Great advances in chemistry were made by Robert Boyle (1627–1691), who has been referred to as the "Father of Scientific Chemistry." He clearly recognized that its purpose was neither the transmutation of metals nor the preparation of medicines, but the observation and generalizations about certain phenomena. This denied validity of the alchemical view regarding the constitution of matter. It also presented the definition of an element in chemistry. Boyle's Law concerned the interrelationship between the pressure and fixed weight of gases. Boyle published *The Sceptical Chymist* in 1661. Jos. Black, Jos. Priestly, and Scheele likewise did important work in the study of gases.

One of the earlier textbooks of chemistry was written by Nicholas Lemery (1645–1715) in 1675, entitled, *Cours de Chemie*. It contained most of the then known facts of chemistry, and was systematic in presenting and dealing with the chemical substances under the headings of mineral, vegetable, and animal. He was one of the first to distinguish between vegetable and mineral, or organic and inorganic chemistry.

In the meantime, George E. Stahl (1660–1734), and others retarded the advance in scientific chemistry by their "Phlogiston" theory of combustion. While their work did explain some things, it failed to account for others.

Later the nonvalidity of the "Phlogiston" theory was demonstrated by Antoine Lavoisier (1743–1794). William Hale in his *Chemistry Triumphant* stated:

"In 1774 occurred that most farreaching discovery by Antoine Lavoisier, in Paris, of the principle of combustion. Up to that day no one understood the nature of changes brought about in the burning of a substance (calcination) or its reverse (reduction), the return of a metallic oxide or calx into original metal. It marks the beginning

# SYLLABUS

### Of a COURSE

### O F

# LECTURES

### O N

# CHEMISTRY.

*By Benjamin Rush M.D.*
*1770*

PHILADELPHIA : Printed 1770.

13 Title-page of Rush's *Chemical Syllabus,* 1770

of chemistry as a science, and still more it opens the door to metal-lurgy and mechanical engineering. Our modern civilization cannot antedate this discovery."

In 1789 he published his *Traite Elementaire de Chemie*, which was a modern text-book of chemistry. This book helped clear up the confusion that had existed regarding chemical theory and nomenclature. At least one other great chemical contribution was to come (1808), when John Dalton (1766-1844) developed the atomic theory as a basis for the correct interpretation of chemical reactions. Of course, many other discoveries affecting chemistry have been made since.

*Chemistry in American medical schools.* After studying under Black, the eminent chemist in Edinburgh, Benjamin Rush returned to Philadelphia, and accepted the chair of chemistry in the newly founded medical school there in 1769. The next year he wrote *Rush's Syllabus*, the first American-written chemistry book. It really was a compendium of facts stated in topical outline form. Many of these facts were really notes copied from Black's lectures. His work apparently was the first teaching of chemistry in America.

Other medical schools followed. The Harvard Medical School introduced chemistry in 1782, and Dartmouth in 1798. Colleges proper were somewhat slower in introducing chemistry, but gradually it became an established subject in them. Princeton was the first academic college to establish a separate chair for chemistry.

*Chemistry teaching in American secondary schools.* Since the early Latin grammar schools failed to offer courses in science, it was in the academies that chemistry was first taught. Philadelphia Academy, founded by Benjamin Franklin in 1851, has generally been given credit as being the first secondary school to offer work in science. It is doubtful, however, whether a regular course in chemistry was offered there in its beginning. However, some chemical content could well have been included in other science courses.

According to Frank Clarke's *Report on the Teaching of Chemistry and Physics in the U.S.*, issued by the Bureau of Education in 1881, Nazareth Hall, Nazareth, Pennsylvania, introduced instruction in chemistry and physics in 1790. This apparently was a secondary school. According to S.R. Powers' *Hiistory of Chemistry in the Secondary Schools of the U.S. Previous to 1850*, Onondaga Academy, New York, was the first to do so in 1813. Other secondary schools that early introduced chemistry were Dwight's Home School for Girls, Clinton, New York in 1815; Hartwick Seminary, Hartwick, New York, in 1815; and Cook Academy in Havana, New York, in 1815, Others soon followed. According to

Stout's study of midwestern high schools, roughly two-thirds of them taught chemistry between 1860 and 1900.

## A. *Earliest American Used Chemistry Books*

*Introduction.* Other than Rush's *Syllabus* (1770), which really was not a regular textbook, the earliest chemistry textbooks published in the United States were reprints of foreign texts, either English or translations from the French. Mangery analyzed 69 chemistry textbooks published in America.[1]

When considering the earliest books it seems very difficult now to know just in what types of schools they were used. In none of the twelve earliest books Mangery analyzed was there a mention of "For Use in Schools." Five of these twelve mentioned "For the Student," and five for "Friends of General Patronage." Likely several of these books were used in American medical schools and colleges. Most of these were too technical and large for secondary school use. Too, records seem to show that academies did not teach chemistry until the second decade of the 1800's. However, historical records are often incomplete on these matters. For example, Paul Monroe's *A Brief Course in the History of Education* mentions that only five chemistries had been published by 1832. Mangery's list includes 23 before 1832, and the writer has two additional early books not in his list. Thus at least 25 were published here before 1832 and likely more.

*Early French chemistry texts.* Two of the six oldest analyzed were written by French authors. In 1790 Antoine Lavoisier's *Elements of Chemistry* was published in a translated edition in Boston with 479 pages. Then M.I.A. Chaptal's *Elements of Chemistry* was published here in 1801. This was a large book, and appeared in a number of editions. Likely these were used in American colleges rather than in academies, both because of their volume, and because they were published before academies taught chemistry.

*Early English written chemistry textbooks.* One of the first of these was written by William Henry, entitled, *An Epitome of Experimental Chemistry,* and edited here by B. Silliman of Yale. In his notes to the first American edition of 1802 Silliman listed the colleges and universities then teaching chemistry. Evidently he expected some of them to use Henry's book. The second American edition of 1810 was a reprint, with added notes, of the fifth English edition. It was a large book. Many later authors acknowledged the use of Henry's texts for help.

Of the English reprints the one which became most popular, and apparently was widely used in American academies, was Mrs. Jane Marcet's *Conversations on Chemistry*. It apparently was first published in England in 1806, and in 1809 a reprint appeared in New Haven. Reference in the previous chapter was made to Mrs. Marcet's ability to write popular science books for youth. She wrote three popular books in conversational form: Chemistry, political economy, and natural philosophy. It has been claimed that 160,000 copies of the chemistry text in its various editions were sold in America before 1853.

The 1813 American edition consisted of 337 pages of conversations, to which were added sections, not in conversational form, dealing with alkalies, mineral waters, dyeing, tanning, and currying. The body of the text consisted of XXIII Conversations carried on among Mrs. B., Emily, and Caroline. For example:

"Hydrogen is derived from two Greek words, the meaning of which is to produce water.

*Emily.* And how does hydrogen produce water?

*Mrs. B.* Water is composed of 85 parts, by weight, of oxygen, chemically combined with 15 parts of hydrogen gas, or inflamable air.

*Caroline.* It must be a most extraordinary gas, that will produce both fire and water."

This method was informal and a great improvement over the old catechetical method. Of course, it did not involve many actual experiments.

Later her book was revised and republished by several American editors. In 1822 J. L. Comstock republished it by rearranging several conversations and adding several others; also adding 15 pages of questions for exercise, 17 pages of "A Vocabulary of Chemical Terms," and a list of 48 experiments. With these additions a more thorough course in chemistry could be given. Comstock's edition appeared in numerous reprints.

In 1831 Thomas P. Jones published the *New Conversations of Chemistry*, "adapted to the present state of that science." This was a rather radical revision of Mrs. Marcet's original work. Eight more conversations were included, many of the original ones were revised, more pictures of apparatus were included, descriptions of experiments incorporated into the conversations, and questions placed at the bottom of all pages. Again this edition was an improvement over the previous ones. Thus the American editions of Mrs. Marcet's *Chemistry*, as well as of her *Natural Philosophy*, became popular in American schools.

In 1810 *The Rudiments of Chemistry* by Samuel Parkes was printed in Philadelphia based on the 1809 London edition. This was a small book of 291 pages and not bound in leather like other early ones. It first presented 20 pages of plates of chemical apparatus, with explanations of them. The principal facts were printed in larger type, and numbered, which were to be "considered as axioms to be treasured up in the mind, as a foundation for superstructure of all his future chemical attainments." Then the illustrations and experiments were given in smaller type. In the back there were 19 pages devoted to explanations and definitions of common chemical terms.

Also in 1810 an even smaller text was reprinted in Philadelphia. It was Sir Richard Phillips' (pseudo Rev. D. Blair) *A Grammar of Chemistry*, edited and revised here by Benjamin Tucker. In 1817 it was slightly revised and reprinted. Tucker urged its use in seminaries. The text contained 133 pages of rather fine print, followed by 16 pages of questions and 31 pages of a glossary of chemical terms. Its principal facts appeared in numbered paragraphs in larger type, followed by illustrations in smaller print. It was reprinted again in 1819.

In 1817 there was published in London the third edition of a book entitled, *Chemical Amusement*, "comprising a series of curious and instructive experiments in chemistry," by Frederick Accum. This edition was reprinted here. Its more than 400 pages explained 192 experiments, which could be "easily performed, and unattended by Danger." Whether this book was used in schools here is not certain. Nevertheless this type of book could help popularize chemistry as a field of study.

In 1827 Edward Turner published his *Elements of Chemistry* in Edinburgh, which soon was republished here. This contained 471 pages of text, plus 27 pages of tables and an index. It later appeared in a larger edition. Its use in secondary schools may be doubted, yet a number of later American authors who wrote texts for secondary schools borrowed heavily from him, particularly Comstock and Gray.

Also in 1827 there was published in Boston the *Elements of Chemistry* for "Schools and Academies" by Andrew Fyfe of Edinburgh, which was edited and revised by John W. Webster of Harvard. The text consisted of 370 pages, with 24 pages of additional matters in the back. On pages 384-385 there appeared a list of 50 authors who were referred to somewhere in the book on such matters as bleaching, brewing, distilling, dyeing, as well as other authors of chemistry texts.

*Other imported texts.* It is not here attempted to mention all of the chemistries that were written in Europe and later reprinted here, but a few additional ones may well be listed. Among them were: James Parkinson's *Chemical Pocket-Book* (1802); Sir Humphrey Davy's *Elements of Chemical Philosophy* (1812); James Cutbush's *Philosophy of Experimental Chemistry*, I, II (1813); Jeremiah Joyce's *Dialogues in Chemistry* I, II (1818); D. B. Reid's *Rudiments of Chemistry* (1837); and Justus Liebig's *Chemistry* (1840).

## B. *Early American Chemistry Textbooks, 1820–1860*

THE earliest attempts by American authors to publish chemistry textbooks was to reprint or revise and reprint books from across. Even when they began to write textbooks, they still leaned heavily on foreign works for reference.

*J. L. Comstock* (1789–1858). Comstock, who was author of the first popular American written natural philosophy, also was one of the first Americans to write in the field of chemistry. Mention has already been made of his republication of Mrs. Marcet's *Conversations on Chemistry*. In 1822 he rewrote and enlarged David Blair's *A Grammar of Chemistry*. In this book the questions appeared at the end of sections rather than at the end of the book. Both ended with a glossary. Apparently this rewriting provided the experience Comstock needed later to write his own texts.

In 1831 he published the *Elements of Chemistry*, "in which the recent discoveries in the science are included, and its doctrines familiarly explained, and designed for use in schools and academies." Although this was Comstock's book, he acknowledged his debt to such authors as Thompson, Henry, Davy, Gray, Ure, Accum, Faraday, and particularly Turner. The text consisted of 345 pages, followed by a long table of Equivalents, and an index. Questions appeared at the bottom of all pages. The book was organized into parts. They were: Part I, Imponderable Agents; Part II, Ponderable Bodies; Part III, Organic Chemistry; and Part IV, Analytical Chemistry.

In 1839 it was republished as the 30th edition without change, except the addition of Part V, Chemical Mineralogy, and Part VI, Miscellaneous Facts and Experiments, consisting of more than 70 added pages. Evidently the first edition was criticised for too few experiments, and so they were added in Part VI. In 1846 it was considerably revised and recopyrighted. The experiments were incorporated throughout the body of the text instead of at the end of the book. Many new plates were introduced. The 1849 reprint was the 54th edition. It is evident that Comstock's texts in chemistry were the first to become really popular in U.S.

*Lewis C. Beck, M.D.* Beck, who was Professor in the University of the City of New York, in 1831 published *A Manual of Chemistry*, intended "for Medical Schools, Colleges, and Academies." It contained 441 pages of rather fine print, and no cuts. It did not appear very appealing or teachable. However, a second edition was published in 1834.

*Mrs. Lincoln Phelps.* She, like Mrs. Marcet of England, developed a flair for writing science books in popular terms for youth. Ultimately she wrote texts in botany, geology, natural philosophy, and chemistry. While teaching science in Troy Female Seminary, of which her famous sister, Mrs. Emma Willard, was principal, she had the girls conduct certain experiments and report on them. These experiences prompted the writing of a simple chemistry text.

In 1834 Mrs. Phelps published a *Chemistry for Beginners*. This was one of two texts thus far discussed that was not bound in leather. It contained 216 pages of text. The paragraphs were numbered. Unlike most texts, the chemical facts and the explanations of experiments were printed with the same sized type. Questions were printed at the bottom of the pages. Simple cuts accompanied the explanations. One edition appeared as late as 1852.

Later Mrs. Lincoln became the principal of a female institute in Maryland. Apparently she soon became aware that her first book was too simple even for girls' secondary schools. So in 1838 she published her *Lectures on Chemistry*, "for the use of Schools, Families, and Private Students." In the preface she stated:

"Chemistry is a most comprehensive science;—while it instructs philosophy in the constitution of matter, it teaches how to perform the most common operations in the business of life, such as the preparation of food, the warming and ventilation of apartments, soap making, washing, etc. The arts of dyeing, glass making, engraving, and of preparing medicines, have their foundation in chemical science."

In brief, she attempted to give chemistry a woman's touch. Lecture I was introductory. Then Part I, dealing with Imponderables, consisted of five lectures. Lastly, Part III, Organic Chemistry, included six lectures. The text contained 383 pages. The paragraphs presenting the topics were numbered. The explanations of the experiments were in smaller type. Cuts of the apparatus to be used appeared with explanations. Questions and comments appeared at the bottom of the pages. A second edition appeared in 1844.

*L. D. Gale.* In 1837 Gale published the *Elements of Chemistry* for "Schools and Academies." Its five parts dealt with Imponderable Agents, Non-metallic Bodies, The Metals, Vegetable Chemistry, and Animal Chemistry. It was a small and attractive leather bound book of 294 pages, and included more than 100 engravings and questions at the bottom of the pages. It soon appeared in a second edition.

*Alonzo Gray.* In 1840 Gray published his *Elements of Chemistry*, which was intended for academies, high schools, and colleges. He, like Mrs. Phelps, attempted to combine the "*scientific* with the *popular* and *useful* parts of the subject." The table of contents consumed 14 pages. After the Introduction, Part I, Imponderable Agents, dealt with caloric, light, and electricity. Part II, Chemical Affinity, was rather brief. Part III, Ponderable Bodies, treated nonmetallic elements, metals, salts, natural substances, animal chemistry, and analytical chemistry. The print and the organization of the book made the various topics and matters stand out clearly. It contained a good glossary and an extensive index of 12 pages. It soon appeared in numerous editions, and evidently had wide secondary school use.

In 1848 the book in parts was revised and recopyrighted. The chapter on Natural Substances was changed to Organic Chemistry, and Animal Chemistry dropped as a chapter, but retained as a topic. In all it was enlarged by more than 50 pages. Since his first book was used in some colleges, it may be that the revision was enlarged to make it even more attractive for colleges. The 1848 book mentioned it to be the 40th edition.

*John Johnston.* In 1842 Johnston published *A Manual of Chemistry*, "on the basis of Dr. Turner's Elements of Chemistry, . . . designed for a text book in colleges and other seminaries of learning." While he primarily wrote this as a college text, yet in the preface he stated that he attempted to "adapt the work for the use of the younger class of learners." So likely it was used in some secondary schools. The four parts dealt with the Imponderable Substances, Inorganic Chemistry, Organic Chemistry, and Analytical Chemistry. The 1848 reprint was the fourth revised edition and the eleventh thousand. The book was well organized and attractively printed. In the back there were 28 pages of review questions.

*John W. Draper.* Draper published *A Textbook on Chemistry*, "for Use of Schools and Colleges" in 1846. He was a professor at the University of Maryland, where he prepared a careful series of lectures on chemistry. These he published in book form. The book was not organized in parts or chapters, but presented 89 topics or lectures. It included many illustrative cuts and questions at the bottom of the pages. Since the text consisted of only 399 pages, it may also have been used in secondary schools. In 1848 the sixth edition appeared. In 1853 it was slightly revised and recopyrighted. The book contained 16 pages of advertisements of other textbooks by the publisher.

*Edward L. Youmans.* In 1851 Youmans published *A Class-Book of Chemistry* for "Academies and Schools." After an Introduction, Part I dealt with Inorganic Chemistry, Part II with Organic Chemistry—Vegetable Chemistry, and Part III with Animal Chemistry. In order to keep the book to reasonable size he omitted the treatment of light, heat, and electricity, which were to be left to natural philosophy. The topics were numbered and printed in italics, so as to guide the study of them. Guiding questions were printed at the bottom of the pages. The body of the text consisted of 336 pages. Youmans was also the author of a *Chart of Chemistry*. Five pages of testimonials by leading chemists regarding the use of the chart in the front and the back of the book were included. Twenty additional pages of advertisements of other textbooks also appeared in the back. In 1863 Youmans revised and considerably enlarged the *Class-Book*, with a change on the title page saying that it was designed for use in "Colleges and Schools." It contained more than 300 illustrations.

*John A. Porter.* In 1856 Porter published the *Principles of Chemistry*. Earlier he had written a *First Book of Chemistry*, which sold for 50c. The 1859 print of the *Principles* contained numerous testimonials concerning the successful use of Porter's texts in academies and high schools. Part I of the *Principles* devoted 139 pages to Physics. Part II treated Chemical Philosophy. The other two parts dealt with Inorganic and Organic Chemistry. It was an attractively organized and printed book. The paragraphs were numbered, headed by a topic title, and accompanied on the side with a question or an instruction as to what was to be done. In the back an appendix of 28 pages listed formulae and chemical tables. In 1864 he revised and greatly enlarged this book and mentioned that it was designed for "Colleges and Schools." Both the earlier book and the 1864 revision appeared in a number of editions.

*David A. Wells.* Wells published his *Principles and Applications of Chemistry* in 1858, for the "Use of Academies, High-Schools, and Colleges." It began by devoting four chapters to matters of physics covering 155 pages. The remainder of the book devoted eleven chapters to inorganic chemistry, and ten chapters to organic chemistry. Four different kinds of type were used to show the headings, the topics, the statements of the principles, and the explanations and experiments. Cuts and questions accompanied the textual matter. It appeared in several editions.

*Other chemistry textbooks, 1820–1860.* A few other chemistry textbooks were

ANTOINE LAURENT LAVOISIER :
Born in Paris, August 26th, 1743; died on the scaffold in Paris, May 8th, 1794.

14  A picture taken from J. H. Appleton's *Chemistry*, 1884

15 J. Dorman Steele, author of science books, on chemistry,
natural philosophy, and physiology

published during this period. However, some were primary in nature and others were very large and advanced, which meant that their secondary school use was unlikely. Among these were Richard W. Green's *First Lessons in Chemistry* (1845); Benjamin Silliman's *First Principles of Chemistry* (1846), used in Yale; James Renwick's *First Principles of Chemistry* (1855); and George Fownes' *A Manual of Elementary Chemistry* (1859), containing 600 pages. Likely there were others not known to the writer.

## C. *Chemistry Textbooks, 1860–1900*

NATURALLY some of the texts first published before 1860 would appear in later editions during this period. So in this section only those texts which were first published after 1860 will receive attention. Little publishing was done in the early 1860's, due to the Civil War. Consequently reprinted editions of earlier texts evidently then continued in use. It will soon be noted that several new texts first appeared in 1868.

*Henry E. Roscoe.* In 1868 Roscoe published his *Lessons in Elementary Chemistry; Inorganic and Organic.* This was a text of 383 pages, of which 24 pages in the back dealt with "Questions and Exercises upon the foregoing lessons." The content of the book was presented in the form of 41 lessons. Less attention was paid to matters commonly related to physics than was true in earlier books. The print was rather small and in general the book was not very attractive. However, the characterizations and explanations of the various chemical elements were very clear. Evidently these features helped its circulation. It was revised and recopyrighted in 1875, 1877, and 1885. The 1885 edition was 75 pages larger than the first edition. Many of the topics were reworded, more pictures of apparatus were introduced, and the printing became more attractive. A reprint of 1892 was the same as the edition of 1888. The fact that Roscoe's books remained in use for at least 25 years is evidence of their merit. In 1873 Roscoe also published a small chemistry text of 103 pages to serve as a science primer.

*W. J. Rolfe and J. A. Gillet.* In 1868 these authors published a *Handbook of Chemistry* for "School and Home Use." This was a well organized and rather attractive small text. Its principal parts dealt with the following: Non-Metallic Elements, Metals, Chemistry of the Atmosphere, Destructive Distillation and its Products, Fermentation, and an Appendix covering numerous practical matters of chemistry. It can be seen that these thopics were different than in most books. The authors stressed practical applications. For example, in the

K

preface they stated that *metals* have been "grouped more according to their uses than according to their chemical relations, with a view to make the subject less dry and more practical." Its second edition appeared in 1871, and in 1874 it was recopyrighted but without revision. It likely was used only in the smaller secondary schools where the apparatus would be limited.

*J. Dorman Steele* (1836–1886). Steele, who was also the author of other popular science books, in 1868 published his *Fourteen Weeks in Chemistry* textbook. His texts in natural philosophy, astronomy, geology, and physiology also bore the *Fourteen Weeks* titles. In the preface he stated that no originality was claimed. Rather he endeavored to "express, in simple, interesting language, a few of the principles and practical applications of Chemistry," which could be taught in one term. He desired its truths to become to the student "household words." He omitted those elements often taught with chemistry that related to plants, natural philosophy, and physiology. The text mainly dealt with Nomenclature, Non-Metallic Elements, Metals, and Organic Chemistry. The treatment of these basic topics consumed 225 pages. In the back 61 pages dealt with many practical problems, experiments, additional nomenclature, and many pages of review questions. It was a rather attractively printed book with many pictures and illustrations. It soon appeared in reprinted editions.

Due to a demand for the admission of the new nomenclature, Steele revised his text in 1873. In it he claimed that his earlier book had been introduced into hundreds of schools not having taught chemistry before. This was printed even more attractively than the 1868 edition. It introduced many interesting footnote comments, and interspersed lists of practical questions throughout the book. Directions for extensive experiments appeared in fine print in the back, together with a section dealing with qualitative analysis. This book was 25 pages larger than the earlier edition, and appeared in many reprints.

Another revised edition was published in 1887, one year after Steele's decease, with the title changed to *A Popular Chemistry*. Its features and organization were similar to the earlier books. Since the regular textual material was printed in larger type, the book was somewhat larger. It is evident that Steele's chemistry textbooks helped popularize chemistry as a study during the latter half of the 19th century.

*Leroy C. Cooley*. In 1869 Cooley, who also had written a natural philosophy, published *A Text Book of Chemistry* for "High Schools and Academies." He claimed three features for it: (1) It contained no more than can be mastered by average classes, (2) it was systematic, and (3) it was written in accordance with modern theories. From these statements it is evident that he kept in mind the learners. Its contents dealt with the composition of bodies, chemical attraction, chemical groups, decomposition in presence of air, decomposition in absence of air, decomposition by ferments, chemical action of light, and conservation of force. It can be seen that this organization, as was true of Steele's texts, was different than the earlier chemistry texts. The presentation of the material seems to indicate that the experiments were to be demonstrated by the instructor rather than to be performed by the students. In the back there were 26 pages of examination questions. These were of two kinds: First, those to be drawn from the text; and second, those requiring practical application of principles. The latter type were printed in italics. This book appeared in numerous editions.

In 1881 Cooley published *The New Text-Book of Chemistry*, which was a revised and enlarged edition of his 1869 text. It contained more pictorial illustrations, listed in the back 30 pages of classroom experiments, and 9 pages of review questions. Cooley had also written an *Elementary Chemistry* in 1872, which was revised and republished in 1886 as, *A Guide to Elementary Chemistry*. These latter were for beginners first studying chemistry.

*William R. Nichols.* In 1872 *An Elementary Manual of Chemistry* was published, which was an abridged edition of the *Manual of Inorganic Chemistry* written earlier by C. W. Eliot and F. H. Storer. This abridgment was a book of 296 pages of text, plus 45 pages of appendix material, most of it dealing with experiments. It was a rather clearly written book with very specific directions. It was recopyrighted in 1877 and in 1880. It was revised and republished by Storer and W. B. Lindsay in 1894.

*John H. Appleton.* In 1884 Appleton published a *Beginners' Hand-Book of Chemistry*. The contents were presented in 28 chapters, most of which dealt with particular chemical elements. The main text consisted of 254 pages. It was interestingly illustrated with fine pictures, some of which were portraits of great scientists. Many of the pictures were in color, which was not common in chemistry texts. It appeared in several editions. Apparently this book was meant for adult reading, as well as for schools, for it was published for the Chautauqua Literary and Scientific Circle by the Chuatauqua Press. Appleton also published a manual for laboratory use, and the *Laboratory Year-Book*.

*James H. Shepard.* In 1885 Shepard published his *Elements of Inorganic Chemistry*. This he claimed to be an elementary treatise based upon "plans and methods which have been employed in the author's laboratory throughout a series of years." Then he suggested four methods that might be followed: The Didactic, the Laboratory, the Working-Laboratory, and the Scientific method. It is clear that he favored the last, which embodied the good features of all. The directions for the experiments were incorporated in the body of the text. The contents were presented in nineteen chapters, each dealing with a chemical element or group of elements. The body of the text contained 340 pages, with 24 pages in the back detailing the nature of the laboratory, its general fixtures and apparatus, and the chemical materials needed for the experiments. It appeared in a number of editions.

*Ira Remsen.* Remsen, who was a professor at Johns Hopkins, became one of the more prolific writers of chemistry textbooks in the latter part of the 19th century. In 1886 he published *An Introduction to the Study of Chemistry.* He had definite ideas about what was weak of much of the work in this field. He stated that it was difficult to provide books that were fully systematic. Most books failed to show the connections between the numerous facts about the various chemical elements. Next, a mistake was to present the profoundest theories before the student was ready for them, and lastly to give directions for experiments without making it clear why the experiment was to be performed. His text consisted of 26 chapters and 382 pages. Each chapter began with a general discussion of the chemical facts involved, which was followed by directions and treatment of related experiments. Everything was clearly stated. In all, 183 numbered experiments appeared throughout the book. It appeared in a number of editions.

Remsen also published two other chemistries, which were much more technical and theoretical. These likely were intended for college use. They were: *An Introduction to the Study of the Compounds of Carbons or Organic Chemistry,* and *The Principles of Theoretical Chemistry.* Some of these books were revised and republished even after 1900.

*Other chemistry textbooks, 1860–1900.* Many different chemistry textbooks were published during this period, but only a few attained wide circulation. Among the texts appearing, other than those heretofore discussed, were: Worthington Hooker's *First Book in Chemistry* (1862), Henry and Leeds Morton's *Students' Practical Chemistry* (1865), Josiah Cooke's *First Principles of Chemical Philosophy* (1868) and *The New Chemistry* (1873), Charles W. Eliot and Frank H. Storer's *Qualitative Chemical Analysis* (1869), George F. Barker's *A Text-Book of Elementary Chemistry* (1870), Elroy M. Avery's *Elements of Chemistry*

(1881), Thomas R. Baker's *Short Course in Chemistry* (1883), and *Practical Methods of Organic Chemistry* by Ludwig Gatterman (translated by W. B. Schober and V.S. Basinian in 1896).

*Chemistry manuals.* While the use of separate chemistry manuals did not become too common until after 1900, because most texts provided instructions for the experiments either in the body of the text or in the back of the book, however, a few books in the nature of manuals were published. One was George W. Rains *Interesting Chemical Exercises in Qualitative Analysis* (1879), which consisted of 59 pages. In 1883 John T. Stoddard's *An Outline of Qualitative Analysis for Beginners*, containing 60 pages was published. Henry Leffman's *A Compend of Chemistry; Inorganic and Organic* (1888) really was a Quiz Compend. One of the best ones was a *Laboratory Manual of General Chemistry* first published in 1888 by R. P. Williams. It provided directions for experiments to be used with "any text-book of chemistry." He was an instructor in chemistry at Boston's English High School, so he knew what could be done in a secondary school in this field. It appeared in several editions. John Appleton also published a manual in the 1880's.

### D. *Characteristics of Chemistry Textbooks*

THUS far the treatment has been to describe in general those texts which apparently gained widest acceptance as evidenced by the appearance of numerous editions. However, it has been a problem in the writing of this chapter to know just what texts were used in secondary schools. It was further complicated by such statements on the title pages, as "for schools and colleges." Thus the writer was forced to judge by the size of the book, the nature of its content, and its apparent teachability as evidenced by its organization, questions, clear directions, and so on. All of these texts, except a few of the smallest, published before 1850 were bound in leather.

*General characteristics.* The earliest chemistry books used here were reprints of those first written in Europe, particularly in England, France, and Germany. Usually some American acting as editor would revise a book by abridging it or by adding questions, experiments, and/or pictures, and then publish it here. In general the foreign texts would be rather technical, many of them large, and with few learning aids in them. After the publication of Comstock's American written *Elements of Chemistry* in 1831, only a few additional reprints of foreign texts appeared here. However, most of the authors of American written texts for a number of decades continued to acknowledge their debts to foreign written books from which they borrowed ideas amply.

The American written books tended to be less technical and theoretical, emphasized the practical values, and paid much attention to making the books more teachable. Among these matters were the addition of questions, either at the bottom of pages or beside the topics; numbering the paragraphs for ready reference; printing the different matters in different kinds of type, such as printing the directions for the experimets in smaller type; and including better illustrations and pictures of apparatus. The size of the different texts varied greatly. Evidently this was in part because secondary schools were not yet standardized, and their curriculum offerings would vary greatly. Thus chemistry was offered in different years of the school, and not always five days per week for a year. Thus different schools wanted different kinds and sizes of books.

*Contents.* As was true of textbooks in other fields, through the years many changes took place in the contents of chemistry textbooks. These changes are shown in the accompanying table as constructed from the findings by Mangery[3] in his analysis of 69 old chemistry textbooks. The only topic treated in all texts was metals. The following topics were treated in sixty or more textbooks: Matter, water, hydrogen, oxygen, nitrogen-compounds, acids-bases-salts, sulfur-compounds, carbon-compounds, halogens, and phosphorus- compounds. Chemical calculations appeared only in 15 books. Combustion was treated in 33, organic chemistry in 35, and electricity in 37 books.

Next, attention should be given to the changes in the amount of space devoted to the various topics during these periods. Since many of the early chemistry textbooks were more inclusively general books on science, they often included topics logically belonging to other fields of science. This was true of certain topics belonging to natural philosophy (physics) and others to biology. A glance at the table will show that the space given to heat, electricity, and atmosphere (air), which belong to physics, during the later periods declined. Likewise matters dealing with animal and vegetable chemistry, really matters of biology, received less space in later texts. The space given to acids-bases-salts also was reduced. The other topic greatly reducing its space was the one called miscellaneous. During the first period nearly ten percent of the space was given to various matters not included in the 22 standard topics, while in the last period it was less than three percent.

On the other hand, as the topics of the textbooks became more standardized,

TABLE VII: *Percentage Distribution of Space Devoted to the Different Topics in Chemistry Textbooks by Periods, 1784–1890*

| | NUMBER BOOKS MENTION- ING TOPIC | PERIODS | | | |
|---|---|---|---|---|---|
| | | 1784 –1815 | 1816 –1840 | 1841 –1865 | 1866 –1890 |
| Number of Books by Periods | | 12 | 18 | 18 | 21 |
| 1 Chemical Nomenclature | 48 | 1.2 | 1.2 | 1.5 | 2.8 |
| 2 Matter | 61 | 1.3 | 1.8 | 2.4 | 1.9 |
| 3 Molecules—Atoms | 46 | .007 | .6 | .61 | 1.7 |
| 4 Caloric—Heat | 56 | 4.5 | 9.3 | 12.2 | 2.4 |
| 5 Light | 49 | 2.8 | 2.4 | 2.3 | 2.4 |
| 6 Electricity | 37 | 3.9 | 4.7 | 7.7 | 1.9 |
| 7 Atmosphere | 55 | 5.2 | 1.3 | 1.4 | 1.9 |
| 8 Water | 61 | 2.8 | 1.1 | 1.2 | 3.0 |
| 9 Hydrogen | 67 | 1.0 | 2.4 | 2.5 | 2.8 |
| 10 Oxygen | 66 | 2.0 | 1.9 | 1.8 | 3.6 |
| 11 Nitrogen-Compounds | 65 | 2.9 | 3.3 | 3.4 | 5.0 |
| 12 Acids—Bases—Salts | 66 | 15.2 | 11.2 | 8.7 | 5.0 |
| 13 Sulfur-Compounds | 64 | 2.0 | 2.0 | 2.3 | 4.2 |
| 14 Carbon-Compounds | 65 | 2.3 | 4.6 | 4.4 | 8.5 |
| 15 Biochemistry (Animal-Vegetable) | 47 | 10.1 | 16.1 | 13.3 | 5.7 |
| 16 Organic Chemistry | 35 | | | 8.1 | 10.3 |
| 17 Halogens | 61 | 1.1 | 3.5 | 3.4 | 5.0 |
| 18 Chemical Affinity-Valence | 55 | 3.5 | 3.6 | 1.9 | 2.3 |
| 19 Metals (Light-Heavy) | 69 | 23.5 | 22.6 | 16.0 | 20.0 |
| 20 Phosphorus-Compounds | 65 | 1.3 | 1.5 | 1.3 | 2.0 |
| 21 Combustion | 33 | 3.1 | 4.0 | 1.0 | 2.1 |
| 22 Chemical Calculations | 15 | | 0.62 | 0.27 | 1.05 |
| 23 Miscellaneous | 58 | 9.6 | 2.7 | 3.0 | 2.9 |
| 24 Average pages per book | | 345 | 319 | 406 | 261 |

many matters received more attention in the later books. Among these matters were: Chemical nomenclature, molecules-atoms, hydrogen, oxygen, nitrogen, sulfur-compounds, carbon-compounds, halogens, phosphorus-compounds, and organic chemistry, which virtually received no attention in the first two periods.

*Demonstrations, experiments, and apparatus.* In the earliest texts there were marked variations in these matters. Of the twelve oldest books analyzed by Mangery only four contained demonstrations, but no experiments; four others included experiments, but no demonstrations; and four contained neither. After 1816 all texts, except two by Turner, contained either demonstrations or experiments or both. The 69 texts on an average suggested 30 demonstrations and 67 experiments per book. The 21 texts of the last period (1866–1890) averaged 22 suggested demonstrations and 67 experiments. The books averaged 13 pictures of apparatus per text. However, eleven books contained no pictures.

*Learning and teaching aids.* Mangery found at least 16 different aids employed. The number of such aids used in one textbook ranged from four to twelve. The only author using as many as twelve aids was in Steele's *Popular Chemistry* (1877). In general the use of aids increased from period to period. For example, the use of indexes did not become common until 1819. Only six of the earliest 16 books had indexes. All 69 books referred to other scientists or chemistries as having been consulted or mentioned for further reference for study. Of the other aids, they were employed as follows: Table of contents, in 66 books; illustrations, 65; prefaces, 64; footnotes, 59; tables, 59; indexes, 55; appendixes, 43; summary questions, 39; introductions, 39; bibliographies, 34; diagrams, 32; instructions to students, 23; charts, 10; and graphs, 1. The later authors became more conscious of the learner, while the earlier authors apparently were more subject-matter minded.

*Concluding statement.* Most of the major changes in the evolution of chemistry textbooks occurred by 1840. In other words, the content, the organization of subject matter, the presentation, aims of authors, the teaching and learning aids, displayed only minor departure in the textual norms from 1840 to 1890. However, texts were made more attractive and teachable from decade to decade as the authors became more pedagogically conscious.

---

[1] Bruno A. Casile, "An Analysis of Zoology Textbooks Available for American Secondary Schools Before 1920." (Unpublished Ed. D. dissertation, University of Pittsburgh, 1953).

[2] Paul L. Shank, "The Evolution of Natural Philosophy (Physics) Textbooks Used in American Secondary Schools Before 1880." (Unpublished Ph.D. dissertation, University of Pittsburgh, 1951)

[3] Peter W. Mangery, "An Analysis of Chemistry Textbooks Used in American Secondary Schools Before 1890." (Unpublished Ed. D. dissertation, University of Pittsburgh, 1959).

[4] Peter Mangery, Ibid.

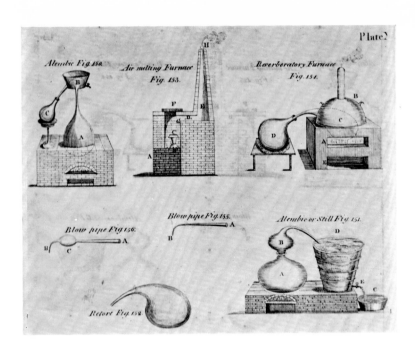

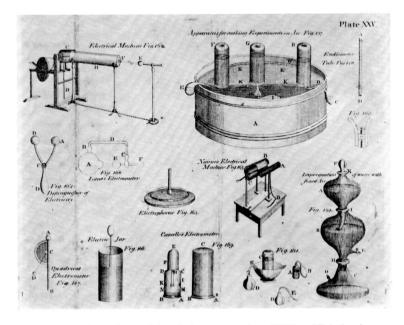

16–17  Illustrations of chemical apparatus from William Nicholson's
*Natural Philosophy*, 1788

## CHAPTER IV

# Foreign Languages

TRADITIONALLY the two languages most commonly taught in the secondary schools of the western world for more than two thousand years were Latin and Greek. They have been generally referred to as the classical languages. Then in more modern times two other languages began to attract attention in U.S. as well. These were German and French, the modern languages. These four then will be given treatment in this part. It is true that other foreign languages are now also taught in some secondary schools, such as Spanish, Russian, and even Chinese, but since our treatment of old textbooks terminates in general at 1900, the last three named foreign languages will not be given treatment. Their introduction in our schools has taken place largely since 1900.

### SECTION ONE

# LATIN

### *Introduction*

THE importance of the Latin language is evidenced by the fact that it was the language of one of the civilizations of|the|world, became the official language of the Catholic church, became the mother of the Romanic languages (Italian, French, Spanish, and Portugese), was the literary language of western Europe for centuries, was the repository for much rich literature of the past, was for some time the language of law and diplomacy of Europe, and has been one of the important instruments in the development of modern civilization. Even today a classical education implies a mastery of Latin.

Latin as a language evolved through a number of changes. Originally it was only the oral language of one of the Roman tribes. About 240 B.C. it also began to take some literary expression. The Romans apparently borrowed an alphabet from the Aeolo-Doric variety of Greek. At first the influence of the Greek on the Roman language was very gradual, but beginning with the second century B.C., the Romans took many learned Greeks as captives and used them as teachers. This greatly hastened the process of enriching the Roman language with many Greek roots and words. As one poet stated, "The captives took the captors captive."

Still later many Roman writers, though not without opposition by some patriotic Romans, such as Cato, further enriched Latin with more Greek compounds and derivatives. In this process Cicero (106–43 B.C.) played a major part in Latinizing Greek terms. His writings ever since have represented Latin at its best. A study[1] of the words in the glossary of a popular third year Latin text used in many high schools in Ohio in the 1930's revealed that 69% of these words were derived or related to Greek. Thus when one studies classic Latin he also learns the meanings of important Greek words, but in Latinized form.

Some of the greatest Latin prose writings were by Terence, Nepos, Caesar, Cicero, Sallust, Livy, Tacitus, Seneca, and Pliny. The leading poets were Horace, Virgil, and Ovid. It will later be shown that writings of all of these Roman writers were studied in some American schools.

With the fall of the Roman Empire and the deadening effect of the Dark Ages the importance and the purity of Latin greatly deteriorated. Then during the Renaissance there was a revival in the study of the best writings of the past, both Greek and Roman. Soon the pure Latin and Greek were taught in the many Latin grammar schools that arose during the Renaissance. For the next 400 years the study of Latin and Greek classics largely constituted the curriculum both of the secondary schools and of universities of western Europe. After the discovery and settlement of America, Latin grammar schools were likewise introduced here.

*Latin in American secondary schools.* It has been generally recognized that the Boston Latin School was the first secondary school in what is now United States. It was founded in 1635. In 1670–1671 Ezekiel Cheever became its headmaster. Writings by such men as Cotton Mather, who had studied under Cheever, indicate that the students were required to study Cheever's *Accidence* (an elementary Latin grammar), Lily's grammar, Aesop's *Fables* in Latin form, the *Colloquies* by Corderius, the *Aeneid* by Virgil, Caesar's *De Officiis* and his orations, Cato, and Ovid's *Metamorphoses*. These were all in Latin. Even as late as 1883 the following Latin was studied there: Latin vocabulary, Ceasar, Ovid, Virgil, Sallust, and Cicero. However, there were also taught there at that time some courses in English, geography, history, natural science, mathematics, Greek, and French. The curriculums of other early American Latin grammar schools were very similar to that of Boston.

The story of the curriculum in the academies was somewhat different. The first well recognized academy was the one founded by Benjamin Franklin in Philadelphia in 1751. His view was that the academy was to offer a broad non-classical curriculum, which was to prepare youth rather directly for the problems and activities of life. However, due to pressure of certain prominent Philadelphians, Franklin eventually consented to have Latin offered as an elective. Later as academies began to replace Latin grammar schools, particularly in New England, the offering of Latin greatly increased in them.

In 1818 Phillips Exeter Academy offered two curriculums: Classical, and English. In the classical department the following were the Latin requirements during the four years: First year—Adam's *Latin Grammar, Liber Primus, Viri Romani* or Caesar's *Commentaries*, Latin prosody, and Exercises in making Latin. Second year—Virgil, Cicero's *Orations, Delectus*, and Roman history. Third year—The same Latin authors, and Sallust. Advanced class—Q. Horatius Flaccus, Titus Livius, Terence's *Comedies, Excerpta Latina,* and Roman antiquities. In 1856 Wesleyan Seminary required Latin every term.

Although America's first high school in 1821—the Boston Classical English School—did not offer Latin, it was not long before other high schools at least offered Latin as an elective. As it became the common practice in most high schools to offer parallel curriculums, Latin was required in the classical course. This practice continued until after 1900.

*Latin in College entrance requirements.* All of the early American colleges required certain attainments in Latin and Greek as a condition for admission. For a student to enter Harvard in 1734 he was to be "able *extempore* to read, construe, and parse Tully (Cicero), Virgil, or such like common classical Latin authors, and to write true Latin in prose, and be skilled in making Latin verse, or at least in the rules of Prosodia, . . . " In 1745 at Yale the student was to be "able Extempore to Read, Construe and Parce Tully (Cicero), Virgil and the Greek Testament; and to write true Latin in Prose and to understand the Rules of Prosodia, and Common Arithmetic." King's College (now Columbia) rules in 1754 were similar, but specified three of Tully's *Orations,* and three books of Virgil's *Aeneid*. In 1786 King's College required a mastery of Caesar's *Gallic War*, four *Orations* of Cicero, four books of Virgil's *Aeneid*, and the Gospels in Greek. It should be noted here that these latter Latin requirements are the same as the Latin offering in most large secondary schools even today. Incidentally it may be added that the Latin and Greek requirements for college entrance were not dropped during most of the 1800's, but other requirements were added. Harvard added geography in 1807, algebra in 1820, geometry in 1844, and ancient history in 1847. Princeton added English grammar in 1819. Immediately after the Civil War certain colleges added modern history in 1869, physical geography in 1870, English composition in 1870, physical science in 1872, and English literature in 1874.

It can be seen from the foregoing that secondary schools, if they expected their graduates to be able to enter college, would virtually be compelled to teach what the colleges required for admission. During the latter part of the 19th century the secondary schools began to resent this virtual dictation from the colleges. The outcome was the formation of regional accrediting associations composed of both secondary schools and colleges. Gradually more cooperative relations between them have been established. Also, the College Entrance Examination Board was formed to provide examination services for those colleges desiring them.

### A. *Latin Grammars Written in England*

As WAS true of the textbooks in nearly all subject matter fields, the earliest used in America were brought here from England, and a few from other countries. This certainly was true of Latin texts. At first these were brought here for direct use, but later it was more common to reprint them for use here. The writer's collection contains 60 Latin texts published before 1800, most of them were first written in England. All of these the writer obtained in the U.S. So even though the earliest apparently were never reprinted here, likely they were used here. Our discussion then will begin by dealing with some that likely were not reprinted here, but evidence is clear that they were used in some American Latin grammar schools.

*William Lily* (1468–1522) It is well to begin the treatment of Latin books written in England with Lily. He studied at Oxford and in Rome. On his return to England he was ranked with Grocyn and Linacre as an English authority of Greek and Latin. About 1512 he was appointed headmaster of St. Paul's School in London. While there he began writing a grammar. About that same time Latin grammars were being written by John Colet, William Linacre, Erasmus, and Cardinal Wolsey, and others had been written earlier. This confusion of Latin books led King Henry VIII to proclaim in 1540 that "his tender goodness towards the youth and childhood of his realm tendeth to have it brought up under one absolute and uniform sort of learning." As a result in 1542, twenty years after Lily's death, the so-called Lily's *An Introduction of the Eight Parts of Speech and Construction of the Same* was published. Henry commanded this to be used in all Latin schools in England and "none other." Thus it became the most commonly used Latin grammar of England for some time. Cotton Mather in his poem written to the memory of Ezekiel Cheever said:

> "He taught us *Lilly,* and he *Gospel* taught."

Thus we know that it was taught in America's first Latin grammar school. Nevertheless, many other Latin grammars were written in England. Solomon Lowe in his *Grammar of the Latin Tongue* in 1726 listed 186 writers of Latin grammars whose books had been or were in use in England.

The writer's collection contains two copies of Lily's book, both printed in England one in 1721 and the other in 1758. These editions really contain three Latin books in one volume. The first part was *A Short Introduction of Grammar* (Latin) of 60 pages. In a later slightly revised edition this was recognized as Ward's *Latin Grammar,* and was used in the Boston Latin Grammar School in 1776. The second part was the *Brevissima Institutio; Seu, Ratio Grammatice* of 130 pages. The third was Lily's *Rules Construed,* of 92 pages. In addition the 1721 edition contained 16 pages of "Omnium Nominum," and in the back 29 pages devoted to "Prosodia Construed." The first book dealt with the eight parts of speech, together with rules and examples in English governing their use. The second book had four parts: Orthographia, the parts of speech, Syntaxis, and Prosodia. These were treated largely in Latin. In the third, Lily's *Rules Construed,* the treatment was very different. The Latin words were construed or translated by interspersing their meanings in English. To illustrate:

> "Multa Nomina *many names* virorum *of men in* a, dicuntur *are called* mascula *mas culines;* ut *as,* scriba *a secretary,* assecla *a page,* scurra *a scoffer, . . .*"

This method was used throughout the 92 pages of Lily. It was a modified application of the method favored by Comenius, who presented the Latin text parallel with a vernacular. Of all the Latin grammars written in England, Lily's was the best known, appearing in reprints for more than 200 years. The first book, *A Short Introduction,* appeared as a separate volume in 1733.

*Humph Hody.* Many attempts were made in England to improve on Lily's work. One of these was Hody's *The Royal Grammar Reformed into a More Easie Method, for the Better Understanding of the English; and More Speedy Attainment of the Latin Tongue* in 1695. The grammar part consisted of 94 pages, syntax of 50, and prosody of 20. Interestingly under prosody musical notes were used to assist in reading verse orally. Another peculiar feature was the use of many sizes and kinds of type in the printing of the book.

*John Stockwood.* In 1738 *The Treatise of the Figures* (examples of Latin) by Stockwood was published in London. This was a small but well organized book of 76 pages, but rather technical. He followed the Lily method of interspersing the Latin with English. The following illustrates both the method and the figures:

Figurae Figures Dictionis of a word.

| | | |
|---|---|---|
| Figurae *figures* dictionis *of a* *word* sunt *are* sex *six*. | Prothesis Aphaeresis Epenthesis Syncope Paragoge Apocope | There are more, but these may suffice for young Beginners. |

Likely the book did not attain wide circulation.

*John Clarke* (1687–1734). Clarke, who had been a master in the Public Grammar School in Hull, wrote *An Introduction to the Making of Latin,* which apparently became very popular in England. In 1786 Isaiah Thomas, the great American printer, reprinted this book here "carefully corrected; and diligently revised by the twenty-fourth London Edition." It was again reprinted by I. Thomas in 1803, and by James Oram, Trenton, in 1806. Likely other editions appeared as well.

In the preface of the 1786 American edition it was stated that "many obvious Defects in those Treatises that have hitherto been published for the Instruction of young Boys in the making of Latin," so he found it necessary to lay them aside and write one of his own. The approach was not to translate Latin into English but the English into Latin. Then he presented the grammar part of the book in 28 brief chapters of 138 pages. Each chapter dealt with the application of some particular rule. For example, Chapter III dealt with "Verbs Transitive govern an Accusative, according to the Rule." Throughout, the English and the Latin appeared in parallel columns. Thus he followed the Comenius method. This aided the pupils to build a Latin vocabulary without committing lists of unrelated words, and also to observe their grammatical construction. He claimed that the examples were mostly taken from "Classic Authors." In the appendix two additional parts, one a brief history of Greece of 44 pages, and the other of Roman history of 90 pages. These histories likewise appeared in English and Latin in parallel columns. It is evident that the re-printed Clarke Latin books had considerable American circulation. It continued as a model for many Latin grammars until about 1835.

*Alexander Adam.* Adam, who was Rector of the High School of Edinburgh, published *The Rudiments of Latin and English Grammar.* The 1793 edition was the fourth in Edinburgh. In 1818 and also in 1826 it was reprinted in New York, but by different printers. Adam had observed "the hurtful effects of teaching boys Grammar Rules in Latin verse, which they did not understand." The 1818 New York edition was a book of 232 pages and four parts: Orthography, Etymology, Syntax, and Prosody. Adam's approach was to learn or commit long lists of words belonging to the different declensions and conjugations. He said, "As the ancient Romans joined the Grammar of their own language with that of the Greek; so we ought to connect the study of the English Grammar with that of Latin." The rules and instructions were presented in English and then applied to Latin. It became the model for many Latin grammars, particularly after 1835. In fact, the structure and approach of the book was similar to the one the writer studied after 1900.

*John Mair.* In 1797 Mair published *An Introduction to Latin Syntax* in Edinburgh. In 1811 an edition revised by James Hardie was published in New York. It consisted of four parts: The Rules of Syntax; Explanatory Notes; Examples, taken for the most part from Classic Authors; and English Exercises. Throughout, the material was presented in parallel columns of English and Latin. In the back there were 76 pages devoted to ancient history, and an extensive list of historical questions. In 1827 Divid Patterson of New York further revised the A. R. Carson revision of Mair's *Introduction* and published it here. Its general plan remained the same, 200 pages being devoted to the grammar, and 48 pages to Ancient History Epitomized. Again throughout, the contents was in parallel English and Latin. This edition appeared in a number of reprints.

*Richard Lyne.* Lyne, who had been a master of a grammar school, wrote *The Latin Primer,* which was reprinted in Boston in 1801. It was different in structure than most other Latin grammars. After presenting 24 rules in English the remainder of the book was nearly entirely in Latin only. It was claimed that most of the sentences and extracts were from Latin poets.

*Other Latin grammars written in England.* No attempt is here made to present a list of all of the Latin grammars written in England before 1800. However, a few others that were also reprinted in America are here mentioned in the chronological order in which known reprints appeared here: Nathan Bailey's *English and Latin Exercises* (1720), Francis Gregory's *Nomenclature Bevis Anglo-Latino in Usum Scholarum* (1735), John Read's *A Latin Grammar* (1736), Robert Ross's *A Complete Introduction to the Latin Tongue* (1752), Thomas Ruddiman's *The Rudiments of the Latin Tongue* (1776), and P. Davy's *Ad miniculum Puerile* (1778). Evidently there were others.

## B. *American Written Latin Grammars*

LATIN grammars written in America appeared earlier than in other secondary school subjects. This was true because of a number university trained emigrants from England came here for varied reasons, particularly to New England. As a consequence most of the earliest American textbooks were written there. It may be added that the writer obtained most of his oldest textbooks in old bookshops in New England.

*Ezekiel Cheever* (1614–1708). Cheever was born in England, where he attended Cambridge University before coming to America in 1637. The next year he settled in New Haven, where he soon opened a Latin school. In 1650 he was invited to head the grammar school at Ipswich. In 1661, after making that school well-known, he was invited to direct the school in Charlestown. Then in 1670 he was called to the headship of the famous Boston Latin Grammar School, which position he held for 38 years. In all, he taught school for 70 years, during which time he trained students who later became the greatest leaders of church and state in New England. As was stated, "he taught their children and their children's children, unto the third and fourth generation." He has been referred to as America's greatest colonial school master.

In addition to his reputation as a teacher, Cheever also wrote a small Latin grammar entitled, *A Short Introduction to the Latin Tongue; For the Use of the Lower Forms in the Latin School Being the Accidence*. It is supposed that he wrote it while at New Haven about 1650. It continued to appear in edition after edition, and likely was used in most of the Latin grammar schools in New England. The writer has three copies dated 1771 (15th edition) and two of 1781 by different printers (one of them is listed as the 18th edition). Thus it had circulation for more than a century. Cotton Mather, who had been a student under Cheever, said of the text, "His Accidence was the wonder of the Age." The

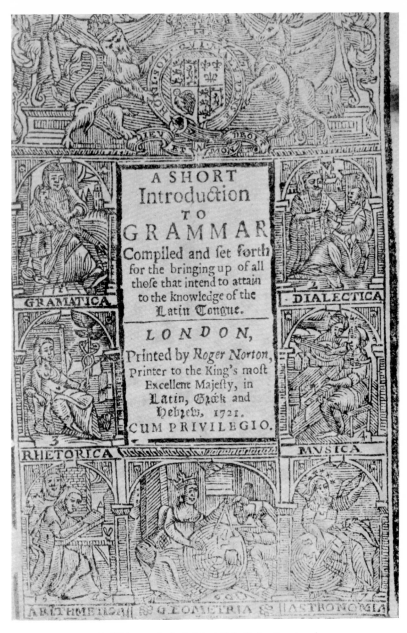

A SHORT
Introduction
TO
GRAMMAR
Compiled and set forth
for the bringing up of all
those that intend to attain
to the knowledge of the
Latin Tongue.

LONDON,
Printed by *Roger Norton*,
Printer to the King's most
Excellent Majesty, in
Latin, Greek and
Hebrew, 1721.
CUM PRIVILEGIO.

GRAMATICA

DIALECTICA

RHETORICA

MVSICA

ARITHMETICA & GEOMETRIA & ASTRONOMIA

18  This was included in Lily's *Rules Construed*,
representing the Seven Liberal Arts

# THE
# ROYAL GRAMMAR

Reformed into

## A more Eafie Method,

### FOR THE

## *Better Underftanding*

### OF

# 𝕿𝖍𝖊 𝕰𝖓𝖌𝖑𝖎𝖘𝖍:

### AND

## *More Speedy Attainment*

### OF THE

# LATIN TONGUE.

*Nullum Munus afferre majus meliúfve poffumus, quàm fi eru-
diamus Juventutem, iis præfertim moribus atque tempo-
ribus, quibus ita prolapfa eft ; ut omnium opibus refræ-
nanda & coercenda fit.* Cic.

IMPRIMATUR,

March 6. 1694.

*Humph. Hody.*

---

#### LONDON,
Printed by J. Heptinftall, for A. and J. Churchill, at the
Black-Swan in Pater-Nofter-Row, MDCXCV.

---

19 A combination text of English and Latin.
Note the spelling and forms of type

earlier editions, since they were printed by several printers, varied in the number of pages. However, most of the later editions contained 72 pages. Its contents were well organized, and plainly and tersely stated. It was used to precede the study of larger Latin texts, most of which at that time were brought here from England. For example, the first class in the Boston Latin Grammar School as late as 1789 studied:

Cheever's *Accidence*
Corderius's *Colloquies*—Latin and English
Nomenclature
Aesop's Fables—Latin and English
Ward's *Latin Grammar*, or Eutropius.

Although Cheever's *Accidence* dealt with the eight parts of speech, the treatment of the adverb, conjunction, preposition, and interjection totalled only $2^1/_3$ pages. Nevertheless, it must be said that the *Accidence* was an important text during the colonial period. Cheever's funeral was attended by many of the most important officials and citizen's of Massachusetts, including the governor.

*Academy of Pennsylvania Latin text.* In 1762 *A Short Introduction to Latin Grammar* "For the Use of the University and Academy of Pennsylvania in Philadelphia" was published. This book appeared in successive editions in 1773, 1786, and so on, The 7th edition was published in 1799. The number of pages in these varied from 108 to 137. The third edition of 1786 contained 116 pages. The first 88 pages consisted of grammar, the next 18 pages were devoted to Sententiae Pueriles in double columns of English and Latin, and the last ten pages of Colloquia Scholastica in Latin. The grammar was very technical, consisting of many rules and exceptions dealing with the eight parts of speech. The declensions and conjugations were given much attention.

In 1814 this grammar was republished under the name of James Davidson, Professor of Latin and Greek at the University of Pennsylvania. The grammar and the Sententiae were the same as the earlier editions. However, a vocabulary list of Latin and English, and an appendix dealing with rules of syntax were added. The fact that this book appeared in so many editions between 1762 and 1814 indicates that it likely was used in a number of schools.

*Edward Rigg.* In 1784 Rigg published *The New American Latin Grammar*. It was formed from the "most approved writings in this kind by the late Presidents, Burr, Finley, and others." It soon appeared in numerous reprints. The earlier editions contained 123 pages, while the 1807 edition 140. It consisted

L

mainly of rules and their applications. It also included a Table of the Kalends, Nones, and Ides, which was the way the Romans reckoned the days of a month, and a table of Roman numbers. The book lacked a preface, table of contents, and an index.

*Caleb Alexander.* In 1794 Alexander published *A Grammatical Institute of the Latin Language.* The next year his *A New Introduction to the Latin Language* appeared. It was an "attempt to Exemplify the Latin Syntax, and Render Familiar to the Mind the Grammatical Construction of this Useful Language, Containing Critical and Explanatory Notes on all the Rules of Government and Agreement." This all appeared on the title page. This book was modelled after Clarke's *Introduction,* which had been written and was popular in England and was reprinted in America. In a preface of nine pages Alexander discussed the value of studying Latin grammar, what improvements were made over Clarke's book, and that this was "the first of the kind, that was written and published in the United States."

The main text consisted of 44 chapters and 182 pages. Each chapter began with the statement of a rule and then was followed by illustrative content taken from classic authors and other Latin grammars printed in two parallel columns of English and Latin. In the back the Appendix of 33 pages contained further explanatory notes in English relating to the various rules of the text by chapters.

*James Ross.* Ross, was a teacher of Latin and Greek in the Franklin Academy in Chambersburg, Pennsylvania, and later in a school in Philadelphia. In 1798 Ross published *A Practical, New Vocabulary Latin and English,* consisting of more than 2000 "Nouns Substantive, Appellative and Proper," with an appendix of adjectives.

More important, he published also in 1798 *A Short, Plain, Comprehensive, Practical Latin Grammar.* In the preface he argued for the thorough mastery of Latin, claiming it to be essential for the proper understanding of English. This book was divided into the traditional four parts of orthography, etymology, syntax, and prosody. It later appeared in numerous editions, the 1835 edition was the ninth. This edition also contained 18 pages of two columns of Latin vocabulary. To one who would look at this book today likely would say it was very technical and forbidding, yet that was what Ross meant by thoroughly mastering Latin.

*Cummings and Hilliard* (Publishers). In 1813 *The Latin Tutor* was published. It was an introduction to the making of Latin. It was "Accommodated to Adam's

Grammar, and Smith's N. H. L. Grammar." There is no evidence given as to who prepared it. Acknowledgments were given to Clarke's *Introduction,* Ellis' *Exercises,* Lyne's *Latin Primer,* and W. Willymott. The first part, An Introduction to the Making of Latin, was similar to Clarke's *Introduction.* It consisted of more than 150 pages of English and Latin sentences classified under specific rules, always referring to the number of the rule in Adam's and Smith's texts. Next a section dealt with rules for adapting the English to the Latin idiom. The third section dealt with the use of English particles exemplified in sentences to be translated into Latin. The last section dealt with the position of words in Latin composition. The book was reprinted in 1818 and 1819. The 1819 edition contained 280 pages. In the back more than 300 books were advertised for sale by the publishers.

*Joseph Dana.* In 1818 (the preface was dated 1815) Dana published his *Liber Primus, or A First Book of Latin Exercises.* It was somewhat different than any book thus far described. The first 22 pages dealt with the more important rules of grammar, referring in each case to the number of the rule in Adam's and Smith's texts, and then presenting sentences involving these rules both in Latin and English. Then 86 pages were devoted to presenting Exempla Miscellanea in Latin. These were brief selections in both prose and poetry. The last 68 pages of the volume constituted a Dictionary which was arranged in double columns. It was an attractively bound book in leather with red and gold trimming.

*Benjamin Gould* (1787–1828). Gould, who was a master of the Boston Latin Grammar School, revised Adam's *Latin Grammar* in 1825. This was one of the first Latin grammars published here to have a table of contents. It consisted of the four traditional parts, with the rules presented in English and then applied to the Latin. Long lists of Latin words with their English meanings were given in connection with the declensions of nouns and the conjugations of verbs. There were two appendices: one following syntax, and another at the end of the book. The last one contained many Roman tables of time, weights, coinage, and measures. It was a very thorough and technical book of nearly 300 pages. It appeared in numerous editions.

*Frederick P. Leverett* (1803–1836). From 1828 to 1831 Leverett was head master of Boston Latin School. In 1829 he published *The New Latin Tutor,* or "Exercises in Etymology, Syntax, and Prosody." In large part it dealt with exercises of changing English into Latin. Most of them were presented in parallel form of English and Latin. Nearly 100 pages dealt with idioms. The part dealing with prosody was more extensive than in most other Latin books. It later appeared in reprints.

## C. *Latin Grammars, 1830–1860*

BEFORE 1830 most American written Latin grammars were either revised editions of books first written in England or were strongly modelled after them During this period there will remain some borrowing, but considerable deviation and independence will be evidenced.

*Chauncey A. Goodrich.* Goodrich wrote textbooks in several other fields before writing in the field of Latin. In 1832 he published his *Lessons in Latin Parsing.* The idea for this book came to him while he was teaching one of his own children Latin. This really was a rather simple Latin grammar with interspersed illustrative exercises between rules in both Latin and English in parallel columns. The grammar part of 164 pages was followed by 14 pages of dialogues and stories in Latin. In the back a good vocabulary list of double columned pages appeared. It was reprinted in several editions.

*E. A. Andrews and S. Stoddard.* In the preface the authors stated that they first planned to revise Adam's *Grammar,* but soon discovered that too many additions and corrections were demanded. They claimed that rapid advances in philology suggested many changes. So they wrote a new book, but followed the plan of Adam. It was *A Grammar of the Latin Language* in 1836. The main part covering the four traditional divisions plus one on orthoepy and the eight parts of speech under etymology covered 296 pages. The rules and applications were very detailed. The word lists and most of the comments were printed in rather small type. The appendix listed in very fine print more than 70 grammatical figures, such as prosthesis, aphaeresis, epenthesis, syncope, etc. There also appeared various miscellaneous Roman matters, including lists of Roman writers of the Golden, Silver, Brazen, and Iron Ages. It was one of the first Latin books to contain both a table of contents and an index. This edition was bound in leather. With the exception of a few corrected errors it was recopyrighted and reprinted in 1849. The 1854 reprint was the 54th edition. In 1857 it was revised, enlarged by more than 80 pages, and recopyrighted. All of these three copyrighted editions appeared in numerous reprints. The 1865 reprint claimed to be the 93rd edition. The later editions used six pages of fine print to advertise the Andrews' Series of Latin School Books. The 1849 and 1857 texts were not bound in leather. These books were used in some colleges as well as in secondary schools.

Apparently there was complaint that his first text was too difficult, so in 1838 Andrews published the *First Lessons in Latin,* which was "An Introduction to Andrews and Stoddard's *Latin Grammar.*" Its plan was the same, but the topics were more briefly and simply treated. In the text proper the rules were given in English and then applied to Latin. Questions in fine print appeared at the bottom of the pages. Then about 30 pages of exercises appeared in parallel form in Latin and English. These were followed by more than 20 pages of brief reading lessons in Latin. In the back more than 30 double columned pages in fine print were devoted to vocabulary. This book appeared in numerous reprints. In 1853 it was slightly revised and recopyrighted as the 19th edition. In 1858 the 28th edition was printed.

In 1848 Andrews published *A First Latin Book.* In size this was between the *First Lessons* and the *Grammar of the Latin Language.* The syntax was enlarged over the *First Lessons,* and the derivation of the words in the vocabulary was in most cases given. Much attention was given to pronunciation. More exercises were included. These exercises were commonly in two parts: The first consisted of a series of Latin sentences, then the second would be in English and in Latin in parallel form. In the back there were listed 20 anecdotes, 36 pages of vocabulary, and a comparative view of the conjugations. The 1854 edition was its sixth. From these descriptions it is evident that the Andrews books were the most popular of any American written Latin books up to his time.

*Charles Anthon.* Anthon was Professor of Greek and Latin at Columbia College and Rector of the Grammar School. In 1838 he published his *First Latin Lessons.* This, however, was not a small book. Its aim was to acquaint the student at each step with those portions of grammar essential for the work of translation, thus avoiding the acquirement of a "disrelish for the language." One unusual feature of the book was to include rather long lists of ungrammatical Latin to be converted into grammatical, so as to suit the English words in a parallel column. In the back about 80 pages constituted a Latin-English Dictionary. In connection with each word its part of speech was given, and with nouns their declension and with verbs their conjugation. The 1846 edition was its sixth.

Anthon also published a revised and corrected book of a translated edition of *A School Grammar of the Latin Language* by C. G. Zumpt, Professor in the University of Berlin. The translation had been made by Leonard Schmitz, Rector of the Edinburgh High School.

*John M'Clintock and George R. Crooks.* These authors, who were professors of languages at Dickinson College, published *A First Book in Latin* in 1846. This was a rather large book, which it needed to be in order "to contain within itself Grammar, Exercises, Reading-book, and Dictionary; in short, all that the pupil will need before commencing the regular reading of Caesar or any other easy Latin author." The book was prepared on eleven principles, which were really guides for the teaching and learning of Latin. They were strong believers in the mental disciplinary value of learning Latin. More exercises involving double translations were included than in most grammars. Prosody was given only brief treatment in the appendix. In the back there were sections on word building, brief reading lessons, Latin-English and English-Latin vocabularies, and review questions. In comparison with other Latin grammars of that period one gets the impression that it provided a strenuous year's work. It appeared in numerous reprints at least until 1870.

*Albert Harkness* (1822–1907). Harkness was a professor at Brown University and one of the founders of the American Philological Association. In 1851 he published a revision of Arnold's *First and Second Latin Book*, written in England, which was entitled *Arnold's First Latin Book* by Harkness. It followed the Ollendorff Method of instruction. After discussing the Continental and the English method of pronouncing Latin, he followed the former. The main part of the book was divided into 88 brief but well organized lessons, which dealt mostly with nouns and verbs. Then more than 30 pages dealt with paradigms, and a section with syntax. In the back there were two vocabulary lists: Latin-English, and English-Latin. Twenty-six pages were devoted to books for sale by the publishers. The book appeared in many editions for about 30 years.

In 1864 Harkness published his own *Latin Grammar*. It was his "desire to promote the cause of Classical study," and aimed to present Latin "to the learner in a form at once simple, attractive, and philosophical" The book was presented in the traditional four parts: Orthography, etymology, syntax, and prosody. The material was presented in 720 numbered sub-sections. In general, the rules, explanations, applications, headings, and so on, were presented in different sizes of type to make them stand out. As was common in most Latin grammars, the first verb to be conjugated was *amo*. In the back was an Index of Verbs, and a long Index of Subjects. It soon appeared in many reprints.

In 1874 the first two parts of the *Latin Grammar* were rewritten. So it was re-copyrighted and published under both dates of 1864 and 1874. The pages of the new book were somewhat smaller but the total number of pages the same.

The chief changes involved Latin forms and inflections, due to later findings in philology. This edition also was reprinted often.

In 1881 the book was again revised. "To a large extent, indeed, it is a new and independent work," he claimed, but the paradigms and rules of construction were only slightly changed. Many footnotes explained the important results of linguistic research, particularly in Germany. In all, the 1881 edition was about 70 pages larger. The general organization, however, remained the same in all three copyrighted editions. The 1881 edition also appeared in numerous reprints, and was also printed in Toronto, Canada.

In 1866 Harkness published *An Introductory Latin Book*. It was intended as an elementary drill-book, and as an introduction to the Harkness *Grammar*. Its three parts dealt with orthography, etymology, and syntax. It consisted of 435 brief lessons, many of them providing for exercises of translating Latin into English and English into Latin. Many footnotes helped explain matters for a better understanding of the rules. In the back there were 16 pages of vocabulary. Like the other Harkness texts, it appeared in a number of reprints.

Finally, when Harkness was an emeritus professor, he published *A Complete Latin Grammar* in 1898. It was designed "at once as a text-book for the classroom and a book of reference for study." In the preface he acknowledged the assistance and criticism of many leading Latin authorities. Instead of the traditional four parts this book was somewhat different. Part I dealt with phonology, and Part II with morphology. The last three parts were the traditional ones of etymology, syntax, and prosody. It was a larger book than his others. Truly, the grammars by Harkness gained wide circulation. The writer's collection contains 18 different copies.

*Peter Bullions.* Bullions, at one time professor of languages at Albany Academy, busied himself in writing English grammars, and both grammars and readers in Latin and Greek. He held that the fundamental principles of teaching grammar in all these languages were somewhat the same. When he published *The Principles of Latin Grammar* it was more or less based on the "foundation of Adam's *Latin Grammar*." This soon appeared in many reprints. In 1853 it was revised and recopyrighted, but was mentioned as the 49th edition. This edition was somewhat larger than the earlier one, but the plan and approach were the same. It presented the conventional four divisions, plus an appendix which dealt with such matters as Roman computation of time, Roman names, divisions of Roman people, Roman civil officers, weights and measures, and the ages of Roman literature. In all, it contained 344 pages.

The rules and principles were printed in large type, while the explanations and notes appeared in much smaller type. This (1853) edition continued to be reprinted at least until 1867.

Bullions also teamed up with Charles D. Morris to write the *Latin Grammar*. Later in 1866 this was abridged by Morris alone in the *Latin Lessons*, which was reduced to fewer than 250 pages. Prosody was omitted. It was an attractively printed book. The topics and exercises were numbered, and questions appeared at the bottom of many pages. Brief reading lessons and a vocabulary were added in the back. It also appeared in reprints.

*Other Latin grammars, 1830–1860.* A few other works published in America during this period may be mentioned. Among them were: J. Schipper's *Practical Grammar of the Latin Tongue* (1832), Baynard Hall's *A New Compendium of Latin Grammar* (1836), N. C. Brooks' *First Lessons in Latin* (1845), Raphael Kühner's *Elementary Grammar of the Latin Language* (from the German, 1845), Leonard Schmitz & Charles Authon's *A Grammar of the Latin Language* (1846), Wm. Mann's revision of Thomas Ruddiman's *The Rudiments of the Latin Tongue,* and I. N. Madwig's *A Latin Grammar* (1857). Likely there were others.

### D. *Latin Grammars, 1860–1900*

As was true of textbooks in most subject fields, few books were published in the early 1860's, due to the Civil War. However, a number were published in the late 1860's. It will be seen that some changes will be made in the books during this period.

*William Bingham.* It was Bingham's intention to write a *"practical first book in Latin,* simple enough for beginners, and yet full enough for advanced students.' This he did in his *Grammar of the Latin Language* in 1866. To do this he placed considerable material commonly in the main body of a text in the appendix. Thus such material could be omitted for those who desired a simpler treatment. He omitted orthography entirely and placed prosody in the appendix. So the text proper only dealt with etymology and syntax, the more basic divisions. The explanations of the rules and principles were very clear. Wherever lists of vocabulary appeared the Latin words were diacritically marked to assist the student in the pronunciation. There were exercises to be translated into English and others into Latin. Frequent remarks were made to amplify rules or to present exceptions. In the back there were both a Latin-English and an English-Latin vocabulary. The 1870 and the 1881 reprints bore copyright dates of both 1866 and 1870.

# A SHORT

# INTRODUCTION

## TO THE

# LATIN TONGUE:

### For the USE of the

### LOWER FORMS in the LATIN SCHOOL.

#### BEING THE

# ACCIDENCE,

Abridged and compiled in that moſt eaſy and accurate Method, wherein the famous Mr. EZEKIEL CHEEVER taught, and which he found the moſt advantageous by Seventy Years Experience.

To which is added,

A CATALOGUE of Irregular NOUNS, and VERBS, diſpoſed Alphabetically.

---

*The* FIFTEENTH EDITION.

---

BOSTON:

Printed by ISAIAH THOMAS, for JOHN PERKINS, in Union-Street. MDCCLXXI.

1771

20  Claimed to be the first Latin grammer written in America, this book was popularly known as "Cheever's *Latin Accidence*"

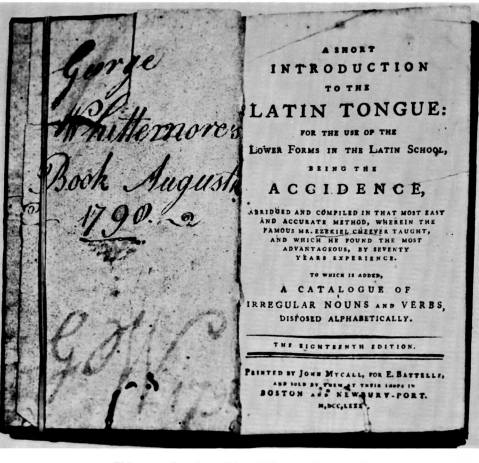

A SHORT

**INTRODUCTION**

TO THE

**LATIN TONGUE:**

FOR THE USE OF THE

LOWER FORMS IN THE LATIN SCHOOL,

BEING THE

**ACCIDENCE,**

ABRIDGED AND COMPILED IN THAT MOST EASY
AND ACCURATE METHOD, WHEREIN THE
FAMOUS MR. EZEKIEL CHEEVER TAUGHT,
AND WHICH HE FOUND THE MOST
ADVANTAGEOUS, BY SEVENTY
YEARS EXPERIENCE.

TO WHICH IS ADDED,

A CATALOGUE OF
IRREGULAR NOUNS AND VERBS,
DISPOSED ALPHABETICALLY.

THE EIGHTEENTH EDITION.

PRINTED BY JOHN MYCALL, FOR E. BATTELLE,
AND SOLD BY THEM AT THEIR SHOPS IN
BOSTON AND NEWBURY-PORT.
M,DCC,LXXX.

21  Title-page of another edition of Cheever's *Latin Accidence*

*Joseph H. Allen and William F. Allen.* In 1868 the *Manual of Latin Grammar* of 139 pages was published, the study of which was approved as sufficient to qualify a student for admission to Harvard and Yale. Its rather small size is evidence that it avoided "prodigious" details so often found in Latin grammars. Many testimonials were secured regarding its merits.

In 1869 their *Latin Lessons* was published. It was adapted to the *Manual*. Part I of nearly 50 pages included 60 brief lessons involving the development a vocabulary largely taken from Caesar's *Gallic Wars* and some exercises of double translations. Part Second told the story of the Helvetian War in Latin, together with extensive notes to assist in the translation. Part Third dealt with examples of scanning and word distinctions. In the back there were the customary two vocabulary lists. This book represented a definite attempt to prepare the student for an easier study of Caesar the following year.

In 1872 Joseph H. Allen and James B. Greenough published *A Latin Grammar*. It was "Founded on Comparative Grammar." Its aim was to provide a complete grammar "to be used from the beginning of the study of Latin until the end of a college course." It was to be used for constant reference. It provided a thorough treatment of etymology, syntax, and prosody in about 250 pages. No vocabulary list was included in the back, as was usual in most grammars. The 1875 edition was the same as the one of 1872 except it included a Supplement, which dealt with an Outline of Syntax. Ten pages of advertisements were included in the back.

In 1877 the *Latin Grammar* was revised and enlarged. The matters of each part were cast in chapters, with its sub-divisions numbered. These changes improved the book pedagogically. Several portions were expanded, and prepatory notes were introduced before several topics of syntax. This edition appeared in a number of reprints. In the beginning of the book the works of 24 authorities of Latin grammar were listed for technical reference. More than half of these were German.

In 1888 the *Latin Grammar* was again revised and enlarged, but it was done by Greenough and George L. Kittredge. The numbers of the sections remained about the same, but many additional explanations and suggestions were added both in the text and foot-notes. The simple index of the earlier edition was changed to extensive indexes of verbs, and of words and subjects. It appeared in a number of reprints. The 1888 edition was slightly revised by Greenough, Kittredge, A. A. Howard, and Benjamin L. D'Ooge in 1903. The arrangement and the appearance was somewhat improved, and some of the material in the back reduced. The Allen and Greenough books were evidently widely used during the last 30 years of the 19th century.

*R. F. Leighton.* In 1872 Leighton published his *Latin Lessons,* "adapted to Allen and Greenough's *Latin Grammar.* The rules of pronunciation both of the "English Method" and the "Roman Method" were carefully explained. Then 72 lessons covering 94 pages involving double translations were presented. The earlier lessons also included brief vocabulary lists. Each lesson referred to a particular section in Allen and Greenough's text for the grammatical rules involved. Frequent footnotes further explained certain rules. The second part consisted of fables, short stories, and biographies written in Latin to be translated, with nearly as many pages of notes about them explaining rules and difficulties. Then in the back were questions for review, and the usual two vocabulary lists.

In 1876 Leighton only slightly revised the body of the *Latin Lessons,* but added greatly to the features in the back. The Latin-English vocabulary was increased to 104 pages. In the back more than 20 pages of parallel references to the grammars written by Harkness, Gildersleeve, and Andrews and Stoddard, were added. This book appeared in several reprints.

*A. M. Cook.* In 1885 Cook published in London a *Latin Course; First Year.* In 1886 it was abridged and published both in London and New York. This edition appeared in many reprints. The body of it consisted of 63 sections of brief Latin selections involving the application of the various declensions and conjugations. The conjugations and two vocabulary lists appeared in the back. In 1892 this was revised and considerably enlarged by J. C. Egbert, Jr. This was primarily done to make it more acceptable for use in American schools. Its general plan, however, was not greatly changed.

*William C. Collar and M. Grant Daniell.* Apparently the last Latin grammars to have gained considerable circulation before 1900 were written by Collar and Daniell. Collar was Head-Matser of the Roxbury Latin School, and Daniell was Principal of Chauncy-Hall School, Boston. In 1886 they published *The Beginner's Latin Book.* The purpose of this book was to "serve as a preparation for reading, writing, and, to a less degree, for speaking Latin." It introduced the Roman and English methods of pronunciation, presented about 25 simple Latin dialogues added to as many chapters, and included easy selections for translation extracted from Nepos, Ovid, Catullus, Caesar, and Cicero. In the back there were the two vocabulary lists, and a Glossarium Grammaticum. It soon appeared in reprints.

In 1894 these authors published their *First Latin Book*. They claimed this was not a revision of their earlier book, but one that would not require the amount of time and practice to complete. The reduction was largely by shortening the exercises for translation. However, a more complete set of tables of declensions and conjugations, and a list of rules of syntax, appeared in the back. Vocabulary lists appeared before most lessons. The body of the 1896 text was the same, but a few changes were made in the back.

In 1901 Collar and Daniell published their *First Year Latin*, which was the book used by the writer when he began his study of Latin. In general, the plan of this book was similar to the two earlier ones, but several changes were made. It began with a 13 page review of English grammar. It followed only the Roman Method of pronunciation. Some of the exercises for translating into Latin were shortened, and review questions were frequently interspersed. Diacritical marks were used to aid in the correct pronunciation of most Latin words. In all, the book was well organized and the work clearly presented as a grammar.

*Other Latin grammars, 1860–1900.* A few other texts published during this period may be mentioned. Among them were: B. L. Gildersleeve's *A Latin Grammar* (1867), and *A Latin Primer* (1875); P Henn's *Ahn's First Latin Book* (1879; Thomas Chase's *A Latin Grammar* (1882); Harry T. Peck's *Latin Pronunciation* (1890); Hiram Tuell and Harold N. Fowler's *A First Book of Latin* (1893); and Charles E. Bennett's *A Latin Grammar* (1895).

### E. *Latin Classics and Readers*

EVIDENCE is rather strong that in most secondary schools in America before 1900 wherever Latin was taught it generally began by teaching a Latin grammar. The evolution of grammars has been rather extensively discussed. But what followed grammar? It may be well to deal with this matter by types of schools.

### F. *Latin in Latin Grammar Schools*

*Boston Latin Grammar School.* Since the Boston Latin school was the first and was generally considered the most important one in America, it may be well to consider what Latin books were taught in it. Table — presents the Latin offering in the Boston school for the years 1700, 1776, 1820, 1860, and 1883. It can be seen that at least until 1820 a very wide offering of Latin was presented. Scattered evidence indicates that other Latin grammar schools, particularly in

New England, provided similar Latin programs. It may be seen that, except in grammar, most of the books were classics written by famous Roman authors. Apparently in the selection of these writings two criteria obtained. First, they should represent good Latin style, and second, they should involve what may be considered moral instruction, even though they dealt more with the old Roman virtues rather than the Christian. Next brief considerations will be given the writings of these authors.

*Maturinus Corderius* (Cordier). (1479–1564) Corderius (he was not a Roman) was a French Protestant teacher, who later became a follower of Calvin and taught under him in Geneva. After writing a Latin book "for the purification of corrupt speech," he published the *Colloquiorum Centuria Selecta* in 1564. It really consisted of 100 dialogues between two boys, A and B, dealing with their problems as students as well as such matters as citizenship, religion, and morals. It became very popular, because it was written for boys and dealt with matters of interest to them. It was translated by Brinsley, Hoole, and others into English. The editions by John Clarke, who published the Latin and English in parallel form, became very popular both in England and America. An edition printed here in 1801 by Isaiah Thomas was from the 26th London edition.

It may be injected here that Erasmus (1466–1536), a famous scholar of the Northern Renaissance, also wrote some Latin dialogues. In 1519 he published his *Colloquia Selecta*. These, too, gained wide usage in Europe and to some extent in America. John Clarke's edition printed in Philadelphia in 1801 was the 19th. Its style and appeal was similar to that of Corderius.

*Aesop.* He was an ancient Greek who composed fables. It may be that they circulated orally before they took written form. Many of these were later converted into verse by several poets. The Phaedri *Fabulae* edition, taught in Boston in 1820, was one of these. The writer's collection contains a number of copies of Aesop's *Fables*. These appeared in parallel language form. One of these appeared in three languages. Likely one reason why these fables were taught in so many American Latin grammar schools was because most of them conveyed a moral lesson. Thus they fit into the program of character education.

*P. Ovidus Naso.* Now consideration will be given to the writings of some of the great Roman authors, whose works were studied here. One of these was Ovid. Ovid, next to Virgil, was one of the most widely imitated of the Roman poets. Many of his poems were of an erotic nature, but eventually he turned his

TABLE VIII: *Lation Offering in the Boston Latin Grammar School at Different Dates*

| ABOUT 1700 | 1776 | 1820 | 1860 | 1883 |
|---|---|---|---|---|
| Cheever's Accidence | Cheever's Accidence | *Viri Romae* | Andrews and | Latin forms |
| Lily's Rules Construed | Corderius Colloquies | Phaedri Fabulae | Stoddard's | Caesar |
| Aesop's Fables | Nomenclature | Cornelius Nepos | *Grammar* | Virgil's *Aeneid* |
| Corderius' Colloquies | Aesop's Fables | Ovid's *Metamorphoses* | Andrews' *Latin* | Sallust |
| Virgil's Aeneid | Clarke's *Introduction* | Dana's Latin Tutor | *Lessons* | Cicero |
| Cicero's De Officiis | Ward's *Grammar* | Caesar Commentaries | Andrews' *Latin* | Virgil's *Bucolics* |
| Cato's Distichia | Entropius (History) | *Electa ex Ovidio* | *Reader* | |
| Ovid's Metamorphoses | *Selecta e Vet. Test.* | Sallust | *Vira Romae* | |
| | Castalio's Dialogues | Virgil | Conelius Nepos | |
| | Caesar | Valxry's *Elegantiae* | Arnold's *Latin* | |
| | Tully's (Cicero) | *Latinae* | *Prose* | |
| | *Epist. & Offic.* | Bradley's *Prosody* | Caesar's Com. | |
| | Ovid's *Metamorphoses* | Cicero's De Officiis, | Ovid's *Metamor.* | |
| | Virgil | *De Senectute, De* | Cicero's Orations | |
| | Cicero's *Orations* | *Amicitia and Orations* | Latin Composition | |
| | Horace | Horace Exp. | Virgil | |
| | | Juvenal | | |

attention to story-telling. His best known of these was his *Metamorphoses*, which was studied in the Boston Latin school even as late as 1860. An important American edition was W. Willymotte and T. Ruddiman's *Decepta Ex P. Ovidii Nasonis Metamorphosen* published in 1810. The text consisted of 138 pages followed by 77 pages of notes explaining and translating many of the more difficult passages. These stories were based on ancient Greek legends. Many of these conveyed significant social messages. The *Metapmorphoses* has been considered one of the great story books of the ages.

*Quintus Horatius Flaccus.* (65–8 B.C.) Horace was a Latin poet and satirist. His *Odes* were among his best poems. These were studied in the Boston Latin school in 1776 and in 1820, and at Exeter in 1818. Most of these *Odes* dealt with virtues. For example, Ode V dealt with the virtues of valour, fidelity, and constancy of Regulus.

*C. Sallustius Crispus* (86–34 B.C.). Sallust was one of Rome's better historians. Some of his writings have perished, but some have survived. One of these was *Bellum Catilinarium*, which dealt with the story of the conspiracy of Catiline, and the *Bellum Jugurthinum*, which dealt with the war against Jugurtha. Sometimes the former one was studied in conjunction with the Catilinarian speeches of Cicero. These together with other historical writings were studied in some Latin schools. Sallust was studied in the Boston school in 1820, and in Exeter in 1818. Sallust's *Opera*, which was a compilation of a number of his historical writings, was printed in Philadelphia in 1804. It included the above mentioned works plus several others.

Lhomond's *Viri Romae.* This book was prepared by Charles F. Lhomond of the University of Paris during the latter half of the 18th century. It had considerable circulation in France and Germany. Eventually it was republished here and used in both Exeter and the Boston Latin School. In this country it was used as a stepping-stone for the study of Caesar. It consisted mainly of brief biographical sketches of great Romans, which made it interesting reading for boys. The American editions by Andrews and by D'Ooge had long vocabulary lists in the back.

*Cornelius Nepotis.* Nepos wrote the *Vitae Excellentium Imperatorum* or *Lives of the Excellent Commanders.* This dealt with the lives of 25 Greek and Roman leaders. In some schools it was used instead of Caesar. An American reprint prepared by John Clarke was published in 1810. In this, like in other books by Clarke, the Latin and English appeared in parallel columns.

*Titus Livius.* Livy was a Roman historian. Although his history liekly was studied more often at the college level than at the secondary, Exeter in 1818 included the study of Livy in its curriculum.

*Publius Terentius.* Although brought from Africa to Rome as a slave, he was eventually provided an education and manumitted by his master. Soon he began writing comedies. Some of these were studied at Exeter in 1818. In the light of the fact that the writer's collection contains a number of copies of Terence, likely his comedies were studied in a number of American schools and colleges.

*Selectae E Profanis Scriptoribus.* This was a book containing selections of many ancient Greek and Roman authors whose writings could be used to exemplify the great Roman virtues *De Deo, De Prudentia, De Justitia, De Fortitudine,* and *De Temperantia.* This was taught in the Princeton Latin school.

*Other Latin classics.* The writer's collection also contains writings by T. Lucretius Caris (Lucretius), Caius Cornelius Tacitus, and M. Annaeus Seneca, all reprinted in the U.S.; and those by Gaius Petronius, and C. Plinius Caecilius (Pliny), published in Europe, but obtained in America. Whether these were studied only in colleges is not clear. Some of these likely were read in some Latin grammar schools.

*Comment.* The writer has with design delayed the treatment of the books of Caesar, Cicero, and Virgil, although they were often taught in Latin schools after 1775. However, of these only Cicero's *De officiis,* not his *Orations,* was taught in the Boston Latin School during Cheever's days. Since the writings of these men were not commonly taught during the colonial period, their treatment will be presented in the next section.

### G. *Latin American Academies*

MOST of the better early academies attempted to teach much of what was given in the Latin grammar schools, but more. The latter aimed primarily only to prepare boys for college, while the academies aimed to do that too, but also to offer enrichment and practical courses not required for college admission. During the early colonial period Harvard and Yale required only a mastery of Latin and Greek for admission. In 1745 Yale expected the student to be found "able Extempore to Read, Construe and Parce Tully (Cicero), Virgil and the Greek," and to understand common arithmetic. Harvard did not require arithmetic until 1803. On the other hand, most of the academies gradually introduced courses in mathematics, science, other foreign languages, English grammar, and rhetoric.

Apparently the entrance requirement adopted by King's College (Columbia) in 1786 did more to set the future pattern for college entrance in Latin than any other action, when it required a mastery of Caesar's *Gallic War*, four *Orations* of Cicero, and four books of Virgil's *Aeneid*. Although the Boston Latin school was teaching these at that time, many of the academies were not. Evidence clearly shows that the Latin schools, and at least the better academies, began to include these three authors in their Latin offering, even though many of them continued for a time to offer additional Latin writings as well. By 1860 even the Boston Latin school offered only Ovid in addition to the above three. In other words, gradually the standard Latin offering in secondary schools became Latin grammar, possibly a Latin reader, Caesar, Cicero, and Virgil, which standard has continued more or less until the present.

According to Harriet W. Marr's *The Old New England Academies*, the number of students taking Latin in academies was smaller than often thought. The catalogues of some academies starred the names of pupils taking Latin. At Wilbraham, Massachusetts, 40 of 101 male students took Latin, and of these only eight continued it the next year. In 1804 at Randolph, Vermont, only 19 of 151 students took Latin. At Westfield, Massachusetts, in 1832, 37 of 136 males took Latin or Greek, and only 11 of 217 females took Latin. Some of the female seminaries did not even offer Latin. The strangle hold that Latin and Greek had held on the secondary schools of Europe and on the colonial Latin grammar school here was gradually being broken after 1800 in the American academy.

*Caius Julius Caesar* (102–44 B.C.). He was the son of a Roman praetor. His marriage to a daughter of a bitter enemy Sulla cost Caesar his rank and nearly his life. When he went to Rhodes to study he was taken prisoner by pirates. After buying his release he armed a ship and conquered them and ordered them crucified. Later he was elected a priest of Jupiter and a praetor. A command in Spain soon followed. Upon his return he was nominated a consul. Then he was appointed to command in Gaul. Upon the death of Crasus mutual jealousy between Pompey and Caesar led to civil war. After defeating Pompey he spent some time conquering Egypt. After defeating Pompey's partisans in Africa and Spain he returned to Rome in triumph. His excessive assumption of honors and powers led many of the Roman senators to fear him, which eventuated in his assassination under the leadership of Brutus.

Of Caesar's writings apparently only his *Commentarii de Bello Gallico* and a few others have survived. Caesar was a man of action rather than a man of

M

literary attainment. Until the action by King's College in 1786 Caesar was read, if at all, in connection with history rather than as literary Latin. Why then was Caesar's *Commentaries* required for entrance? Apparently some professors there considered them easier, employing a more limited vocabulary than Nepos, Sallust, Terence, and Livy. Nevertheless reading Caesar has proven difficult following one year of grammar study. This difficulty has been largely due to the complexity of the periodic sentence, the word order, and the insertion of speeches involving indirect discourse. The length of these speeches in the first book has led some teachers to begin with the second book.

Since the study of Caesar became the standard second year's work in Latin in American secondary schools, many editions of Caesar have been reprinted or published here. One of the earlier ones was by Johannes Godvinus printed in Philadelphia in 1804. In the same year an edition by John Mair (from England), revised by James Ross, was printed in Lancaster. Then in 1813 Thomas Clark published a further revision of the Godvinus edition of Caesar in Philadelphia. In the preface Clark commented that the editors of Latin classics wrote for men "already well versed" in Latin rather than for schools by making all their comments and explanations in Latin rather than in English. Thus in this edition the military terms, allusions to the manners and institutions of the Romans and Greek, as well as vocabulary terms and expressions, were explained in fine print at the bottom of the pages. Clark's book was a large one. It presented the Gallic War in eight books (parts) and 187 large pages. Then he presented Caesar's *Bello Civill* in three books in about 100 pages, the Alexandrian War in 30 pages, the African War in 37 pages, the Spanish War in 17 pages, plus some historical fragments about Caesar. A number of folded maps appeared in the book. It is evident that not all parts of this book could have been studied by second year Latin students in one year.

A much more attractive edition of the *Commentaries* was published by Fred P. Leverett in 1829. The main text of eight books was printed in rather large type in 272 pages. The paragraphs were numbered. Then in the back there were 45 pages of notes of explanation referring to particular books and paragraphs, and 16 pages of a geographical and historical index of terms.

In 1844 E. A. Andrews published an edition of seven books of the *Commentaries* in 152 pages. A fine dictionary of 144 pages followed. In the back 59 pages of notes on the text and a brief life of Caesar appeared. The dictionary apparently made this a very usable book. It appeared in a number of reprints.

In 1870 Albert Harkness published an edition very similar to the one by

Andrews. Again only seven books were included. In the back were notes and a dictionary. An edition re-edited by Greenough, D'Ooge, and Daniell published a very attractive edition of Caesar in 1886. It contained many pictures and other interesting features. Other editions of Caesar were published by Charles Anthon in 1838, William Duncan in 1844 (a translation), Peter Bullions in 1847, J. A. Spencer in 1848, George Stuart in 1867, Allen and Greenough in 1874, Francis W. Kelsey in 1886, and William Collar in 1891. Likely there were many others. In addition many Latin readers contained sections of Caesar.

*M. Tullius Cicero* (106–43 B.C.). Cicero was the son of a Roman knight. He had the privilege of studying under outstanding scholars of rhetoric, oratory, and law in Rome. After briefly serving in the army, he entered political life. After a brief experience as a legal pleader, he temporarily retired to study philosophy at Athens and Rhodes. After returning to Rome he again resumed his public career. The political turmoil of the times inspired the writing of many of his famous orations. He was advanced from one important public office to another until he was elected to a consulship. However, the changing political climate of Rome at that time periodically led him to retire to his villa for literary work. Even then his political entanglements during the brief ascendency of Mark Antony led to his proscription and death, since he was a republican patriot. However, it was amazing how much literary work was done by Cicero in spite of his many political activities, even though most of his orations were related to political matters.

In his writings Cicero greatly enriched the Latin language by Hellenizing or Grecianizing it. He Latinized many Greek words, so now when we learn Latin we also learn the meanings of many Greek words or roots as well. He developed a style which was far richer and superior to any other Roman writer. Consequently his writings became models for the study and composition of Latin. His works later were so widely studied and imitated, particularly during the Renaissance, that the practice became known as Ciceronianism.

Cicero's writings covered many subjects. His philosophical writings were tinged with Grecian thought. His *De Oratore* was educational in nature. Among his minor works may be mentioned *De Senectute*, on old age, and *De Amicitia*, on friendship. Both of these were written in a charming style. More than 700 letters have been collected that Cicero wrote to various friends and acquaintances. At least 57 of his orations have been found extant. The most famous were the four against Catiline, the 14 of the so-called Philippics against

Antony, one on behalf of Archias, one on behalf of L. Murena, one for Marcus Caelius, and two of legal import. It is now believed that not all of these were actually orally delivered. Some took the form of tracts. Too, not all of these were originally in their present literary form. Cicero often re-edited his writings for further perfection.

The orations were not the only works of Cicero studied in American secondary schools. The Boston Latin School about 1700 taught only the *De Officiis* by Cicero; in 1776 his *Epistolae* (letters), *De Officiis*, and *Orations:* in 1820 his *De Officiis, De Senectute, De Amicitia,* and *Orations:* but in 1860 only his *Orations.* The grammar school at Princeton did not teach Cicero about 1785, and Exeter taught only the *Orations* in 1818. Much evidence has been uncovered revealing that during most of the 1800's mainly only the *Orations* were taught in American secondary schools. However, some editions of Cicero's other works were published in America after 1800. The writer's collection contains a copy of Ciceronis *Selectae Quaedam Epistolae* edited by M. L. Hurlbut in 1836; a *De Officiis* by Thomas A. Thacher in 1850.

Since Cicero's *Orations* were commonly taught in the Latin schools and the academies, and later in the high schools, many editions of them appeared prepared by different editors. One of the earlier ones to appear in several editions was by Charles Folsom. The second edition was published in 1811, the fourth edition in 1828, and another appeared as late as 1848. The 1828 edition contained three orations with notes against Catiline and notes and synopses for one on the Manilian Law, one for M. Marcellus, one for the poet Archias, one for T. A. Milo, and one against M. Anthony.

In 1869 George Stuart published the *Select Orations of Marcus Tullius Cicero.* This later appeared in many editions. This, like Folsom's, also contained many orations in addition to those against Catiline. In the 1883 edition the orations consisted of 202 pages, the notes of 110 pages, and the lexicon of 125 pages.

Other editions of Cicero's *Orations* were prepared by John Smart (1826), by Hilliard, Gray, Little & Wilkins (publishers) (1828), Charles Anthon (1836), Hubert Holden (1854), Austin Stickney (1860), E. A. Johnson (1871), E. P. Crowell (1871), A. Harkness (1873), Joseph and William Allen (1873), Francis Kelsey (1882), William Underwood and Thomas Clark (1885), Martin Kellogg (1889), A. P. Montague (1890), and J. B. Greenough (1896). These dates may not all be first editions. Likely there were many other editions of Cicero's *Orations* published.

*Publius Vergilius Maro* (70–19 B.C.). Vergil was born near Mantua in northern Italy. Here he spent a somewhat sheltered youth during the stormy times of the later years of the republic. His poetic genius was first evidenced in the writing of a series of pastoral poems (*Eclogues* or *Bucolics*), while he still was somewhat under the influence of Theocritus. Partly for reasons of health and partly for political considerations he moved to Rome. Soon Maecenas placed him in affluent circumstances. Then at the suggestion of Maecenas he wrote the *Georgics* or *Art of Husbandry*, a farming treatise of four books. This was done to idealize and revive rural and farming life. This confirmed his position as the foremost poet of the age. In the meantime he had moved to a villa near Naples. At the insistence of Augustus he devoted the last eleven years of his life to writing the great national epic, the *Aeneid*. It did much toward idealizing the highest and best of the history and attainments of the Romans. Although it was roughly finished before his death, he suggested that it be burned because it was not sufficiently polished or refined. Fortunately this was not done. Some refinement was done on it later by others. Thus Vergil has gone down in history as Rome's greatest poet, and possibly next to Homer, as the greatest epic poet of antiquity.

Vergil was listed for study in all of the five dates of the Boston Latin School curriculum. It was likewise offered in the Princeton school about 1785 and in Exeter in 1818. Evidently this was true because Harvard and Yale required it for entrance.

Likely most of the editions of Vergil used in the colonial schools were books published in Europe and brought here. The writer's collection contains a number of these. One of the earliest editions published here was Reverend J. G. Cooper's *Publii Virgilii Maronis Opera* in 1815. (Spellings of Virgil vary in different books). It was designed for the use of "students in the colleges, academies, and other seminaries in the U.S." It soon appeared in numerous editions. The 1844 edition was the ninth. This edition included the endorsements of the presidents of Columbia and Harvard, and of a long list of college professors and 23 principals of academies. This book contained Eclogae Decimae (ten eclogues) of *Bucolia*, four books of *Georgics*, and twelve books of the *Aeneis*. In all it contained 615 large pages. The poems were printed in Latin on the upper part of the pages with every fifth line numbered, while the notes and comments were printed below in double columns in very fine print in English. In general the notes occupied about two-thirds of most pages. Before each book of poems there was an introduction in English. Evidently Cooper's was one of the more commonly used editions of Vergil before 1850. However, likely not all of the poems were studied in any one academy.

In 1870 Thomas Chase published *Six Books of the Aeneid of Virgil*. After a brief biography of Vergil, the six books were presented in Latin. These were followed by about an equal number of pages of notes and comments in English. In the back there was a vocabulary of about 125 pages. Thus the text occupied about one-third of the book, while the notes and vocabulary the remainder. This book appeared in later revised editions.

In 1881 J. B. Greenough published the *Greater Poems of Virgil*. Volume I contained the pastoral poems and six books of the *Aeneid*. The first 29 pages contained the pastoral poems in Latin, the next 150 pages the *Aeneid*. Then there were 64 pages of notes, comments, and pictures about the pastoral poems, and more than 200 pages about the *Aeneid*. In the back there was a vocabulary list of 307 pages in double column. This list was a virtual Latin dictionary. The book appeared in later reprints.

Among other American published editions of Virgil the following may be mentioned: Francis Bowen's *Virgil* (1842), Edward Searing's *First Six Books of Virgil's Aeneid* (1869), Theodore Buckley's *Works of Virgil* (1872), Levi Hart and V. R. Osborn's *The Works of P. Virgilius Maro* (1882), T. E. Page's *P. Virgili Maronis Bucolica* (1891), J. Conington's *Publi Vergili Maronis Opera* (1896), and Edward H. Cutler's *Ninth Book of Vergil's Aeneid* (1896). Likely other editions were published.

*Latin readers.* In addition to books dealing only with particular Latin authors, such as Caesar, Cicero, and Virgil, many Latin readers containing selections from many authors were also published in America. However, some of the earliest were merely reprints of those first written in Europe. Latin readers apparently were used either in conjunction with the study of grammar to help enlarge the Latin vocabulary and reading ability of students or used following the study of grammar before beginning the study of Caesar. In fact, comments in the prefaces of a number of these readers indicated these uses.

Apparently the earliest readers to become popular in America were written by F. Jacobs and F. W. Doering in Germany. In the early 1820's the Cummings, Hilliard & Co. reprinted *The Latin Reader—First Part*, and *Part Second* in Boston as separate books. These were for "Use of Schools, Academies, Etc." The *First Part* contained exercises in simple sentences, some of Aesop's *Fables*, mythology, outlines of Roman history, and a brief historical treatment of the nations of antiquity, all of which were in Latin. These extracts were followed by notes translated into English. Then in the back there was a dictionary of about 125 pages. In 1825 *Part Second* was published here from the fourth German edition. It contained select fables from Phaedrus, extracts from Cicero and Livy, and about 100 pages devoted to an abridgment of Justin. These selections were only in Latin. No notes or dictionary appeared in this volume. The 1828 edition contained 30 pages of advertisements of other textbooks sold by the publishers. Both of these *Parts* soon appeared in a number of reprints.

Apparently the popularity of these readers by Jacobs and Doering prompted certain American Latin professors to re-edit them with certain revisions and to republish them. One of these was by John D. Ogilby, Principal of the Grammar School of Columbia College. In 1830 Ogilby published the two Parts in one volume, but amplified the notes and reduced the dictionary after the *First Part* and added notes after *Part Second*. Ogilby's edition appeared in a number of reprints.

In 1837 E. A. Andrews also republished the *First Part* of Jacobs and Doering's *Reader*. However, he made two changes. At the bottom of the pages of the Latin text he listed references to the sections and subdivisions of the Andrews and Stoddard's *Latin Grammar*, which would explain or illustrate the grammatical rules or constructions involved. Too, he enlarged the dictionary in the back. This edition contained no notes. However, the 1849 edition added nearly 30 pages of notes in the back. These editions continued to be reprinted at least until 1867.

In 1846 Peter Bullions likewise republished *Part First* of the Jacob's book, but adapted it to Bullions' *Latin Grammar*. The plan used for references was similar to the one used by Andrews. After the dictionary he included exercises in Latin composition instead of notes. The 1868 edition added more than 40 pages of Latin idioms in the back. These editions appeared in many reprints. Thus it can be seen that modified reprints of the Jacobs and Doering's *Latin Reader—Part First* continued to appear until in the 1870's. Apparently American authors were hesitant about departing from the highly accepted selections of these two German authors.

One of the first Latin readers, which was not primarily based on Jacobs, to attain much circulation was Albert Harkness's *A Latin Reader* in 1865. Part First of 40 pages was devoted to a review of Latin grammar. Part Second of nearly 60 pages consisted of brief Latin selections comprised of fables, anecdotes, and historical extracts. Some of the readings were the same as in Jacobs. In the back were extensive notes and a Latin-English vocabulary. It was recopyrighted in 1875, 1877, and 1882. The writer's collection contains eight different reprints of the Harkness *Reader*, which is evidence that it must have had considerable acceptance in the academies and high schools for several decades.

A number of other Latin readers were published here, particularly after 1865. Among these were S. C. Walker's *A New Latin Reader* (1829), Allen H. Weld's *Latin Lessons and Reader* (1845), John M'Clintock's *A Second Book in Latin* (1853), William Bingham's *A Latin Reader* (1869), William and Jeseph Allen's *A Latin Reader* (1869), and George Stuart's *A Latin Reader* (1882).

### H. *Latin in High Schools*

THE first American high schools, the Boston English Classical School, founded in 1821, did not offer Latin. However, a law passed in Massachusetts in 1827 required towns of over 4000 population to provide a teacher for Latin, Greek, history, rhetoric, and logic. Thus two types of education were to be given in high schools: the college preparatory, and the advanced English branches for practical life. Evidence seems to indicate that the law was not enforced for about ten years. In 1859 the law was changed to require every town of 500 families or more to maintain a school in which a broad offering of subjects was to be given, including Latin.

According to Kandel's *History of Secondary Education* the high school in Hartford offered Latin in 1848, Providence in 1855, and Lockport, N.Y. in 1850. By the 1860's most high schools were offering multiple curriculums, with the classical curriculum offering Latin. Then as the high school commonly also assumed the college preparatory function, it would offer the Latin required for college admission. By that time most colleges required preparation in Latin grammar, Caesar, Cicero, and Vergil.

### I. *Some Characteristics of Latin Grammars*

*General characteristics.* Until after 1840 nearly every Latin grammar was bound in leather. Commonly the earlier books failed to include either a table of contents or an index. One of the first to include a table of contents was Gould's in 1825. In most garmmars the first verb to be conjugated was *amo*.

*Two major methods.* An analysis of Latin grammars soon made it evident that two very different methods or approaches were followed in the earlier books. The one method was that advocated by the famous educator, Jan Comenius. He favored teaching Latin with its vernacular counterpart. In its application

14. Quid hoc ? ferisne, O Timon ? Antestor O Hercules ! hei ! hei ! in jus voco te de vulnere ad Areopagum.

16. Clavum fortunæ veteres dedere ; et basin globosam pedibus subjecerent; oculis etiam (eam) privarunt.

# CHAP. XXIV.

Verbs of *asking*, *teaching*, *clothing* and *concealing ;* also verbs of *giving*, *hurting* and *accusing*, with their contraries, govern two accusatives.

1. The wicked always work some evil to those who are nearest them.

Ο πονηρος αει κακος τις[ne] εργαζομαι ὁ εγγυτατω αυτος ειμι[g].

2. The king said to the maid, Ask of me what (thing) you will, and I will give it you.

Ειπον ὁ βασιλευς ὁ κορασιον, Αιτεω[s] εγω ὁ εαν (χρημα) θελω, και διδωμι συ.

3. Come then, if I buy you, what will you teach me ?

Φερω δη, ην πριαμαι συ, τις εγω διδασκω[3] ;

4. It is fit that men should bear such things as they have done to others.

Αναγκη ὁ ανθρωπος τοιουτος πασχω, διοσπερ αν ὁ αλλος δραω.

5. They have passed a decree to demand Pagasæ from him, and have prevented him to fortify Magnesia.

Και γαρ Παγασαι απαιτεω αυτος ψηφιζω[p], και Μαγνησια κωλυω τειχιζω.

6. I never said nor did any thing to him, for which he was ashamed.

Ουδεπωποτε αυτος ουτε ειπα ουτε ποιεω ουδεις, επι ὁς[d] αισχυνω[s].

7. They teach their servants arts, frequently spending much money upon them, but they neglect themselves.

Ο μεν οικετης εκδιδασκω[m] τεφνη, παμπολυς πολλακις εις αυτος αργυριον αναλισκω, και ἑαυτου δε αμελεω.

22  A page from Neilson's *Greek Exercises,* 1809. Note the parallel method of learning to read Greek

this approach took three forms: The vernacular interspersed among the Latin words, the vernacular and the Latin presented in parallel columns, and the interlinear form so commonly used clandestinely by students for the last 100 years. Lily and Stockwood interspersed the vernacular with the Latin. Then when John Clarke wrote *An Introduction to the Making of Latin* in England, which was republished here by several printers, he used the parallel column form. Its popularity influenced many other authors to use it. Among them who used it largely or in part were John Mair, Caleb Alexander, Cummins and Hilliard (Publishers) in *The Latin Tutor*, Joseph Dana, Chauncey A. Goodrich, and Frederick P. Leverett.

The other approach was the purely grammatical approach, commonly presenting grammar under the four divisions of orthography, etymology (with the eight parts of speech), syntax, and prosody. Usually the book would be organized into brief lessons presenting particular rules or principles with their applications to Latin. Many of these lessons would contain short vocabulary lists to be committed. Thus the Latin words, rules, declensions, and conjugations were to be committed. This was in contrast to the Comenius method, in which an understanding of the Latin words would be developed from their use in context. An early Latin grammar that became the model for the grammatical approach was Alexander Adam's *The Rudiments of Latin and English Grammar* written in Edinburgh, Scotland. In 1818 it was reprinted here. It was not long before other authors followed this approach. After about 1835 nearly all used the grammatical method. This approach was favored by those who believed in the "formal discipline" theory of psychology. This theory became dominant, not merely in Latin, but in many other subject fields as well. However, certain authors in other fields began using the inductive approach just about the time when the formal approach in Latin became common. This was true of certain texts in arithmetic and in English grammar.

## J. *Characteristics of Latin Classics and Readers*

UNTIL nearly 1800 the books to be read in Latin were not standardized, except that Harvard and Yale rather early required mastery of Cicero and Vergil for entrance. However, this did not necessarily mean Cicero's *Orations* or the *Aeneid*, for other writings of Cicero and Virgil were read in many Latin grammar schools. The *Colloquies* by Corderius were very popular for some time. Other classsical Latin books read in some schools were Ovid's *Metamorphoses*: the *Odes* by Horace; history by Sallust, Nepos, and Livy; comedies by Terence;

and occasionally writings by Lucretius, Tacitus, and Seneca. Apparently the writings containing moral lessons were favored.

Apparently the Latin offering in secondary schools began to standardize after 1786, when King's College (Columbia) began requiring a mastery of Caesar's *Commentaries*, four *Orations* of Cicero, and four books of *Vergil's Aeneid*, for entrance. Since Latin grammar schools offered much Latin, they generally taught several other classics as well. However, as other subjects began to be offered in them, the Latin offering gradually was reduced to these three Latin classics. This was still true when the present writer took Latin after 1900.

## SECTION TWO

# GREEK

### Introduction

*The language.* Greek and Latin of all the languages have had the greatest influence on the development of western civilization. Greek belonged to the Indo-European family of languages. As has been true in nearly all geographical areas, different dialects developed in the Greek world. Just how old the Greek language is has been a matter of conjecture. It is not even certain just when it began to take written form, but some think about 1000 B.C. The alphabet was borrowed from the Phoenicians. The classical Greek language came to have 24 letters.

The two chief dialects were the old Ionic and the Attic. The old Ionic was used by Homer and Herodotus. The Attic became the language of the larger and later portion of Grecian literature. Then the conquests of Philip of Macedon and Alexander the Great tended to spread the fused language of the Macedonians and Greeks into Asia and parts of Africa. All this resulted in the development of Hellenistic Greek. The Septuagint and the New Testament were written in this form of Greek. Alexandria, Egypt, became the center of this new Greek culture. Later when the Greeks were conquered by the Romans considerable Greek was absorbed by the Romans. Cicero borrowed many Greek words to form so-called Ciceronian Latin.

*Literature.* The earliest form of Greek literature was the epic or narrative poem. The epics by Homer became the best known. The second form was that of lyric poetry, such as the lyrics of Sappho, Alcaeus, Anacreon, and others. Some took choral or religious form. The third was the development of the drama. This form was used in connection with the inculcation of the ideas of democracy, particularly in Athens. During the period of democracy there also developed the production of histories, philosophy, and orations. That was the golden period of Athenian culture. Greek literature was based on or dealt mainly with Hellenic characteristics and virtues. Among these was great attention to characteristics of the physical body—strength, fitness, skill, and beauty of form. The more idealistic concerns were reverence, moderation, social obligation and justice, and a love of beauty of art and expression.

*Grammar.* The development of systematic Greek grammar was a long process. Plato began by drawing a distinction between the subject and the predicate. He also recognized number and the tenses of verbs. Aristotle recognized only three parts of speech—the noun, verb, and conjunction. Later the Stoics did much to clarify grammar. The so-called famous grammarians at the Alexandrian Library did much to improve the analysis of structure of the Grecian language. Famous among these were Aristophanes of Byzantium and Aristarchus of Samothrace. It was finally at Rhodes, where Cicero later studied, where the first Greek grammar was written by Dionysius Thrax (born about 166 B.C.). When in printed form it consisted only of 16 pages, yet it remained a standard for a long time. The earliest lexicographic attempts were made at Alexandria, which were later transferred to Constantinople. The labors there relating to grammar consisted chiefly of commentaries on the work of Dionysius. Possibly the first western grammar using Greek type was written by Constantine Lascaris published in 1476 in Milan, which remained the standard for several centuries.

*The study of Greek.* Greek was not commonly studied in western Europe during the middle ages. However, during the early Renaissance a considerable revival of the study of Greek took place in Italy. As scholars from England and Germany went to Italy to study both the pure revived Latin and the Greek, these languages were introduced by them into northern Europe. Of these countries it was in Germany where Greek came to be studied most extensively. Later it was in Germany where the best studies of Greek were written and published.

*College entrance requirements in Greek.* The colonial colleges required a considerable mastery of Greek for entrance. About 1643 Harvard expected a student to be able to "decline perfectly the Paradigms of Nounes and Verbes in ye Greek tongue; then may hee bee admitted into ye College." Then in 1655 the requirement was changed to read, the "Greek Testament, Isocrates, and the Minor Poets or such like." Yale in 1745 required ability to be "able Extempore to Read, Construe and Parce . . the Greek Testament." It was not until after 1850, when many colleges began to grant the B.S. degree, that one could enter many colleges without competence in Greek. For the A.B. degree Greek generally continued to be required for entrance in many colleges for some time.

### A. *Foreign Written Greek Textbooks*

SINCE few textbooks were printed in America during the colonial period, the earliest Greek books studied here would have been brought from Europe. Apparently only rarely would all the students possess the same textbooks. Mention was made in Ironside's book in 1799 that the school "for several years past has suffered much inconvenience, . . . from the variety of Latin and Greek grammars used by the students, in consequence of that diversity to which, under different instructors, they have been accustomed in their preparatory course; . . ." A number of these foreign written Greek grammars that were likely brought here are in the writer's collection.

*Claude Lancelot* (1615–1695). One of these was written by Lancelot, who was one of the distinguished Pt. Royalists of France, so well known for the development of excellent teaching methods and for authorship of outstanding textbooks. He, with the aid of his brethren wrote *A New Method of Learning with greater Facility the Greek Tongue* (1655). The writer's copy translated from the French was published in Dublin in 1747. It contained the rules for the "declensions, conjugations, resolution of verbs, syntax, quantity, accents, dialects, and poetic licence digested in the clearest and concisest order." Throughout, the rules were stated and thoroughly explained in English (translated from the French), and then applied to the Greek. It appeared in repeated editions abroad. Much testimony was given of its "superior excellence." It consisted of nearly 450 pages.

*Westminster text.* Another old text was the *Institutio Graecae Grammatice* published in London in 1784. The seven liberal arts were illustrated with pictures on the title page. This was a rather small book of 196 pages bound with home spun linen. The rules and explanations were in Latin, and then applied to the Greek. Its four parts dealt with Orthographia, Etymologia, Syntaxi, and Prosodia.

*Edward Wettenhall, D.D.* In 1789 a copy of Wettenhall's *Graecae Grammatice Institutio Compendiaria in Usum Scholarum* was reprinted in Philadelphia. This was even smaller than the Westminster text, having only 95 pages, but very similar to it in treatment. It too, presented and explained the rules in Latin, then applied them to the Greek.

*George Ironside.* In 1799 Ironside published in New York *A Grammar of the Greek Language,* which was originally written for the College-School of Gloucester. It was recommended by the University of Cambridge (Mass.) "to be used by those who are intended for that Seminary." The 3rd American edition appeared in 1815. This book somewhat followed the plan of Ward's and the Eton Editions of Cambden's Greek texts, both of which had wide usage in England, but claimed to contain a number of improvements. The improved parts dealt with "Declension and Comparison of Adjectives, the Rules of Augment, and of Formation of Tenses, and particularly those of Syntax and Prosody." The rules and explanations were in English. Just half of the book was devoted to the regular text, while the latter half constituted an Appendix, which dealt with "Observations, Schemes of Heroclites, Patronymics, Diminutives, Possessives, Verbals, Lists of Anomals, Tables of Dialects, etc."

*William Neilson, D.D.* In 1809 the Principals of Baltimore College republished Neilson's *Greek Exercises* here. It was originally published in Edinburgh. It was for the "use of colleges, academies and schools." It covered syntax, ellipsis, dialects, prosody, and metaphrasis. It was very different from the above discussed books. It began by presenting and illustrating 63 rules of syntax in 12 pages. These were followed by 53 brief chapters illustrating particular grammatical rules in parallel contexts in English and Greek. For example, Chap. III's rule was: "A verb signifying actively governs the accusative." Sentence one to illustrate it was: "1. For ye *have* the *poor* always, but ye *have* not *me* always." Its equivalent Greek was beside it. A Key of 71 pages was in the back.

An identical edition in regards to content was published in New York in 1810 directly under Neilson's name and claimed to be the first American edition; from the second Edinburgh edition. However, its pages and print were smaller. The Key was not included in the back. Neilson tried to do in a Greek book what John Clarke had done in his popular Latin text earlier; namely, to follow the Comenius method in teaching a foreign language by means of developing a vocabulary through parallel usage of both languages instead of committing it. Its 7th edition was printed in 1824, and a new edition in 1846.

*Caspar F. Hackenberg and C. A. Goodrich.* In 1814 Goodrich secured an American copyright to republish Hackenberg's *Elements of Greek Grammar*. This was first published in Utrecht, Holland, in 1792. This was a technical Greek grammar, dealing with the four parts of orthography, etymology, syntax, and prosody. It attempted to do in a Greek grammar what the famous Alexander Adam text had done for Latin. It was opposite in approach to the book by Neilson. It contained 317 pages. Like most early Greek grammars it contained neither a table of contents nor an index, however it had a rather long preface.

*R. Valpy and Charles Anthon.* In 1805 Anthon republished Valpy's *Elements of Greek Grammar*, which was a well known text in England. The material was presented in the traditional four parts. The rules and explanations were presented in English, and applied to Greek. More space was devoted to prosody than in most books, which dealt with position, contraction, composition and derivation, of feet, of metres, dactylic measure, iambic measure, trochaic measure, and anapaestic measure. More than 30 pages were devoted to appendix material. The sixth edition appeared in 1827. Its index was in the beginning of the book.

*Philip Buttman* (1764–1829). Buttman wrote a number of Greek texts in Germany. In 1822 his *Greek Grammar* in translated form was reprinted in Boston. This was a book of 292 pages. In 1826 a revised edition of 336 pages was printed here. Part I dealt with accidence and etymology. Part II dealt with syntax. It contained an index but no lexicon. In 1833 it was again enlarged. Although it contained 493 pages, it was intended for "high schools and universities." This was translated by Edward Robinson. Its three parts dealt with orthography and orthoepy, grammatical forms and flexion of words, and syntax. In the back was an appendix of 30 pages and two indexes. In 1851 again an enlarged edition of 517 pages was translated and published here by Robinson, which was based on the 18th German edition. Its parts were similar to the 1833 edition. This was reprinted as late as 1872. It is evident that the Buttman Greek grammars enjoyed an extended circulation.

## B. *American Written Greek Grammars Before 1850*

APPARENTLY Greek grammars were not written in America as early as those of Latin. In part this may have been due to the fact that not as much Greek was taught in the Latin grammar schools and academies as Latin. This limited the sale of Greek texts. Too, the printing of the Greek characters may have been a problem for colonial printers. So Greek texts continued to be imported to a later date. Then even after American authors began to write Greek texts, they borrowed heavily from European authors.

*Caleb Alexander.* Alexander, who also published grammars in Latin and English, in 1796 published *A Grammatical System of the Grecian Language.* In it were listed the names of eight other Greek grammars which he consulted in its preparation. The rules were given in English, but immediately followed with Greek applications. The text proper consisted of 135 pages followed by 70 pages of appendix material. Among the appendix contents he briefly discussed the Attic, Ionic, Doric, Aeolic, Boeotic, and Poetic dialects of Greek. It was bound in homespun linen. It failed to contain a preface, table of contents, or an index.

*John Smith.* Smith, who was Professor of the Learned Languages at Dartmouth College, in 1809 published his *Grammar of the Greek Language.* This was a more attractive book than Alexander's and was bound in leather, as were most Greek texts before 1840. It was clearly organized into the four traditional parts and an appendix. The text consisted of 204 pages, plus 64 pages in the appendix. There were many explanatory footnotes. It contained an excellent and detailed table of contents, but no index.

*Chauncey A. Goodrich.* Goodrich, who wrote textbooks in many fields, also entered the field of Greek. Reference has been made of Goodrich's reprint of Hackenberg's *Grammar* in 1814. Then in 1828 Goodrich revised it considerably, but published it as a Fourth Edition, Enlarged and Improved. A testimonial by President Jeremiah Day of Yale stated that candidates for admission were examined in Goodrich's *Greek Grammar.* Goodrich suggested that the leading principles be committed to memory, which were briefly stated. Remarks and exceptions immediately followed the rules in smaller type. The paradigm of the verb was reduced to tabular form. In plan of presentation he claimed to follow Adam's *Latin Grammar.* Other authors were also mentioned as authorities. Most of the appendix was reprinted from Valpy's text. The treatment of prosody also appeared in the appendix. Its table of contents appeared in the back. A slightly enlarged edition was printed as the fifth in 1831.

*Benjamin F. Fisk.* In 1830 Fisk published *A Grammar of the Greek Language.* He claimed that he wrote it due to the many complaints of the then current Greek grammars. In this book he attempted to overcome these complaints. Its organization was largely conventional, dealing with the letters, the parts of speech, syntax, prosody, and a number of Greek dialects. Rules and explanations were in English with their applications to Greek. A slightly revised 2nd edition was published in 1831. The 29th stereotyped edition of this book appeared in 1846. This is evidence of its circulation.

In 1831 Fisk published his *Greek Exercises*. This book of 171 pages was modelled on John Clarke's Latin book. Each exercise began with a statement of a grammatical rule, which was followed with applications and usages both in English and Greek in parallel columns. In all there were 61 rules or sections and 1270 sentence applications or illustrations. Many of the sentences were quotations from or about great Greek writers. It was intended for use with the grammar. All these books were bound in leather and were attractively printed.

*Alpheus Crosby*. In 1841 Crosby, who was professor of Greek at Dartmouth, published *A Grammar of the Greek Language*. This was a much larger book than Fisk's. Its books dealt with orthography, orthoepy, etymology, and syntax. It contained three tables of contents: a general table of contents; contents of the tables of declension, numerals. and conjugations; and contents of the syntax. He claimed that as a good English grammar would not deal with the grammar of Chaucer and of other old periods of English, so a Greek grammar should deal primarily with Attic Greek, rather than with the many types of older Greek. Its organization was rather detailed. It was divided into books, the books into chapters, the chapters into heavy numbered sections, and the sections into numbered paragraphs. It was one of the earlier Greek grammars to contain two indexes: a Greek index and an English one.

In 1846 he revised his book. All of the tables, instead of appearing throughout the book, were placed in the beginning, covering nearly 90 pages. Then the remainder was organized into the traditional four books or parts. In all, it contained 750 sections and the Greek and English indexes, but was slightly smaller in volume than his earlier book. Both of these appeared in a number of reprints.

In 1849 Crosby published a small book of *Greek Lessons*, consisting mainly of brief selections from Xenophon's *Anabasis*. These were printed fully in Greek, but there were profuse footnotes referring to particular rules in his grammar. Apparently he, like Fisk, intended the exercises to be studied in connection with grammar. However, Crosby's *Lessons* were very different from Fisk's *Exercises*. Fisk attempted to have the students learn how to change English into Greek, while Crosby apparently intended the student to translate these selections into English. These *Lessons* appeared in numerous reprints.

*Raphael Kühner*. In 1844 an English translation of Kühner's *Grammar of the Greek Language* was published here. It was translated by B. B. Edwards of

Andover Theological Seminary and S. H. Taylor, Principal of Phillips Andover Academy. Kühner was connected with the Lyceum at Hanover, Germany. He was the author of numerous Greek and Latin books. This book was first published there in 1836.

Although on the title page it was stated that the book was "for use of high schools and colleges," it was a large book of 603 pages bound in leather. It consisted of only etymology and syntax, but each was very extensively treated. In the back there were three indexes: Of subjects, of Greek, and of the forms of the verbs. In 1852 it was republished in slightly revised form and bound in linen. It was reprinted in 1853. Although it was also intended for high schools, it is doubtful whether it was used in very many secondary schools, due to its size.

In 1846 Taylor published a translation of Kühner's *An Elemntary Grammar of the Greek Language.* This was a book of about 350 pages bound in linen. It consisted of etymology, syntax, and an appendix of Homeric dialect. It also contained a Greek and English vocabulary and two indexes. Apparently its much smaller size made it more acceptable for secondary school use. The 1853 reprint was its 13th edition.

*Peter Bullions* (1791–1864). Bullions, who was a professor of languages at Albany Academy, wrote grammars in English, Latin, and Greek. In the early 1840's his *Principles of Greek Grammar* was published. By 1847 the 12th edition appeared. In 1853 it was revised and recopyrighted. In 1859 the 42nd edition was printed. It appeared at least as late as 1868. The 1860 edition contained 26 pages of advertisements of textbooks in the back and was bound in light colored leather.

The 1853 book was organized in the traditional four parts. In turn, the parts were divided into numbered sections and sub-sections. The definitions were clearly stated. Bullions claimed that "time and experience have only strengthened the conviction, that no system of Grammar will answer a good purpose" unless the leading facts and principles were presented "as to be easily *committed to memory,* and so to be always ready for immediate application when necessary." Its many editions evidenced its wide circulation. Bullions also wrote the *Greek Lessons for Beginners.*

*Other Greek grammars before 1850.* Among other Greek grammars published before 1850 may be mentioned Alexander Negris's *Grammar of the Modern Greek Language* (1828); Thomas Arnold's *First Greek Book* was revised by J. A. Spencer, and E. A. and A. M. Sophocles' as a *Greek Grammar* (1838); John

N

M'Clintock and George R. Crook's *A First Book of Greek* (1848); and William Veitch's *Greek Verbs* (1848). Many other authors of Greek grammars were mentioned in the prefaces of most of the books here discussed, but most of them were of European authorship.

### C. *Greek Grammars, 1850–1900*

A RATHER large number of Greek grammars were published in America during this period, but only a limited number of them seemed to have received wide acceptance. One reason may have been because the academies began to decline and the high schools increased in number, but many high schools did not teach Greek. Treatment will be given only those books most commonly used.

*James Hadley.* Hadley was a professor at Yale. In his teaching he became versant with George Curtius's *Griechische Schulgrammatik,* first published in Germany in 1852. It soon appeared in successive editions there. At first Hadley merely intended to translate this book and publish it here. However, he soon realized some changes were necessary "to adapt it to the wants and habits of instructors in our country." So he published this *Greek Grammar* in translated and revised form under his own name, but acknowledged his debts to Curtius. Its four parts dealt with orthography and euphony, inflection, formation of words, and syntax, plus an appendix which dealt with versification. It may be noted that the organization was very different than most other Greek grammars. In the text he largely followed the Attic dialect, but frequently made applications to other dialects in fine print at the bottom of the pages. In the back there appeared both Greek and English indexes. This edition appeared in a number of reprints.

After Hadley's death Frederic de Forest Allen revised the book in 1884. The main parts remained the same but a number of the sections were rearranged, and numerous other technical matters were revised. These matters increased its volume by about 50 pages. Part of this space was devoted to a table dealing with the "Corresponding Articles in the Two Editions." This edition likewise appeared in a number of reprints.

*W. W. Goodwin.* In 1860 he published his *Syntax of the Moods and Tenses of the Greek Verb.* Its purpose was to give those who had learned the elements of Greek syntax a deeper understanding of the moods and tenses as "is necessary for writng Greek correctly." In the back were an English and a Greek index. It contained 311 pages. It was revised in 1865, and again in 1870, which appeared as the fourth edition. Editions appeared as late as 1893.

In 1870, when Goodwin was the Eliot Professor of Greek in Harvard, he published *An Elementary Greek Grammar*. This was a small book of less than 250 pages. In 1873 minor changes were made and two indexes added. Its four parts dealt with Letters, Syllables, and Accents; Inflection; Syntax; and Metres. Thus its organization was somewhat similar to that of Hadley's text. Its parts were divided into large numbered sections and the sections into smaller numbered paragraphs. Several reprints appeared.

Apparently the smallness of the first *Elementary* text eventually proved unsatisfactory, so in 1879 Goodwin published a much enlarged *Elementary Greek Grammar*. The part dealing with inflection was largely rewritten and enlarged by about 50 pages. Part III, which dealt with the Formation of Words, was new, and Part V on Versification was almost entirely new. Thus its size was increased nearly to 400 pages. Apparently this edition proved more satisfactory, for it appeared in frequent successive reprints at least until 1890.

Then in 1892 Goodwin again enlarged his book by about 60 pages and published it as *A Greek Grammar*, dropping the word *Elementary* from the title. The parts were the same as in the 1879 edition, but they were somewhat expanded. It was reprinted in 1893. Goodwin also wrote a *Greek Reader* and an edition of Xenophon's *Anabasis*. The writer's collection contains seventeen Greek books of different titles and dates written by Goodwin.

*Albert Harkness.* Harkness, who earlier was author of very popular Latin books, in 1860 published a *First Greek Book*. He based this upon the same philological principles as his Latin books. He bemoaned the fact that the "old method of burdening the memory of the beginner with a confused mass of unmeaning forms, inflections, and rules, without allowing him the luxury of using the knowledge...." After an introduction, Part I dealt with etymology and syntax, and Part II consisted of short Greek selections of fables,, jests, anecdotes, and legends. In the back, there were some notes on the selections, and a Greek and English and an English and Greek vocabulary. It appeared in reprints at least until 1878.

*James M. Whiton.* In 1861 Whiton's *First Lessons in Greek* appeared. They were modeled on Crosby's *Greek Lessons*, and were intended as a companion-book to Hadley's *Grammar*. It began with XV exercises in Greek. Then these same lessons appeared in English. Sixteen pages of Greek selections followed. Twenty pages of notes and references followed. In the back appeared a Greek-English and an English-Greek vocabulary. It soon appeared in reprints.

*John W. White* (1849–1917). In 1876 White published *A Series of First Les-*

*sons in Greek,* which were adapted to the 2nd edition of Goodwin's *Greek Grammar.* These *Lessons* were very different from those by Whiton. Each of the LXXX lessons in the 1880 edition began by referring to certain grammatical rules or principles in Hadley's text and was followed either by brief vocabulary lists of Greek and English or by sentences or brief selections in Greek and English to illustrate the rules. Then more than 40 pages of additional exercises on forms in Greek and English followed. In the back two vocabularies were presented. These books continued to appear in reprints for some time. Later White published a *Beginner's Greek Book* in 1892, and *The First Greek Book* in 1896. The latter book was profusely illustrated with pictures of famous Greeks, and other matters of ancient Greek life and activities. It was one of the most attractive of all Greek grammars discussed in this chapter.

*Other Greek grammars, 1850–1900.* Among other Greek grammars appearing during this period were: N. C. Brooks' *First Lessons in Greek* (1851), Edward Robinson's *A Greek Grammar* (1851), R. F. Leighton's *Greek Lessons adapted to Goodwin's Greek Grammar* (1871), George Curtius's *A Grammar of the Greek Language* (1872), James R. Boise's *Exercises in Greek Syntax* (1874), Joseph B. Mayer and Edward G. Coy's *Greek for Beginners* (1880), Thomas D. Seymour's *Introduction to the Language and Verse of Homer* (1885), Robert P. Keep's *Greek Lessons* (1885), and Thomas D. Goodell's *The Greek in English* (1886). Evidently there were many others.

## D. *Greek Readers and Classics*

ATTENTION must now be given to what Greek books were taught following the study of grammar. As was true in the field of Latin, not all secondary schools taught the same books or classics. Some Latin schools, such as the one at Princeton and Exeter, used the *New Testament* in Greek as a text. Others used readers or various Greek classics. Consideration will now be given to those Greek books which seemed to have been most commonly used.

*Greek readers.* Apparently those early schools that attempted to jump directly from the study of a Greek grammar to a classic found the transition rather difficult. So the practice to follow the study of grammar with some sort of reader ultimately developed. These readers usually included selections from various Greek sources.

Possibly the most widely used early books of this sort were the *Collectanea Graeca Minora* and *Majora* by Andrew Dalzel, Professor of Greek in the University of Edinburgh. In 1791 these began to be reprinted in this country. These

Dalzel books appeared in many editions here by different printers at least until 1833. The *Minora* contained 31 of Aesop's *Fables*, 12 selections from *Palaephato de Incredibilibus Historiis*, 19 *Luciani Dialogis*, some of *Xenophonte de Cyri Institutione*, 10 from *Plutarchii*, 6 from *Sacris Scriptoribus*, and 21 *Excerpta Ex Poetis*. In most editions the Greek text consisted of about 125 pages, the notes of nearly an equal number of pages, and a lexicon of about 75 pages.

The *Majora* was much larger, the text containing about 350 pages and the notes varying in different editions from 170 to 350 pages. However, the notes were in Latin rather than in English as in the *Minora*. The contents of Pars Prima consisted of *Excerpta Heroica of Homero, Hesiodo,* and *Appolonio Rhodio;* Pars Secunda of *Excerpta Tragica of Sophocle* and *Euripide;* Pars Tertia of *Excerpta Buccolica of Theocrito, Bione,* and *Moscho;* Pars Quarta of Excerpta *Lyrica of Odae, Scolia,* and *Paeanes:* and Pars Quinta of *Excerpta Miscellanea of Hymni, Sententiae,* and *Epigrammata.* Both of these books were studied at Exeter in 1818, and likely in many other secondary schools, particularly the *Minora.*

Regular Greek readers eventually began to displace the *Collectanea Graeca Minora* and *Majora* for study following grammar. One of the earliest widely used ones was Frederick Jacobs' *The Greek Reader.* It was first published in Germany. It was republished in Boston in 1823. In Germany it appeared in four volumes, appearing in many editions. The 1829 Boston third edition was from the seventh German. The Boston edition appeared in one volume. It included all of the first German volume, much of the second, and a few extracts of the fourth. In the 1829 edition the first 50 pages contained brief Greek extracts illustrating definite Greek grammatical rules. The next 126 pages contained many fables, anecdotes, matters in natural history, mythological narratives, dialogues, and considerable geography, all in Greek with some comments in English footnotes. The next 74 pages contained extracts from Phutarch's *Lives* and some poetical extracts. In the back there appeared a 116 paged lexicon in double columns.

The first New York edition of Jacobs' *Reader* was published in 1827, and was recopyrighted in 1829, 1836, and 1845. The New York editions were considerably smaller than the Boston one. In the back a vocabulary of proper names preceded the lexicon, which also was smaller than in the Boston edition. The New York editions were edited, corrected, and improved by David Patterson and Patrick S. Casserly. All these volumes were bound in leather. It is evident that the *Reader* by Jacobs attained considerable circulation in America.

In 1839 J. O. Colton published *A Greek Reader* of new selections and notes.

Its main Greek texts of 172 pages dealt with fables, jests, history, mythology, dialogues, odes, and incredible stories. Its notes covered 50 pages and the lexicon more than 100 pages. In 1840 C.C. Felton published *A Greek Reader*, which was being used in the Boston Latin Grammar School in 1860.

In 1861 Peter Bullions published *A Greek Reader*. In the first 90 pages he related brief exercises to grammatical rules. Most of these exercises were both in Greek and English. The next 70 pages were taken from Jacobs' *Reader*, dealing with fables, anecdotes, stories of animals, and mythology. Brief biographies of ancient heroes followed. Then nearly 80 pages of notes and an extensive lexicon of more than 200 pages concluded the book. It was bound in leather.

In 1871 William W. Goodwin and Joseph H. Allen published their Greek *Reader*. It was composed entirely of extracts from four Greek authors. The first 95 pages were given to the Third and Fourth books of Xenophon's *Anabasis*. Then 16 pages of Plato dealing with the trial and death of Socrates were presented. Next 80 pages of history were reproduced from the writings of Herodotus. Lastly, about 20 pages were devoted to the story of Pylus and Spacteria by Thucydides. The authors claimed that the Greek contained in these seclections was important for college preparation in Greek. These extracts were printed fully in Greek, but were followed by 117 pages of English notes dealing with the extracts page by page. It was adapted to Goodwin's Greek *Grammar*, and appeared in reprints.

In 1881 Edward Coy published a *First Greek Reader* containing easy selections with notes and references to Hadley's and Goodwin's *Grammars*. This was a small book of nearly 140 pages dealing with parts of Xenophon's *Anabasis* and extracts from Thucydides. The notes on these were not very extensive.

In 1890 Charles T. Williams published his *Extracts from Various Greek Authors* to accompany the regular lessons in Xenophon's *Anabasis*. It contained selections from 15 Greek authors. In the back there were two indexes, an extensive table of Greek verbs, several maps, a historical chart, and common Greek measures and moneys. Likely other Greek readers were published here before 1900.

*Greek classics.* Of the Greek classics the one whose writings apparently were most often taught in American secondary schools were those by Xenophon. Xenophon (430–355 B.C.) was an Athenian historian, soldier, and philosophical writer. His military experiences were mixed and entangled with Persian, as well as Greek military exploits of his age. Historically he is best known by his writings. These were of three types: Historical, technical and didactic, and politico-philosophical. The *Anabasis* was historical.

The oldest copy of Xenophon in the writer's collection was Xenophontis *De Cyri Institutione* in eight books. This was published in England in 1737 and republished in Philadelphia by Cura Johannis Watts in 1806. The text consisted of 519 pages, followed by 12 pages of Addenda, and two brief indexes. The pages of the text were Greek at the top, Latin under the Greek, and then finer notes in Latin at the bottom. Considering the size of this book, it is doubtful if it was used in many American secondary schools.

It seems that the study of the Xenophon's writings became more common in America after 1840. In 1843 Alpheus Crosby published an *Anabasis* which appeared in a number of reprints. In 1853 R.D.C. Robbins published Xenophon's *Memorabilia of Socrates*. This continued in reprints at least until 1889. The book began with 36 pages on the life of Socrates. The Greek text consisted of 169 pages. More than 200 pages of notes in English followed. Indexes in Greek and English concluded the book.

It seems that there was a stepped up impetus in the study of Xenophon's writings in American schools after 1860. The writer's collection contains 13 different books dealing with Xenophon's writings published between 1860 and 1900, ten of these dealt with the Anabasis. One that appeared in a number of reprints was published by William W. Goodwin and John W. White in 1877. It covered four books. These books dealt with military matters and conflicts of the Persians and the Greeks. Apparently the treatment of these military matters in the study of Greek somewhat corresponded with the study of Caesar in Latin in secondary schools. The textual Greek in the Goodwin and White book covered about 120 pages, the notes about 110 pages, and the lexicon about 150 pages.

In 1889 Francis W. Kelsey and Andrew C. Zinos also published four books of the *Anabasis*. The book was made more attractive by presenting four plates containing about 40 colored cuts relating to ancient military dress, instruments, and equipment. Also a colored map relatng to the places discussed in the *Anabasis* was presented. An introduction in English of nearly 50 pages preceded the Greek text. More than 350 pages of notes, idioms, and vocabulary followed the Greek text.

Other texts of the *Anabasis* were published by James R. Boise (three books, 1863), Asabel C. Kendrick (1872), J. F. MacMichael (1883), and William R. Harper and James Wallace (1893). J. Irving Manatt in 1886 and C. W. Gleason in 1897 published other writings of Xenophon. Likely there were other editions of Xenophon published not known to the writer.

Next to Xenophon apparently the most studied Greek author was Homer. Homer was taught in the Boston Latin Grammar School in 1776 and in 1883. Evidence seems to indicate that the *Iliad* was taught in more schools than the *Odyssey*.

The writer's collection also contains Greek texts containing writings of Plato, Demosthenes, Aeschylus, Isocrates, Aristophanes, and Sophocles. Likely these authors were more often studied in colleges than in secondary schools.

### E. *Charactristics of Greek Grammars*

NEARLY all early Greek grammars were bound either in leather or home spun linen. Some were bound in leather as late as the 1860's. Very few grammars before about 1830 contained tables of contents or indexes. American authors more than the European included these learning aids.

As was true in most subject fields, the earliest textbooks were brought here from Europe. In fact, Greek grammars were not published or reprinted here as early as those in Latin. Likely this was true because Greek was not studied as extensively as Latin, thus limiting the market for Greek books. Too, it may be that colonial printers were not equipped to print books in Greek. Beginning about 1800 European Greek grammars began to be republished here, after some revision by American editors. Even when American authors began to publish grammars, they freely acknowledged their debts to Europeanauthors.

As was true in the field of Latin, two rather opposite approaches were followed. The American reprints of Neilson's *Greek Exercises* followed the Comenius approach of attempting to teach the Greek with English. This approach was also followed by Fisk, and to some extent by Whiton. On the other hand, the American reprints of Hackenberg's *Elements* followed the traditional grammatical approach of committing to memory the rules, declensions, conjugations, and vocabulary words. By far the greater number of grammars followed this latter approach.

It was not until about 1840 before the Greek grammars began to include both a Greek and an English index. American editors or authors tended to include more aids than the European.

### F. *Characteristics of Greek Readers*

APPARENTLY in some early Latin grammar schools attempts were made to read the *New Testament* or some other Greek classics immediately after the study of grammar. Evidently this practice did not succeed too well, for immediately after the colonial period Greek books that may be called readers began to appear. Later they usually bore the title of "Reader." These usually contained brief Greek selections taken from many sources. Commonly they would begin with fables, anecdotes, mythology, and history. These would be followed by brief selections from Greek classics. Most of them included a good lexicon in the back.

Readers apparently were followed by the study of one or more classics. The writings of Xenophon were the most commonly studied, particularly the *Anabasis*. Next most commonly studied were Homer's *Iliad* and *Odyssey*.

While Greek was studied in all early Latin grammar schools, and in most of the better academies, it was not so commonly taught in the high schools. Stout's study of the curriculums of midwestern high schools between 1860 and 1900 shows that fewer than one-third of them taught Greek. After 1900 this decline in the study of Greek continued until now very few secondary schools teach Greek.

## SECTION THREE

# FRENCH

### Introduction

*The language.* French is commonly, together with Italian, Spanish, and Portuguese, considered to be a Romance language. However, this is far from entirely true. The Latin (Roman) language was introduced into Gual during its occupation by the Romans. Since the area now known as France was occupied by many varying groups, each having a dialect, the blending of these with the Latin resulted in further dialects. In the valleys of the Rhone and the Garonne (nearly half of modern France) the language inclined to the Italian and Spanish development of Romance. Later when the power of Paris became sufficiently strong to absorb the Mediterranean area the language absorbed some elements of the southern dialects known as Provencal. With the decline of Roman power the language in France veered further from the Latin. While various dialects continued, the dialect of Paris became dominant in the formation of the French language.

During the twelfth and thirteenth centuries French had gained extensive use in Europe. During the fourteenth and fifteenth centuries its influence declined somewhat. Then it was during the sixteenth century, with the adoption of grammatical rules and the tendency to standardize the vocabulary, that French took established form. It was during the latter part of seventeenth and the early eighteenth century, when France was exerting considerable influence over European civilization, especially during the reign of Louis XIV, that French began to gain status as an international language.

Eventually during the latter part of the nineteenth century further changes or additions to the French language were made. One was due to the rapid development of science. Many scientific terms common to all countries were adopted greatly to enrich the French language. Another was the influence of the cosmopolitan development of the society of the western world, including France. In fact, French became so important as an international language that when the League of Nations was formed after World War I, it became the League's official language.

The present French language is a composite largely derived from Latin stock, from many primitive dialects, a few words of Germanic origin, and from scholarly and foreign origin. However, often the spellings were changed after adoption.

*French influence on American education.* France's alliance with America during the Revolution created a friendly atmosphere here for things French. Benjamin Franklin and Thomas Jefferson greatly aided in introducing French ideas here. New scientific and philosophical societies founded here were modelled largely on the French type. The founding of state universities was another result of France's emphasis on non-sectarian and public control of education. Jefferson's plan for education in Virginia was French in nature. The educational theories and writings of Rousseau, Diderot, Condorcet, and Guizot were considerably read in America. Lastly, the introduction of the teaching of French in our colleges and later in the secondary schools evinced some influence here.

*The teaching of French in America.* It is clear that the teaching of the modern languages was not introduced as early or as commonly in America's secondary schools as the classical languages. However, Miss Marr, in her book entitled, *Old New England Academies,* says that the modern European languages appeared in the academies "with surprising frequency." French was then offered more often than German. Unfortunately, she does not mention the schools or the dates of introduction. It is known that the study of French became more popular in female seminaries than in boy's academies. However, in Franklin's Academy of Philadelphia as early as 1756 French was permitted to be studied in the program of senior study during leisure hours.

Nazareth Hall, a school for boys in Pennsylvania, reopened after the Revolution under Moravian auspices, offered courses in English, German, *French*, Latin, and Greek. A classical school in Charlestown, S. Car., (about 1820 to 1850) offered French taught by a born Frenchman. A school law enacted in California in 1851 provided for the establishment of high schools in places with 400 or more scholars. Among the subjects to be offered were French and Spanish. Stout found that about one-fifth of the high schools in the midwest taught French between 1860 and 1900.

Since it was not until 1875 that a modern language was required for college admission, it was necessary for colleges to offer beginning courses in French and German. This was done rather early. French instruction was allowed in Harvard as early as 1735. The College of William and Mary established a chair of modern languages in 1774, and Columbia provided one in French in 1784. Harvard established a chair in French in 1815. Commonly the study of modern foreign languages was elective. Ultimately this practice led the way for offering other subjects as electives as well. The elective system gained its most common acceptance under President Charles Eliot at Harvard. Many other colleges followed.

## A. *Foreign Printed French Textbooks*

As IN nearly all subject matter fields, the earliest textbooks used here were brought from Europe. Apparently the most likely ones were reprinted here. The writer's collection contains more than 250 French textbooks published before 1900, and of these nearly all appearing before 1850 were either printed abroad or reprinted here from books first written abroad. Most of these were written either in France or England.

Before discussing any of these books it must be said that at this time it is very difficult to distinguish or determine which books were used primarily in secondary schools and which in colleges. Since few students entering college before about 1830 or 1840 had any French upon admission, the colleges offering French would have to start with beginning French, which was usually grammar. On the other hand, those early academies offering French likely used the same or similar French grammars. Thus in dealing with these grammars no serious attempt will be made to determine the level of their offering. These foreign printed books were all obtained in this country, so likely they were used somewhere here.

*Port Royalist French Grammar.* The oldest of these in the writer's collection is the *Grammaire Generale et Raisonnée,* believed to have been originally written about 1660 by Antoine Arnauld and Pierre Nicole, two brothers of the Port Royalist Order. The Port Royalists were well known for their excellent methods of teaching, as well as for their writing of excellent educational books. They favored beginning with the vernacular rather than with Latin, which was then the most common approach. Reason and understanding rather than memory were followed in their teaching. The writer's copy was bound with leather and trimmed in gold. It was printed in Amsterdam in 1703. Première Partie dealt with the letters and their characteristics in writing, and Second Partie dealt with the principles and reasons for the diverse forms in the use of words. Likely, this book, like their other textbooks, had considerable circulation in Europe and possibly some in America.

*Lewis Chambaud.* The writer's copy of Chambaud's *The Treasure of the French and English Languages* was a third London edition published in 1766. The first 152 pages consisted of French vocabulary terms with their English meanings classified under meaningful headings, such as Du Monde (of the world), De l'Homme (of man), Des Alimens (of food), and so on. Then 88 pages were devoted to Common Forms of Speech. Lastly, 43 pages consisted of proverbs and maxims in French and English. It is clear that Chambaud did not believe in teaching French by the grammatical method. Later in 1784 Chambaud's *Fables Choisies* was reprinted in Philadelphia.

*M. Lhomond.* Lhomond was a professor at the University of Paris. The writer has a copy of his *Eléments de la Grammaire Francaise* reprinted in Montreal in 1831. This was a small book of 84 pages. The material was presented in the traditional grammatical approach. Apparently it was not intended as a book from which English speaking people would learn French, but rather as a simple grammar for French speaking people. An earlier edition had been published in Tours, France in 1809. The writer's copy was published in Paris aslate as 1852.

*Others.* Some other foreign printed French texts brought to America were: A. Boyer's *The Compleat French Master for Ladies and Gentlemen* (London, 1753, 17th edition); *Instruction Facile Sur Les Conventions ou Notions Simples* (Paris, 1779); and Nicholas Hamel's *Grammatical Exercises Upon the French Language* (London, 1798).

## B. *Early Reprinted Foreign French Texts*

MANY foreign written French texts were republished here by American printers. A number of them were even republished here in several cities by different printers. The frequency of these attests to the fact that apparently few Americans believed themselves sufficiently competent in French to write such books. However, in a number of cases the foreign books were revised here better to meet American conditions and needs.

*John Perrin.* Apparently the widest circulated French books in early America were first published in England by Perrin. In 1779 Perrin's *A Grammar of the French Tongue* was reprinted in Philadelphia. Later this book was also republished by several New York printers. The first Philadelphia edition consisted of 320 pages divided into four parts. The later editions contained more pages. Part I dealt with pronunciation, an alphabetical list of French adjectives, accents, and familiar and easy dialogues for beginners in French and English. Part II dealt briefly with the parts of speech; the gender, number, and declension of nouns and pronouns; and the conjugations and tenses of verbs. Part III covered the theory joined to practice of rules and observations upon nouns, pronouns, verbs, adverbs, prepositions, and conjunctions. Lastly, Part IV dealt alphabetically with many French irregularities.

The writer has a copy of Perrin's thrid London edition (1777) of *The Practice of the French Pronunciation* (126. pp.). This was republished in Philadelphia in 1780. The first 46 pages presented an alphabetical list of French words (with their English equivalents) in classified sections with suggestions for their pronunciation. Then 40 pages of brief stories in French and English appear. A second list of vocabulary words covered 12 pages. Smart and witty reparties and pleasant stories occupied 20 pages. The last part of the book presented a brief treatment of grammar.

Perrin also wrote the *Instructive and Entertaining Exercises of the French Syntax,* which was reprinted in 1781, and the *Elements of French Conversation* in 1794, both in Philadelphia. The writer's collection contains seven of Perrin's French textbooks. Thus it can be said that his French books apparently were the most popular in early America.

*Mr. Porney.* Mr. Porney was the French master at Eaton College in England. He held strong convictions regarding the method of teaching French. So he prepared several French books to demonstrate his method. In 1791 he published in London his *Models of Letters in French and English.* Later he wrote his

*Syllabaire Français,* or *A French Spelling Book.* This was reprinted in Philadelphia in 1808 and in New York in 1817. The book began with exercises in the pronunciation of letters and then with hundreds of words. These were followed with simple reading lessons interspersed with further word lists. Both the words and reading selections appeared in French and English. Then 34 pages were devoted to French grammar in catechetical fashion. The latter part of the book presented a "Vocabulaire, Français et Anglois." Its several editions of reprints indicates that it likely had considerable circulation. In fact, J. Meier republished one here in the late 1860's.

*M. Blondin.* Blondin, who was the Secretary-Interpreter of the National Bibliothic in France, published his *Précis de la Langue Française* in Paris. Later it was translated into English by C. Hyatt and published in Windsor, Vt., in 1809. This was a rather small book of 155 pages. In fact, it was only equivalent to half that number of pages, since the left hand page was always in French, while the one on the right was in English. It followed the grammatical approach. It would present the definitions or rules and then give examples. It did not contain many vocabulary words. Consequently a child could have learned the grammar without being able to read much French.

*J. H. P. Seidenstuecker.* Seidenstuecker's *An Elementary Practical Book for Learning to Speak the French Language* was originally written in German in 1810. Mrs. Barbara O. Addicks translated it into English and published it in New York in 1831. Its approach was to attempt to teach French to beginners as one learns his mother tongue. It simply followed the method of *learning to read by reading* in easy stages. The first 86 pages consisted of graded reading lessons. Then 18 pages listed the words in double columns involved in the lessons with their English meanings. The Second Part of 26 pages contained a Table of French sounds and articulations with appropriate reading lessons for practice. Fundamentally it followed the direct reading method of teaching. Both the German and American editions appeared in numerous reprints.

*N. Wanostrocht.* Sometime before 1817 there was reprinted in Boston Wanostrocht's *A Grammar of the French Language,* which was first published in England. The fourth American edition in 1817 was reprinted from the 13th London edition. Later editions continued to appear here. This was the largest book dealt with thus far. Its approach was largely grammatical. It devoted a chapter to each of the six parts of speech, plus chapters dealing with participles, idiomatical expressions, and promiscuous exercises. The 1819 edition contained 480 pages. The 1837 edition contained more than 30 fewer pages. It is evident that Wanostrocht's books gained considerable circulation in America, but due to their size likely they were used in colleges more than in secondary schools.

*M. DeLevizac.* DeLevizac's *A Theoretical and Practical Grammar of the French Language* gained wide usage in France and England. Eventually it was revised and published in America by Stephen Pasquier. The edition bearing an 1829 U.S. copyright date was the seventh American. In 1835 it was recopyrighted with very slight revision by Professor J. Mouls. It continued to appear as late as 1847. After covering accentuation and other introductory matters it contained three parts. First, treatment of words and their inflections; second, words considered in their construction; and third, idioms and words in their particular rules. While it gave much attention to grammar, yet the presentation of the material looked attractive. Many of the exercises and explanations appeared in modified interlinear form. Many later American texts borrowed ideas from it, particularly Bolmar.

*Other reprints.* Other French books published here before 1840 were: Mary John's *A New French and English Grammar* (1784), Anthelme Gay's *A French Prosodical Grammar, or Reading Book* (1795), Nicolas Gouin-Dufief's *The French Grammatical Companion* (1795), A Henry de Heusch's *The Teacher, or Practical French Grammar* (1796), Nicolas Hamel's *Grammatical Exercises Upon the French Language, compared with the English* (1798, 2nd ed.), J. B. DeSeze's *The English and French Interpreter* (1813), M. A. Texier De La Pommeraye's *Abridgment of a French and English Grammar* (1822), Mariano Soler's *Le Traducteur Francois* (1826), J. Rowbatham's *A Practical Grammar of the French Language* (1831), and J. L. Jewett's *Ollendorff's New Method of Learning to Read, Write, and Speak the French Language* (1835). Likely there were many others.

## C. *American Written French Textbooks*

APPARENTLY few Americans believed themselves competent to write French books very early. Even when some began to do so they still learned heavily upon French sources. In this section attention will be given those first published before 1840.

*Francis Benj. Gardera.* In 1829 Gardera's *A Manual of the Difficulties of the French Language* was published in New York. Although he was from Paris, it was particularly prepared for "Use of American Schools." He claimed no originality for the book and stated that it was "a complement to the French Grammar of Ch. C. Le Tellier." It was not a regular grammar, but rather an "alphabetical collection of barbarisms, neologisms, and solecistic expressions" used daily by those having an incorrect knowledge of French. In addition three fourths of the book dealt with participles, exercises in cacography, grammar, and idioms. It contained 270 pages. Likely its circulation was limited.

*Bernard Tronchin.* Tronchin was professor of languages in the city of New York. In 1829 he published *A New Pronouncing French Primer.* This was a small book bound in paper board. Most preceding books were bound in leather. It claimed to contain the "elements of the French Language according to the best usage," particularly according to Girand Duvivier. Its vocabulary lists were presented in groups relating to particular topics, such as "Of a school," "Of a church," "Of Sciences and Arts," "Of commerce and trades," and so on. Exercises on phrases together with their English meanings were also given. The book was intended to be used in connection with the author's *New French Theoretical and Practical Grammar.*

*A. Bolmar.* Bolmar, who for years was the principal of the West Chester Academy, published *A Collection of Colloquial Phrases* in 1830. This book began with such fundamental French words as the days of the week, the months, the cardinal and other numbers, and then thousands of simple everyday phrases and expressions in double column of French and English. These were classified as relating to varied experiences of life.

In 1834 Bolmar published his *Theoretical and Practical Grammar of the French Language,* which largely was a reprint of Levizac's *French Grammar.* After an introduction the book was divided into three parts. Part I dealt with words considered in their nature and inflections; Part II dealt with the syntax of words considered in their construction; and Part III dealt with idioms or words in their particular rules. Many of the exercises were in a somewhat interlinear form. This book appeared in many editions at least as late as 1866. The 1865 edition consisted of 294 rather large pages, with 175 pages added in the back presenting a "complete treatise on the genders of French nouns, as also . . . all the French verbs, both regular and irregular."

Bolmar also published *A Book of the French Verbs, A Collection of One Hundred Fables, Les Adventures de Télémaque,* and other French books. The writer's collection contains twelve books by Bolmar. It is evident that he was the first American author whose French books attained a rather wide circulation, even though he borrowed heavily from European books. They appeared about the time when French became more or less accepted as a language to be taught in the American schools.

| | | | |
|---|---|---|---|
| ve-nai-ſon, | *veniſon.* | veſ-ti-ge, | *a footſtep.* |
| ver-du-re, | *greenneſs.* | vo-liè-re, | *a great bird-cage.* |
| ver-get-te, | *a little iron rod.* | u-ſa ge, | *uſe.* |
| ver-get-tes, | *a bruſh.* | u-ti-le, | *uſeful.* |

# FIRST LESSON.

*In which the longeſt Words do not exceed Three Syllables.*

## *The* FABLE *of the* CROW *and the* FOX.

UN corbeau s'étoit per-
ché ſur un arbre, pour
manger un morceau de fro-
mage qu'il tenoit en ſon bec.
Un renard, qui l'apperçut,
fut tenté de lui enlever le
fromage. Pour amuſer le
corbeau, il commença à le
louer de la beauté de ſon
plumage. Le renard voyant
que le corbeau prenoit goût
à ſes louanges ; ſi votre voix,
pourſuivit-il, eſt auſſi belle
que votre corps eſt beau,
vous devez etre le plus ai-
mable de tous les oiſeaux.

Le corbeau fut ſi content
de ce compliment flateur, &
ſi ſot de croire le renard,
qu'il ſe mit à chanter, &
laiſſa tomber le fromage
qu'il avoit au bec. C'eſt ce
que le renard attendoit. Il

*A* Crow was perching on a
tree, to eat a bit of cheeſe
which he held in his bill. A
fox, that perceived him, was
tempted to take away from
him the cheeſe. To amuſe the
crow, he began to praiſe him
for the beauty of his feathers.
The fox ſeeing that the crow
took pleaſure in his praiſes ; if
your voice, continued he, is as
fine as your body is beautiful,
you muſt be the moſt lovely of
all birds.

*The* crow was ſo well
pleaſed with this flattering
compliment, and ſo ſilly as to
believe the fox, that he began
to ſing, and let fall the cheeſe,
which he had in his bill. It
was what the fox waited for.
s'en

23  A page from John Perrin's *The Practice of the French*
*Pronunciation,* 1777

*William T. Theal.* In 1832 Theal published a beautifully leather bound book entitled, *A Grammar of the French Language*. He looked upon French as being the mother of the English and as having given her "beauteous branches from the parental veins." He claimed that there were 10,357 more words in French than in English. A large part of the book was devoted to tables of the conjugations of verbs. In the back a number of reading selections were presented in interlinear form.

*Francois M. J. Surault.* After having taught Latin and French in Paris, Surault came to America and taught French at Harvard and in the Boston English Classical School. In 1835 he published *An Easy Grammar of the French Language* "for the use of colleges and schools." Part I presented chapter dealing with articles, nouns, adjectives, pronouns, verbs, participles, adverbs, prepositions, conjunctions, and interjections. However, 174 pages were devoted to verbs alone, while only 66 pages to all the other parts of speech. Part II of 45 pages dealt with syntax as related to the various parts of speech. A brief Third Part dealt with versification. It was a well organized book following the grammatical approach. English always appeared with the French either in double columns or in interlinear form. A third edition appeared in 1838. Surault also published *New French Exercises, French Fables,* and *New French Conversations.* In 1831 J. Rowbatham published *A Practical Grammar of the French Language* based on Surault's *Grammar.* It appeared in several editions.

*A. N. Girault.* Girault was the principal of a female seminary in New Jersey. In 1837 he published *The French Guide,* which was an introduction to the study of the French language. He aimed to avoid the extremes of omitting any essential matters and of including some non-essentials involved in learning French. After dealing with such matters as difficult sounds and accents he extensively covered nouns, adjectives, and verbs. Like in many other French texts, the treatment of verbs was much more extensive than of the other parts of speech. In the back about 125 pages were devoted to many Moral Tales "written in an easy French, expressly for beginners." The 1839 edition was its fourth. Girault also published *Vie de George Washington,* and the *Recueil Dramatique.*

*French teaching before 1840.* The teaching of French in American schools was far from stabilized before 1840. Apparently only a small fraction of the secondary schools taught French. Consequently beginning French needed to be taught in the colleges. So separate texts were not commonly written for secondary schools.

O

Likewise there was little standardization in the type and nature of textbooks written. There was great variation both in the approach of presentation and in the emphasis of content. Not many French texts gained real wide circulation. Of the reprinted European texts Perrin's became most popular, and of those written in America Bolmar's apparently had the widest circulation.

### D. *French Textbooks, 1840–1870*

SINCE French became a more or less accepted member of the American curriculum family around 1840, more and more French textbooks appeared. In fact, during the 1840's a rash of such books appeared. Not many of these, however, became real popular. Some of these will now be discussed.

*A. G. Collot.* Collot for some years was a professor at the University of Oxford, but later came to our country to teach French in Philadelphia. In 1844 he published *Progressive French Grammar and Exercises,* based on Levizac's *French Grammar.* After an introduction of about 30 pages the book was divided into two parts. Part I devoted a chapter to each of the parts of speech. More than half of the space dealt with verbs. One table of irregular and defective verbs occupied 17 pages. Part II treated syntax involved in relation to the parts of speech. In the back 22 pages of promiscuous exercises appeared. Later editions of this book continued to appear at least until 1860. Collot also published an *Interlinear French Reader, Progressive French Dialogues and Phrases,* and *French Anecdotes and Questions.*

*J. L. Mabire.* In 1845 Mabire published *The Guide to French Conversation.* This was the first book so far discussed to be definitely based on the conversational approach. The book began by listing more than 500 verbs alphabetically arranged. The book then contained 236 conversations about topics, ideas, and actions. These were presented in parallel columns in English and French. Such topics as dinner, weather, time, and such actions as, to repeat, interrupt, buy, and so on were treated. In the back appeared a list of idioms, and model business notes and letters.

*M. De Fivas.* In 1846 *An Introduction to the French Language* by De Fivas was reprinted here from the fifth English edition. It was planned to accompany Ollendorff's *New Method of Learning French.* Though primarily designed for schools, it was claimed to be acceptable for adult learning. However, it really only consisted of nearly 100 pages of short stories in French, together with 40 pages of a French and English dictionary in the back. It seems that this represented a slow process in learning French unless preceded by some other book. It appeared in a number of reprints.

*J. L. Jewett.* Also in 1846 Jewett published his edition of *Ollendorff's New Method of Learning to Read, Write, and Speak the French Language,* which method was applied to the German language in 1835. The presentation consisted of 86 well-organized lessons, plus an appendix of 82 pages. Most lessons began with some grammatical rule or principle, followed by short expressions in English and French, and by exercises in English to be translated into French. The method was semi-direct in approach. This book was some larger than the editions by De Fivas. Jewett's book rapidly appeared in successive editions for more than a decade.

*H. G. Ollendorff.* To assist the teachers using the texts by De Fivas and by Jewett, Ollendorff himself published in America *A Key to the Exercises* in Ollendorff's *New Method* in 1846. This book merely contained in French translation the exercises which appeared in English in the above books. Likely there was a fear that many American teachers of French were not too competent to translate all these exercises into good French. That is, this was a "pony."

*V. Value.* In 1850 Value also published an *Ollendorff's New Method of Learning to Read, Write, and Speak the French Language,* to which were added Value's "System of French Pronunciation, his Grammatical Synopsis, a New Index, and Short Models of Commercial Correspondence." In all the book contained nearly 600 pages. After an introduction dealing with French pronunciation, the book was divided into 86 lessons. Each lesson began with brief terms or expressions in English and French in parallel form, which were followed by exercises in which these expressions were to be used. Thus it involved much *oral* French. The lessons were carefully and systematically prepared. Apparently the grammar in the back was to be used for reference when necessary. Although De Fivas, G. W. Greene, J. L. Jewett, and Charles Badois also prepared Ollendorff textbooks, Value's seemed to be the most thorough. It appeared in a number of editions.

*G. W. Greene.* In 1851 Greene published his version of *Ollendorff's New Method of Learning to Read, Write, and Speak the French Language.* This was a very much smaller book than the one by Value. The main text consisted of 57 simple lessons according to Ollendorff's method. In the back there were various grammatical matters, and a number of short French dramas. Its third edition appeared in 1866.

*Louis Fasquelle.* Fasquelle was professor of modern languages in the University of Michigan. He became a prolific writer of French books. The writer's collection contains 18 of them. In 1851 he published *A New Method of Learning the French Language*. This was a rather large book, yet became very popular. It appeared in 40 editions by 1859, and was even published in England. Part I of this book presented 100 definitely systematized lessons. These were in some respects similar to the Ollendorff lessons, but instead of having the long exercises only in English to be translated into French, Fasquelle commonly had two rather long exercises, one in French to be translated into English, and the other in English to be translated into French. Part II of neraly 200 pages consisted largely of technical grammar in French and English. A French-English vocabulary appeared in the back. In 1860 it was slightly revised and recopyrighted. Editions continued to appear until in the 1870's. In 1852 he published *A Key to the Exercises of Fasquelle's New French Method*. This merely contained translations of the Exercises of the regular text.

In 1858 he published *A Course of the French Language*, which was to be introductory to his larger book. Like the Ollendorff's books it was divided into lessons and exercises. In all there were 69 lessons and 136 exercises. One half of the exercises were in French to be translated into English and the others in English to be answered in French. This procedure involved the process of translating more than the books based on the Ollendorff method, which was more direct in approach. Fasquelle also wrote French readers and literature books.

*M. Noel and M. Chapsal.* In 1853 Sarah Saymore published an English adapted edition of Noel and Chapsal's *A New System of French Grammar*. This had been written in France about a decade earlier. Its approach was largely grammatical, and the contents of the text proper appeared in French. Most of the rules appeared in question and answer form. Then in the back of the book a Key appeared. It presented in English most of what appeared in French in the text.

In 1857 Noel and Chapsal's *Novelle Grammaire Français* was printed here in a much larger edition. Part I dealt largely with grammair (in French), and Part II with Syntax. The last 160 pages consisted of exercises in French. To the writer this book appears rather difficult for a beginner studying French.

*Louis Pujol and Rev. D. C. Van Norman.* In 1860 these men published *The Complete French Class-Book*, which embraced grammar, conversation, literature, and commercial correspondence. Pujol was a professor at the University of France and Van Norman was the principal of the Van Norman Institute for Young Ladies in New York. This was a large book in four parts. Part I dealt largely with pronunciation and grammar with exercises. Part II dealt with syntax, and with exercises and polite conversations. Part III included conversations embracing more than 100 topics. Part IV presented a course in French literature, followed by commercial and polite correspondence. The appendix contained tables, correspondence models, and an "adequate dictionary" in two parts: French and English, and English and French. Apparently it was intended to be studied more than one year. It appeared in several editions.

*Ferdinand Bocher.* In 1864 Bocher, who was an instructor at Harvard, published his revision of *Otto's French Conversation Grammar.* This was first published in Europe in 1859, after which it appeared in many editions. Part I contained 47 lessons, and Part II 25. The lessons in Part I were very similar to those followed in the Ollendorff books. In Part II most exercises appeared only in English to be translated into French. An English-French vocabulary appeared in the back.

Also in 1864 L. Pylodet published a *French Conversation-Grammar* by Dr. Emil Otto revised by Ferdinand Bocher. This was an exact reprint of the Bocher's book, except that a rather long French-English vocabulary was added.

*Other French books, 1840–1870.* Many French textbooks were published during this period. In addition to those discussed some others were: M. G. Maurice's *Cours Théorique et Pratique de Langue Francaise* (1845); Norman Pinney's *The Practical French Teacher* (1846); B. Granet's *Exercises Upon All the French Verbs* (1848); Guillaume H. Talbot's *Philosophy of French Pronunciation* (1849); Adelbert Doisy and Philippe Gengensbre's *Gengensbre's Method for the French Language* (1851); J. C. Pehlschlaeger's *Abu's Introductory Practical Course to Acquire the French Language* (1854); T. Robertson's System which was revised in America by Louis Ernst and published here as *The Whole French Course* (1858); Gustava Chauquet's *First Lessons in Learning French* (1858); Jean Gustave Keetels' *A New Method of Learning the French Language* (1858); Francis S. William's *English into French* (1860); William I. Knapp's *A Practical Grammar of the French Language* (1863); P. Sadler's *Translating English into French* (1863); Edward H. Magill's *A French Grammar* (1866); Charles Badois's *Ollendorff's New Method for Frenchmen to Learn to Read, Write, and Speak the English Language;* and a similar book by Theodore Simonne. Likely there were many others written during this period.

### E. *French Textbooks, 1870–1900*

As WAS true during the previous period, many French textbooks were published in this period. However, very few became as popular as those by Fasquelle and the Ollendorff adaptations by several American authors.

*F. Duffet and Alfred Hennequin.* Duffet was a professor of languages in France. There he wrote a *Method for the Study of the French Language.* Hennequin revised and adapted this book for "use of American Schools and Colleges" in 1873. Later it was revised and republished as the *New French Method.* Part I began with a thorough treatment of the pronunciation of letters and words in French. This was followed by 25 well organized lessons. Commonly each lesson would contain one or more rules, a list of words and expressions in English and French, and English exercises to be translated into French. Then about 75 pages were devoted to the study of verbs. Part II consisted of 25 additional lessons. These were longer than in Part I. Commonly they would select several verbs and use them in expressions listed in English and French followed by conversational exercises. Generally one would be printed in French and the other in English. The authors evidently aimed to combine several methods. The grammatical, the parallel reading, and the conversational methods were more or less blended throughout the book. It appeared in several editions. Later Hennequin published his *Practical Lessons in Idiomatic French.*

*Dr. P. Henn.* In 1873 Henn began publishing a series of textbooks based on Ahn's method of teaching French. The first one was *Ahn's French Primer.* This was a small but very appealing book. After dealing with the alphabet there followed 100 very brief graded lessons. In the first part the French and English words appeared in interlinear form. The correct pronunciation of the French words was assisted by printing the silent letters in "hairline type." Beginning with Lesson 31 the French exercises appeared in paragraph form, followed by an equivalent paragraph in English. In 1874 the *Second Course* was published.

In 1875 *Ahn's First French Grammar* was published. This was to follow the *Primer.* Also in 1875 Henn published *Ahn's First French Reader.* It contained 75 reading selections in French. In the back there were 40 pages of notes on these lessons in double column, and 37 pages of a French-English vocabulary. In 1878 a *Second French Reader* was published. Henn's books demonstrated a definite attempt to teach French in graded serial form. It is not now certain just on what school levels these books were intended to be used.

*Lambert Sauveur.* In 1875 he produced his *Petites Causeries,* which was printed by several publishers. In the same year he also published *Entretiens Sur La Grammaire.* Then in 1878 his *Grammaire Française* appeared. The first three-fourths of the book followed the grammatical approach. The latter one-fourth contained 82 lessons in French to be translated into English. He also produced a book of fables.

*Dr. James H. Worman.* Worman was a professor of languages at Vanderbilt University. In 1881 he published his *First French Book.* He prepared this with the aid of an accomplished Frenchman, Amedee de Rougemont. It aimed to follow the "Natural or Pestalozzian Method," for "schools and home instruction." The approach attempted to teach the French language with the help of the learner's vernacular. It based the linguistic instruction upon a direct appeal to a pictorial illustration of the object mentioned. Grammar was involved only to assist the student to speak accurately. The alphabet was taught by pictures of objects beginning with the various letters, e.g. R was illustrated with a picture of a fox. After the alphabet there were brief reading lessons illustrated with pictures. In brief, the student was to learn to read French by reading French only. This was the direct reading method. In 1882 Worman published his *Second French Book.* He had also written the *Echo de Paris,* which was a type of Manual of French conversation.

*C. Chardenal.* In 1876 Chardenal's *French Exercises for Advanced Pupils* was published here. Then in 1886 he published his *First French Course.* This, together with certain revised editions, slowly began to become popular in America. After 1900 Chardenal's texts appeared in edition after edition, until by 1920 it became one of the most widely used texts. Its approach was largely grammatical, but provided plenty exercises in both French and English.

*M. D. Berlitz and E. Dubois.* In 1882 these authors published their *Methode Berlitz.* This book followed a purely natural method without translation. It began with object teaching and easy conversation. The Premier Livre was followed by Deuxieme Livre, which consisted of "copious exercises in conversation and composition" grammatically graded. The words were so arranged that their meaning could be understood by context. Much later Berlitz published a *Grammaire Pratique* in four volumes. They were: Vol. I, *Verb Drill;* Vol. II, *Nom. Pronom., Adjectif et Article:* Vol. III, *Adverbe, Préposition, Conjonction et Observations Générales;* and Vol. IV, *Prononciation et Orthographe.* Berlitz published books in many other foreign languages.

*William Dwight Whitney.* Whitney taught several languages at Yale. In 1886 his *A Practical French Grammar* was published. This book was very different than the books by Henn, Worman, and Berlitz. Whitney largely followed the grammar approach. In Part I, after dealing with the alphabet and pronunciation, 42 lessons were presented each dealing with and illustrating some grammatical rule. Part II contained chapters dealing with the various parts of speech. Illustrative sentences showing usage accompanied the treatment of the parts of speech. In the back there were 84 pages of two vocabulary lists— French-English and English-French. It was a rather forbidding and uninteresting book. Whitney also produced a smaller *Practical French* book, and a *Brief French Grammar*.

*M. L. Chapuzet and W. M. Daniels.* About 1887 these men published their *Mes Premiers Pas (Steps) En Francais*. This was a very attractive rather small book. The direct reading method was largely implied together with brief vocabulary lists interspersed. It included many interesting pictures, some of them in color, and a number of songs. A Vocabulaire Alphabetique appeared in the back. It was in extreme contrast to Whitney's grammars.

*Other French texts, 1870–1900.* Some other French grammars that were written during this period were: Dr. C. Ploetz's *Easy and Practical French Grammar* (1871), Emil Otto's *French Conversation-Grammar* (1875), L. H. Buckingham's *Eugene's Students' Comparative Grammar of the French Language* (1881), J. D. Gaillard's *The Modern French Method* (1884), A. Hjalmar Edgren's *A Compendious French Grammar* (1889), M. Gauthier's *French and English at a Glance* (1890). W. S. Lyon and G. De H. Larpent's *A Primary French Translation Book* (1893), and C. H. Grandgent's *A Short French Grammar* (1894). Likely there were others. In addition the writer's collection contains many other French grammars written during this period, but which were published in France or England.

### F. *French Readers*

THE teaching of French commonly began with some sort of grammar book or a primer, although a few beginning French books using the direct reading method gave little attention to grammar. In either case such beginning books would be followed by some sort of reader. Some bore the title of "reader," others bore titles characterizing their content, such as a book of fables, dramas, history, or a classic. Of course, most beginning books, even the grammars, contained considerable reading in the form of short selections or conversations. Thus the beginning students after finishing their first course often could read considerable French. This meant that most readers could contain more advanced reading content. Brief descriptions of some of these readers will now be presented.

*Mariano Cubi Y. Soler.* In 1826 Soler's *Le Traducteur Français* was published in Baltimore, London, and Paris. It represented "A New and Practical System for

Translating the French Language." It contained 156 pages of the "most beautiful and classic selection with which litterature has been adorned." The
selections consisted of moral lessons, anecdotes, narrations, description of portraits, orations, and poetry. Footnotes and different kinds of type assisted in
correct pronunciations and understanding of meanings. A vocabulary of more
than 200 pages appeared in the back.

*A. G. Collot.* He was a professor of French at Oxford in England. In 1844 his
*Progressive Pronouncing French Reader* was published in Philadelphia. In fact, it
was published in two forms, one in French only with emphasis on correct
pronunciation, and the other in interlinear form to help develop the understanding of the French vocabulary. It contained 91 reading selections, beginning with about 30 fables, followed by selections taken from the writings of
many leading French authors.

*M. De Fivas.* In 1846 *An Introduction to the French Language* by De Fivas was
published in New York from the fifth London edition. This contained 54
selections of "Fables, Select Tales, Remarkable Facts, Amusing Anecdotes,
etc.," together with a French-English Dictionary of 40 pages. The selections
were in French only. Thus it required much use of the dictionary.

*Louis Fasquelle.* In 1853 Fasquelle published *The Colloquial French Reader*, or
"Interesting Narratives" in French. It contained 82 brief selections, mostly
taken from the writings of French authors. Most of the selections were followed by a list of colloquial exercises or questions, together with notes and references to grammatical matters to be found in his *New French Method* grammar. In the back a vocabulary list of nearly 90 pages appeared.

*Edward H. Magill.* He published *An Introductory French Reader* in 1867.
Although it was entitled, *Introductory,* it was the largest of all of these readers.
The first 80 pages dealt with grammatical matters in French. Then 60 pages
of familiar conversations followed, but each one illustrating some grammatical rule. About 100 pages of selections from French authors were then
presented. In the back there were 40 pages of notes to the foregoing, and a
dictionary of 160 pages.

*L. Pylodet.* In 1868 Pylodet published his *Beginner's French Reader.* This was
a small book of short and easy pieces in prose and verse with a dictionary.
These pieces seem to have been well graded, beginning with very easy ones
illustrated by interesting pictures. This book was in great contrast to Magill's
rather technical reader. In 1867 Pylodet had published *Leçons de Littérature
Française Classique.*

*Ferdinand Bocher.* Bocher's *Progressive French Reader* appeared in 1870. It included 41 selections taken from the writings of well-known French authors, with the names of these authors appearing at the end of the selections and when they lived. The 40 pages of notes on the selections referred to Otto's *French Grammar.* More than 50 pages of vocabulary also appeared in the back.

*Jean Gustage Keetels.* In 1879 Keetels published *An Analytical Reader,* which was considerably different than most readers. Part I presented 91 very brief French selections followed by: (a) some questions on grammar, (b) an exercise in English to be translated into French, and (c) oral questions in French. Part II contained 61 literary French selections. Nearly 150 pages of notes and vocabulary appeared in the back.

*Paul Bercy.* In 1888 Bercy began to publish a series of readers. These were the *Livre des Enfants* and *Le Second Livre des Enfants.* These contained very simple miscellaneous exercises, a few pictures, and no grammatical notes or dictionary, Likely they were used in the elementary grades.

*Comments.* Evidence indicates that there were many other French readers published. The above readers, however, show the nature and variation of French readers in circulation in America before 1900.

### G. *Other French Reading Books*

IN addition regular readers, which contained many selection from many authors, a number of other types of French reading books were published for use in schools. These included books of fables, dramas, historical books, and classics.

*Fables.* It seems that books of fables were very popular to provide supplementary exercises in French reading. One of the earliest of these books was M. Perrin's *Fables Amusantes* published in 1819, which soon appeared in several editions. This book presented about 150 short fables. Perrin's method of presenting them was unique. The fables were presented in French on the upper part of the page, and then on the lower part it appeared again in French with equivalent English word meanings interspersed. This made it unnecessary to have a dictionary in the back. It was bound in leather.

In 1828 A. Bolmar published *A Selection of One Hundred of Perrin's Fables,* accompanied by an unusual Key. The first 60 pages presented the 100 fables in straight French. Then the Key in the back occupied 120 pages. There the lines of the text appeared in sets of three. The middle line was the French, the lower line the equivalent English, and upper line represented the words spelled out indicating the French proununciation. The writer has not discovered any earlier books like it. It continued to be reprinted as late as 1865.

In 1834 F. M. Surault published his *French Fables,* with a Key. The first 18 pages constituted A Treatise on French Pronunciation. Then 100 short fables were presented in French. In the back the Key was arranged just like Bolmar's; namely, a line of French, one in English, and one with the French pronunciation spelled out in a interlinear arrangement.

In 1864 *Aesop's Fables in French* was published by Frederick Leypolat. It presented 100 fables in French, which were followed by an Alphabetical Dictionary. No aid was given the reader except that he could look up the meanings of the French words.

Evidence indicates that other editions of fables were published, but the above descriptions should suffice to reveal their nature.

*Classical Books.* Apparently to provide more advanced reading experience in French, a number of classical works have been reprinted for use in French classes. Seemingly the one most often reprinted was the *Adventures of Telemachus,* the son of Ulysses. These travels were made popular reading by that famous French scholar, Francois Fenelon (1651–1715), when he published *Les Adventures de Télémaque.* These were later edited, annotated, and republished by a number of American writers. A. Bolmar published an interlinear edition of the first eight books of *Telemaque* in 1827. In 1831 he published 24 books of *Telemaque* in straight French. In 1850 Louis Fasquelle published an edition. This also was in straight French, but footnotes and a Dictionaire were added to provide the students with considerable assistance. Many other editions of *Telemaque* have since been published in America.

Among other literary works republished were: *Corinne ou L'Otalie* by Madame De Stael (1860), *Molière's Le Bourgeois Gentilhomme* by P. Jacquinet (1870), *French Classics* by Gutave Masson (1874), *Nanon by George Sand* by B. D. Woodward (1893), *Jules Verne's Michel Strogroff* by E. S. Lewis (1893), *Victor Hugo's Les Misérables* by F. C. De Sumichrast (1895), and *George Sand's Le Mare ou Diable* by E. S. Joynes (1899). This list represents only a fraction of French works republished for school use.

*Dramas.* Some French dramas were published here apparently for school use. In 1838 A. N. Girault published the *Recueil Dramatique.* This book included seven dramatic works. Girault was the principal of a female seminary in New Jersey. Apparently these plays were used there. In 1893 I. H. B. Spiers published *Le Barbier de Séville* by Beaumorchais apparently for school use. Evidently many others were reprinted here.

*Historical works.* Some of the French reading books were historical in nature. A few that may be mentioned were: A. N. Girault's *Vie de George Washington* (1835), Charles Picot's *Historical Narrations in French* (1844), Thomas Day's *L' Histoire de Sandford et Merton* (1848), Louis Fasquelle's *Napoleon par Alexander Dumas* (1855), Victor Dunny's *Petite Histoire de France* (1883), and A. Cohn and Robert Sanderson's *Histoire de Gil Blas de Santillane by Alain-René Lesage* (1899). Other similar works have been used in our schools.

### H. *Characteristics of French Textbooks*

*Some general comments.* The study of French was much slower in gaining attention in American secondary schools than Latin and Greek. It was not taught in the early Latin grammar schools. Apparently only a few academies taught it before about 1825 or so. Since colleges did not commonly recognize French for admission until about 1875, it never became a universally taught high school subject before 1900.

In examining these old French books the writer found difficulty in attempting to determine which texts were used in secondary schools and which in colleges. Likely many of them were used in both, since colleges also taught beginning French. Thus attention was given indiscriminately to beginning books.

It is the writer's impression that more variation appeared among French textbooks than in any subject field analyzed. There was great variation in regard to content, methods, gradation, use of learning aids, size, and binding. Very few used pictures. Leather binding did continue as long or as late as in most secondary school textbooks. Although most grammars included a vocabulary in the back, these varied greatly in scope, some being only a French-English vocabulary, while others also included an English-French list.

*Methods and approaches.* There was far greater variation in the approaches and methods used in these French books than in any secondary school field. Among the approaches used were the purely grammatical, partly grammatical, the direct method, the semi-direct, the interlinear, parallel French and English by columns or pages, catechetical, and the conversational. However, very few books used only one approach exclusively. For example, the parallel form commonly used the grammatical method with it.

In general, most of the books published before about 1840 followed some approach whereby the French and English words appeared together in some forms, thus enabling the student to learn the meaning of French words in context rather than by committing vocabulary lists. The memoriter method was not very common then. This was during the period in American educational history before the formal discipline theory was greatly emphasized. A few books began using the conversational method, at least in part, about 1835. After 1850 the conversational approach became rather common.

   A number of European textbook authors developed particular systems of teaching modern foreign languages which could be applied to French. These systems were usually identified by their own names. Then it became common for American writers to prepare French books based on these systems. Among the systems reprinted here, many times with some revisions and adaptations, were prepared by J. H. P. Seidenstuecker of Germany (about 1810), M. De Levizac of France (before 1830), Ollendorff's (during the 1840's), Louis Fasquelle (prepared in America in the 1850's), M. Noël and M. Chapsal of France (about 1850), Emil Otto (about 1860). Philippe Gengembre, Ahn (about 1870), and the M. D. Berlitz (about 1880). Most of these systems involved the use of mixed approaches. Very few French textbooks before 1900 were fully written by American authors. Dependence upon European authors lasted much longer than in most other subject matter fields.

SECTION FOUR

# GERMAN

## Introduction

*The language.* German, like most other languages, has resulted from many evolutionary changes. In general, there was the Upper German, which was spoken in certain German states, much of Switzerland, and Austria; the Middle German, which was spoken in Prussia and other middle German states; and Low German, which was spoken in northern Germany, and with considerable modifications in the Netherlands, part of Belgium, and the Scandinavian countries.

   The literary language of modern German has been largely based on Middle German. The importance of modern written German may be traced to the middle of the 14th century, when the Imperial Chancery of Emperor Louis adopted German instead of Latin in its official documents. Other State Chanceries later followed suit. Then when Luther translated the Bible into German he used the midland (High) German. He also wrote hymns, pamphlets, and catechisms in such German. These writings soon gained wide circulation. The reading of these tended to spread and somewhat to standardize the use of the High or Midland German throughout the German Empire. Only relatively minor changes have been made in German since.

*German influence on American Education.* American education has been inflenced by German ideas and practices in a number of ways. Many German settlers came to early America, at first particularly to Pennsylvania, and later to the midwest. In Pennsylvania they soon opened German schools. These were commonly parochial, primarily for teaching German and religion. In fact, the first pedagogical book published in America was written by Christopher Dock (1698–1771), a Mennonite German school teacher. It was written in 1750 but not published until 1770, which was entitled, *Schulordnung*. Many other German books were published in Pennsylvania.

Many favorable reports about the schools in Germany appeared here. Among these were reports by John Griscom (1819), Victor Cousin (translated from French, 1831), Calvin Stowe (1837), Alexander D. Bache (1839), and Horace Mann (1843). Americans whose thoughts were influenced by German literature and philosophy were Edward Everett, George Bancroft, Henry Barnard, Elizabeth Peabody, William T. Harris, Theodore Parker, Charles DeGarmo, and Frank and Charles McMurry.

During the 19th century many American students went to Germany to pursue graduate study at such German universities, as Göttingen, Berlin, Halle, Bonn, Heidelberg, Jena, and Leipzig. Hundreds of these later became professors in American colleges, and thus transplanted German ideas of advanced instruction and methods of research.

*The teaching of German in schools.* Naturally, German was commonly taught in the German parochial schools of Pennsylvania, even during the colonial period. However, since most of these schools taught only the elementary subjects, they will not be given particular attention here.

Apparently German was not taught as early or as soon in many secondary schools as French. Franklin, in his Proposals for the Philadelphia Academy, which opened about 1750, suggested that those studying to be future merchants should take French, German, and Spanish. Nazareth Hall, sponsored by the Moravians in Pennsylvania, taught German when it reopened after the Revolution. This was a secondary school for boys. Miss Marr, in her study of the early academies of New England, apparently failed to find any offering German. Likely German was taught by some private teachers, since the writer has obtained a number of early German textbooks in America.

Later when high schools increased in number, German was taught in many. The first mention of German in a Massachusetts high school was in 1854. Stout, in his study of midwest high schools from 1860 to 1900, found that more than half of them offered German, while only a fifth of them taught French. German was taught in nearly one-fourth of the high schools of the U.S. in 1910. However, the intense anti-German feeling during World War I led to the elimination of the teaching of German in most high schools. Since then it has been reintroduced in a few, but it is not offered as commonly as French and Spanish now.

## A. *Early German Textbooks*

THE writer has numerous small German textbooks, but plainly they were not intended for secondary schools. They bore such titles, as *A B C Büchelein*, *A B C Buchstabier-und Lesebuch*, and *Deutsches Buchstabier—und Lesebuch*. Too, they plainly stated that they were "Für Deutsche Schulen." Thus they do not concern us here.

On the other hand, there were a number of good sized German grammars published here before 1850. They could well have been used by private teachers, academies, or colleges. Some of these will now be discussed.

*John James Bachmire.* In 1788 Bachmire's *A German Grammar* was published in Philadelphia. In the preface mention was made of the frequency of the use of German "in this City; not only among the Germans themselves, but others, especially Young Men of liberal Education." This edition apparently was an abridgment of a larger book likely published in Germany. "The Editor intended it principally for the University of Pennsylvania, where at certain Hours, daily, the Students are exercised in Speaking and Writing German." Its size of only 100 pages indicates that it was likely used in the academy department rather than at the higher level. It first dealt with rules and exercises in pronunciation. The remainder of the book dealt with the nine parts of speech: Article, Noun, Pronoun, Verb, Participle, Adverb, Preposition, Conjunction, and Interjection. The purely grammatical approach was followed. The rules were in English, but all other matters were in German and English.

This volume was bound in leather. In 1804 the third American edition appeared. The writer has two copies of the third edition, one bound in leather and the other in paper boards.

*Charles Follen.* In 1825 Follen was appointed professor of German at Harvard. In 1828 he published *A Practical Grammar of the German Language.* In the preface he acknowledged his debt to a number of other German grammars; namely, those by Grimm, Harnisch, and Heinsius of Germany, and particularly those of Noehden and Rowbothan of England. Follen's *Grammar* was well organized. Book I, Elements, dealt with pronunciation and orthography, and the parts of speech; Book II covered syntax; and Book III dealt with prosody. The appendix included a few brief reading selections and dialogues, and German abbreviations. It followed the grammatical approach. The vocabulary lists were in German and English. In 1831 a second edition appeared with slight revisions, and the third in 1834. In the 1840's other editions were published. The 13th, which contained 308 pages, was published in 1848. All the earlier editions were bound in leather. Without doubt it was one of the most popular early German grammars here.

*Joseph Ehrenfried.* In 1834 Ehrenfried published his *Colloquial Phrases and Dialogues in German and English.* His purpose was to deal with "every topic necessary to maintain conversation; with directions for pronunciation." The first nine pages dealt with rules and principles of pronunciation. The remainder of book of 228 pages presented carefully graded and meaningful phrases, dialogues, and historical and geographical materials in parallel columns of German and English. Apparently it was an interesting book from which to acquire a reading and considerable speaking knowledge of German. It appeared in several editions.

*Heinrich G. Ollendorff* (1803–1865). In the 1830's Ollendorff developed a special system for the effective teaching of the modern languages. Soon grammars were prepared to teach French, Spanish, Italian, and German, according to this system. Captain Basil Hall, of famous memory, said of the system, "Everybody in Paris began to learn German *à la mode l'Ollendorff,* and in all German towns you might find Englishmen and Frenchmen thumbing the 'New Method,' and repeating its thousands of phrases with commendable perseverance." In 1838 it was introduced into England by the publication of the *New Method of Learning to Read, Write, and Speak a Language in Six Months.* It soon acquired a wide circulation. Later George J. Adler, Professor of German in the University of the City of New York, published *Ollendorff's New Method*

A

# GERMAN GRAMMAR,

CONTAINING

## The THEORY of the LANGUAGE

through all the

## PARTS of SPEECH,

By JOHN JAMES BACHMAIR, *M. A.*

To which are prefixed

R ules for *Pronunciation* and *Spelling.*

PHILADELPHIA:

Printed by Charles Cist, in Race-ftreet, M,DCC,LXXXVIII.

1788

24  Title-page from John James Bachmair's *A German Grammer,* 1788

*of Learning to Read, Write, and Speak the German Language* in America. In 1846 its third edition was printed in Philadelphia. Apparently some teachers needed some help in teaching it, so in 1845 *A Key to the Exercises in Ollendorff's New Method* was published. In 1846 Adler published *A Progressive German Reader* to supplement the *Grammar*. Both the grammar and the reader appeared in many editions even as late as 1875.

*Other German textbooks before 1850.* Among other German books published rather early were: M. Billmeyer's *Deutches Buchstabier—und Lesebuch* (1820), Caspar J. Beleke's *A Grammar of the German Language* (1840), and J. G. Schmauk's *Deutsche Schulen* (1840). Likely there were others.

## B. *German Textbooks, 1850–1875*

BY 1850 the study of German in American schools had become much more common, and many more German texts began to be published. A number of these gained rather wide circulation.

*W. H. Woodbury.* At midcentury Woodbury published *A New Method of Learning the German Language.* The second edition appeared in 1851. It embraced both the "Analytic and Synthetic Modes of Instruction; being a Plain and Practical Way of Acquiring the Art of Reading, Speaking, and Composing German." The first half of the book was organized into 70 well planned lessons. Each lesson usually consisted of a number of definite steps and then ended with translation exercises of German and English. For example, Lesson XIII dealing with interrogative pronouns had eight steps dealing with *Wer, Was, Für, Welcher,* and the declension of *Wer* and *Was.* Then examples of their usage in sentences appeared in parallel columns of German and English. These were followed by a German reading selection of 16 lines and an English one of 16 lines. These involved double translations. Following these lessons about 170 pages were devoted to Etymology. The parts of speech were given rather technical treatment. In the back there was a list of idiomatic phrases, some German reading exercises, and two vocabulary lists, German—English and English—German. In all, the book contained more than 500 pages. It continued to appear in later editions into the 1870's. Woodbury also published a *Shorter Course with German,* several *German Readers,* and a book for Germans to learn English.

*F. Ahn.* Ahn, who was a professor at the College of Neuse, prepared *A New Practical and Easy Method of Learning the German Language.* This book became very popular in England. Later it was reprinted in America. The 2nd American

P

edition was printed in 1853. The 1860 edition was from the 8th London edition. It really consisted of a First Course of 88 pages, and a Second Course of 125 pages. After five pages of exercises on pronunciation, Part I contained simple reading exercises in German and English. Vocabulary words were introduced as needed. The exercises in Part II were longer and more difficult, followed by terms in German and English relating to life's experiences and expressions. These exercises were presented without any particular attention to grammar. The Second Course consisted largely of grammar, a chapter being devoted to each part of speech. In the back 60 reading exercises were included, together with collections of words and phrases.

In 1867 Ahn's *Rudiments of the German Language* was published here. This was a small book of 94 pages, and likely was used in elementary schools.

In 1855 Ahn's *New Practical and Easy Method* was published in Philadelphia as revised by J. C. Oehlschlager. In 1869 Oehlschlager published another revised edition. This was considerably larger than Ahn's earlier book. The First Course contained 172 pages, consisting mainly of reading selections, collections of words related to practical matters and experiences, and dialogues. Most reading selections were preceded with vocabulary terms. German and English exercises were alternated. No doubt, the German ones were to be translated into English, and the English ones into German. The Second Course of 73 pages was nearly entirely grammatical in nature. These two courses were bound in one volume. All of Ahn's books appeared in a number of editions.

*Dr. Emil Otto.* Otto was Professor of Modern Languages at the University of Heidelberg. In 1856 he published a *German Conversation—Grammar.* This book with minor revisions continued to appear into the 1880's. The 1864 edition was its 18th. Its Part First covered etymology, and the Second Part syntax. In the back were more than 60 pages of poetical German literature and two vocabulary lists. The grammar part of the book was presented in 51 rather detailed lessons. Each lesson dealt with a particular grammatical matter. For example, the 13th lesson covered determinative adjectives. In subsections of the lesson it discussed and illustrated the use of the demonstrative, the interrogative, the possessive, and the indefinite numeral adjectives. These were followed by seven remarks or comments. Then there appeared a list of words, reading exercises in German and in English, and a list of Sprechübungen. In 1874 it was slightly revised and enlarged by L. Pylodet.

In 1865 Otto's *Materials for Translating English into German,* with grammatical notes and a vocabulary, was published. It included 90 brief anecdotes and stories, 20 model letters, 10 historical extracts, and a dramatic extract. It was revised with fuller grammatical references by Rodes Massie and Edward S. Joynes in 1878. It is very evident that Otto's German textbooks were rather widely used in the United States.

*A. Douai.* He was a teacher of German in Boston. In 1858 he published *A Practical and Complete German Grammar.* In the preface he acknowledged his obligation to grammars written by Heilner, Becker, and Aue, written and published in Europe. Too, he paid tribute to the *"practico-theoretical system"* used by Ollendorff, Ahn, and Woodbury, but he aimed to improve upon their books. He claimed Woodbury's book was too cumbersome. The practical lessons consisted only of 24 instead of 70 as in Woodbury's book. The theoretical part presented the grammar in about 240 pages. Syntax was presented in 90 pages in Part III. Part IV was entitled the "First German Reader," which presented 32 reading selections in German. There was no vocabulary list in the back. Douai believed that the youth must "learn foreign languages, more or less, in the same natural way in which he acquires his own mother tongue." Words were to be learned in usage. It appeared in several editions.

*James H. Worman.* Worman taught languages at Lawrence University. Eventually he wrote a series of seven German and six French books. In 1868 he published *An Elementary Grammar of the German Language.* Apparently this book was intended for secondary school students who had no German in an elementary school. This was a book of 300 pages divided into four parts. Part I contained 50 elementary exercises or lessons involving pronunciation, and considerable attention to declensions of adjectives and nouns. Each lesson consisted of several exercises. For example, Lesson XXII began with a list of masculine and one of feminine nouns, followed by a German reading exercise and a theme in English to be changed into German, and lastly a list of questions in German as a basis for conversation. Part II contained exercises on the verb and other parts of etymology. Part III presented a synopsis of German grammar. In the back two vocabulary lists appeared. The 1873 edition contained fifteen pages of advertisements of other books by the publisher.

Also in 1868 Worman published *A Complete Grammar of the German Language.* This was a large book of nearly 600 pages. This likely was intended for secondary schools where some German had been taught in the grades, or could have been used in beginning German courses in college. After about 20 pages of introduction, it was divided into three parts. Part I covered etymology, covering the parts of speech in 41 lessons. The structure of the lessons was similar to those in his *Elementary* work. Part II covered syntax. The reading selections were much longer in this part. Part III contained lists of different types of verbs, and two extensive vocabulary lists. The author acknowledged that he considerably followed the methods followed by Otto. The fly-leaf contained 46 brief testimonials for Worman's *German Grammars*.

Later he also published a *First German Book* of 69 pages, a *Second German Book* of 84 pages, apparently for the grades, and several German *Readers*. All of these appeared in numerous editions.

*George F. Comfort.* He was professor of modern languages at Allegheny College in Pennsylvania. In 1869 he published *A German Course*, "adapted to use in colleges, high-schools, and academies." This was a rather large book of nearly 500 pages. Part First contained 51 systematically organized "Practical" lessons. Each lesson consisted of from three to five types of work similar to those of Woodbury and Otto. Part Second contained sections dealing with conversations, German and English idioms, examples of synonyms, letters and forms of business, and reading lessons. Most of this part appeared in parallel form in German and English. Part Third was a "Compend of German Grammar," which consisted of 200 pages. Part Fourth presented personal proper names, geographical proper names, abbreviations, various kinds of German measures, classified list of words, German-English and English-German vocabulary lists, and a general index. This book appeared in a number of editions. Later he wrote *A German Primer*, *A First Book in German*, *A Manual of German Conversation*, and several German *Readers*.

*William D. Whitney.* He was a professor of languages at Yale. In 1869 he published *A Compendious German Grammar*. As suggested in the title, it was a somewhat abridged German grammar of 252 pages. He argued that since few Americans learn oral German sufficiently well to speak it proficiently, it was impracticable to attempt German for that purpose. So this book attempted primarily to teach German for translation and reading purposes. He largely followed the grammar approach with a mixture of brief vocabulary lists and German exercises for translation added. What German vocabulary one could learn from it was limited. In the back the vocabulary list for the exercises consisted only of five pages. The 1871 edition included a *Supplement to Whitney's German Grammar* of 51 pages. It consisted mainly of exercises for translating from English into German. Its English-German vocabulary included 18 pages. It continued to appear even after 1900.

In 1885 Whitney published *A Brief German Grammar*, which was even a smaller book, but much more appealing and attractive. In 1882 a *German by Practice* book was published by L. R. Klemm and edited by Whitney. This was a book of over 300 pages and included extensive vocabulary lists and practice. The grammar involved was less technical and detailed. Whitney also published a German *Reader*.

*Other German texts, 1850–1874.* Many other German grammar books appeared during this period. No attempt is here made to include all of them, but a few are here mentioned: Theodore G. Glaubensklee's *Synthetic Grammar of the German Language* (1857), Edward Keller's *New German Method* (1858), Elias Peissmer's *Elements of the German Language* (1865), J. C. Oehlschlager's revisions of Ahn's German grammars, and Hermann D. Wrage's *A Practical Grammar of the German Language* (1872).

## C. *German Textbooks, 1875–1900*

A NUMBER of the popular German books published during the previous period, such as those by Ahn, Woodbury, Otto, and Worman, continued in circulation into this period. Thus the texts first published during this period encountered considerable competition in gaining wide acceptance. While a considerable number were published between 1875 and 1900, none apparently gained the circulation of the above mentioned books. However, a number will be discussed.

*Herman J. Schmitz and J. Adolph Schmitz.* Both being teachers of German, in 1875 they combined their efforts in publishing an *Elementary German Grammar*. From its use and from suggestions given by others, they decided to replace it with *The Elements of the German Language*, Part First in 1888, and Part Second in 1889, separately bound. In part they attempted to follow a process developed by Gottlieb Heness at New Haven in 1866. However, they attempted to adapt their books for more suitable use in "public schools, in academies, seminaries, and colleges." The method was largely inductive. "The living forms of the language are given to the student and explained by objects, association of ideas, translation, etc." Thus the language was to be learned" partly unconsciously, partly consciously."

Part First included 50 lessons and two vocabulary lists in the back, totalling in all 149 pages. The material was attractively presented, each lesson consisting of several parts or exercises. For example, the parts of Lektion 17 were: Sprechübung, Wörter and Ausdrücke, Bemerkungen, and a Writing Exercise.

The Part Second volume was some larger, many of its lessons being longer. Too, it contained 400 Wiederholungs—und Prüfungsfragen (Review—and Examination—questions), and its vocabulary lists were twice as long. The lesson arrangements, however, were very similar to those in Part First.

*Charles P. Otis.* Otis was professor of modern languages in the Massachusetts Institute of Technology. In 1881 he published an *Elementary German* book, which constituted "an outline of the grammar, with exercises, conversations, and readings." About 200 pages were devoted to the treatment of the articles, nouns, adjectives, and the various kinds of verbs. Generally, word lists, and German and English exercises, were included in each lesson. In the back were many brief German selections for translation, and two rather extensive vocabulary lists. This book, in slightly revised form, was recopyrighted a number of times, even as late as 1904.

*Charles Harris.* In 1892, when Harris was connected with Oberlin College, he published his *German Lessons*. It was intended to provide "such knowledge of forms as will adequately prepare the student to read ordinary German." The work was presented in 28 carefully organized lessons. Grammatical principles and rules largely formed the bases for the lessons, but vocabulary lists and German and English exercises were included. A rather extensive appendix of miscellaneous matters appeared in the back. He had also published *Selections for German Composition*. Both of these books appeared in several editions

*Calvin Thomas.* Thomas was professor of Germanic Languages and Literature in Columbia University. In 1894 he produced *A Practical German Grammar* in two parts. Part I aimed to present the fundamentals of grammar "without omitting the essentials or including the unneccessary." After dealing with introductory matters it covered the parts of speech and their variations. Part II largely dealt with syntax in relation to the parts of speech. Toward the back there were 29 exercises in syntax. In the appendix there was a treatment of orthography and the two conventional lists of vocabulary. Its approach was fundamentally grammatical and deductive. It was slightly revised and recopyrighted a number of times, even as late as 1932.

*Arnold Werner-Spanhoofd.* Spanhoofd was the Director of German Instruction in High Schools of Washington, D.C. In 1899 he published the *Lehrbuch der Deutschen Sprache*. It aimed to provide a practical German course for "high school, academy, or college." The material was presented in 35 sectionized lessons. Commonly the lesson would begin with a grammatical principle in German together with reading content involving it. A discussion of the grammar in English and the vocabulary list in German and English followed. Lastly, there were exercises in German and in English for translation. The usual two vocabulary lists were in the back. It soon appeared in later editions. He also wrote several other German textbooks.

*Other German grammars, 1875–1900.* Many other German books were written during this period, but most of them failed to gain wide circulation. Some that may be mentioned were: Adolphe Dreyspring's *Cumulative Method for Learning German* (1883), H. C. G. Brandt's *A Grammar of the German Language* (1884), J. Seybold's *How to Speak German* (1885), Franz H. Kirmayer's *A Simple Method of Learning German* (1886), William C. Collar's *Graded German Lessons* (1887), Edward S. Joynes' *A German Grammar* (1887), and Sophie Doriot's *The Beginner's Book in German* (1889). Evidence indicates that there were many others.

## D. *German Readers and Classics*

As WAS true in the other language fields, after the beginning course, which usually consisted largely of grammar, the students would be introduced to readers. Most of these readers were prepared by authors who also had written a grammar. Often the footnotes in these readers would even make reference to rules in the grammar.

After an examination of a number of these readers the writer is under the impresssion that there was not the sameness in them as there was in the Latin and the French readers, at least this was true of the earlier readers. Now brief treatment will be given a number of these.

*German readers.* The oldest reader in the writer's possession was Johann V. Meidinger's *Angenehme Unterhaltungen* printed in Frankfurt, Germany in 1799 (4th ed.). Likely this copy was brought here by some German immigrant. It consisted of about 125 brief miscellaneous German reading selections, each followed by a vocabulary list of the key words in German and French. The earlier readings were mainly moral stories, such as Der Treue Freund, Der Gute Sohn, etc. Then about two-thirds of the later selections dealt with foreign peoples, cities, and countries. If the vocabulary had been in German and English instead of French, it could have been very useful here.

My next oldest reader was F. P. Wilmsen's *Deutscher Kinderfreund* fur "Schule und Haus." The first Philadelphia edition was printed in 1840 after the 146th original German edition. A number of testimonials for the book were included. Its 90 selections were mostly grouped under certain headings. About half of them were of a moral and sentimental nature, such as Der Ehrliche

Knabe, Die Gute Tochter, etc. Other groups dealt with peoples, the world, health, religion, songs, prayers, and maxims. A large section dealt with the United States.

In 1846 G. J. Adler's *A Progressive Reader*, which was adapted to the American edition of Ollendorff's *German Grammar*, appeared. This was considerably different from the other two readers. Its 87 selections were grouped into five Abschnitte (Parts). The selections of the first group were mostly fables, the second brief classic pieces, the third fairy tales, the fourth poetic pieces, and the fifth mostly about religious topics. Nearly every selection was taken from the writings of famous German authors, such as Lessing, Schubart, Campe, Wagner, Schiller, Göthe (sic.), Herder, Grimm, Körner, Kant, Fichte, and so on.

In 1852 W. H. Woodbury published *The Eclectic German Reader*. This, like Adler's, contained choice selections from the best German writers, but these were not presented in groups. Footnotes referred to rules and principles in Woodbury's *Grammar*. In the back nearly 100 pages were devoted to a list of German-English vocabulary in double column.

In 1857 the Reverend L. W. Heydenreich's *Elementary German Reader* appeared. Four pages of testimonials opened the book. It was prepared on the plan of Jacob's *Greek Reader*. Each of the first 57 very brief selections illustrated some grammatical rule or principle. The 64 selections of the Second Part were from leading German authors, many of them fables. There were 60 pages of vocabulary.

In 1865 Leopold Simonson produced the *Deutsches Balladen-Buch*. This consisted of 297 pages of German ballads, all in poetic form. These had been written by such authors as Goethe, Schiller, Bürger, Uhland, Schwab, Körner, and so on. Most of them were preceded either by a brief biography of the writer or some comments concerning the occasion for the writing of them. Many pages contained explanatory footnotes.

In 1873 James H. Worman published *An Elementary German Reader* of prose and verse. Only about 50 pages consisted of selections, of which a number were dramatic in character. To help in the study of the selections there were 55 pages of notes and references, and 145 pages of vocabulary. It likely was a tedious process to teach these selections.

William H. Rosenstengel published *A German Reader* for high schools in 1881. The 62 selections were both of poetry and prose. It began with fables, which were followed by various types of German literature. A good many of the prose selections were from novels. The Second Part contained the key vocabulary words in German and English of the selections lesson by lesson. The Third Part consisted of Fragen (Questions) on the 62 lessons.

In 1883 L. R. Klemm and W. D. Whitney produced an *Elementary Reader*. Part First consisted of nine descriptive selections, 12 fables and popular tales, and 14 anecdotes and narratives. Part Second contained 14 pieces of lyric poetry, 12 of didactic poetry, eight of epics, and two of dramatic poetry. Part Third presented 43 extracts about America and her interests. Footnotes and an extensive vocabulary were intended for student aid.

The last one to be discussed was *A German Reader* by Edward S. Joynes in 1889. Part I presented 20 very brief selections in interlinear form to help the students get started. Part II contained pieces of familiar prose. Part III introduced 30 easy poems. Part IV contained 15 more difficult prose selections. The last part presented 15 personal letters written by famous German authors. This was the first book here discussed to have contained letters. As usual, there were ample notes and vocabulary helps in the back of the book.

In addition to these, there were many other German readers published. Among them were: George Storme's *Select German Stories* (1869), Jacob and Wilhelm's *Kinder und Hausmärchen* (1881), Und. C. Grebner and W. H. Weick's *Deutsches Drittes Lesebuch* (1886), Carla and Helene Wenckebach's *Die Schönsten Deutschen Lieder* (1885), and H. A. Guerber's *Märchen und Erzählungen* (1896). Evidently there were many others.

*German classics.* In addition to German readers, which usually contained selections from many authors, some German books for school use contained a writing or writings solely of one outstanding author. Among the authors receiving such treatment most often were Goethe, Schiller, Lessing, and Heine.

The writings of Johann Wolfgang von Goethe (1749–1832) most often reproduced for school use were *Faust* and *Egmont*. Among Johann Friedrich von Schiller's (1759–1805) reproduced works were *Die Jungfrau von Orleans*, and *Wilhelm Tell*. The work of Gotthold Ephraim Lessing (1729–1781) most often used was his *Minna von Barnhelm*. Heinrich Heine's (1797–1856) most popularly used writing was *Das Buch der Lieder*. Most of these works were published for school use by American editors who prepared notes and vocabulary lists to assist in the study of them.

### E. *Characteristics of German Textbooks*

GERMAN did not gain acceptance as a secondary school subject as early as

French, but after the popular Ollendorff method of teaching German was introduced here in the 1840's its teaching soon became more common. In fact, after 1860 German was taught in more than twice as many high schools of the midwest than French. This popularity continued until World War I, after which most high schools dropped the teaching of German. Only relatively few have reintroduced it.

The purposes for teaching German were not too often specifically mentioned in the texts, but the nature of the purposes usually were implied. The three most common purposes seemed to be: (1) Formal discipline, (2) ability to read German, and (3) ability to speak it. The fact that so many beginning German texts largely followed the grammatical approach indicates that certain mental disciplinary training was implied. The predominance of so much German textual material to be translated into English, both in the grammars and even more so in the readers, indicates that the development of the ability to read German for meaning was the dominant purpose. A number of the books also included conversational exercises indicating that the development of the ability to speak German was also a purpose.

German was not an easy language to teach to non-Germans. Hence the teaching of German did not become at all common here until certain methods or systems of teaching it effectively were developed. This was done by several professors in Germany. The methods most commonly accepted by American textbook publishers were those of Heinrich Ollendorff, Emil Otto, and F. Ahn. Their books, commonly after minor revisions by American editors, became very popular here. Even the so-called American written German texts were based considerably on one or another of these systems. This was true of Woodbury's books, which became very popular here.

The usual feature of these systems was that the work was presented in carefully prepared lessons consisting of a number of steps. For example, most lessons in Otto's system consisted of an important grammatical rule illustrated with examples, a vocabulary list, a brief German selection for translation, an English selection to be changed into German, and conversational exercises.

Few books indicated the grade level at which they were to be used. One of the few to do so was Spanhoofd's in 1899, when he stated it to be for "high school, academy, or college." Likely the same books used in the secondary schools for beginning German were also used in beginning German classes in many colleges. Testimonials and advertisements appearing in the back of many books intimated this to be true.

The content of the German readers varied more than in the Latin, Greek, and French readers. There was very little standardization of the content, except that most readers used only the writings of German authors. Evidently there was a spirit of German nationalism exhibited in this. Too, the existence of so much excellent German literature made it tempting for the authors of the readers to do this. A few of the German readers did contain a few reading selections about America, but their authorship generally was also German.

# CHAPTER V

# Social Studies

SOCIAL studies, as such, were not taught in the early Latin grammar schools, although a number of the Latin and Greek books used contained considerable content related to history and governmental matters. Many of the academies soon after 1800 began to teach universal or world history, and the early high schools later followed suit. Some of the secondary schools also taught separate history courses dealing with the ancient Greeks, the Romans, or the English. American history was not so commonly taught in the early secondary schools as is true today. Too, since my other book, *Old Textbooks*, contains a chapter on American history, no treatment will be given it here. Such courses as problems of democracy, sociology, and economics have been largely introduced into secondary schools since 1900, no attempt is made to deal with their textbooks.

## SECTION ONE

## WORLD HISTORY

### *Introduction*

*Nature of history.* If history is a record of the past, then in a sense it must have begun as soon as writing was developed. However, good history should be more than a mere chronological record of the past. It is now commonly considered to be a narrative story showing the development of events of a particular classification or field. Thus there are many kinds and types of history such as the religious, legal, governmental, literary, economic, sociological, educational, scientific, and so on. Here we are concerned primarily with what has been commonly called world or universal history, but which has dealt primarily with the history of races, nations, cultures, and political and religious leaders.

*The study of history.* The first writing of creditable history, like the beginnings of so many other academic matters, can be traced to the Greeks. Herodotus, often referred to as the "Father of History," Thucydides, and Xenophon were among those whose writings were historical in nature. Among the Romans who wrote historical works were Caesar, Sallust, Nepos, and Tacitus. Josephus, who spent considerable time in Rome, wrote an extensive history of the Hebrews. Even though these writings were extant, the subject of history, as such, was rarely taught in the schools, either among the Greeks or Romans. Likewise, it was not taught as a formal subject in the medieval universities. History was not included in the Seven Liberal Arts, which constituted the core of the medieval university curriculum. However, some historical content appeared in some of the classical writings. During the Reformation some attention began to be given to the history of the middle ages.

The formal teaching of history came somewhat later. Oxford founded the Camden Professorship of Ancient history in 1622. The Regius Professorship of Modern History began in Cambridge in 1724. Soon thereafter a number of continental universities began to teach history. In America a professor of ecclesiastical history was appointed at Yale in 1778, but the first professorship of history in a general sense was not created until 1839 at Harvard. Later other American universities followed.

Just when history first began to be taught in American secondary schools seems to be uncertain. It is known that Franklin, in his "Proposals" for the Philadelphia Academy, emphasized the study of readings in history. He said, "If history be made a constant part of their reading, . . . may not almost all kinds of useful knowledge be that way introduced to advantage?" However, it is doubtful just how much history was actually taught in the early years of the academy, since Franklin later complained that the school had discriminated in favor of the classical studies. Nazareth Hall, a school for boys in Pennsylvania, when it was revived after the Revolution, included history in the curriculum. The curriculum of Phillips Exeter in 1818 taught modern history in the third year of the English Department, and ancient history in the advanced class of the Classical Department. Evidently many other academies soon began to teach history. The first American high school, in Boston, in 1821, offered several courses in history. In 1826 Massachusetts enacted a law requiring towns of 500 families to teach history. Russell[1] made a study of the history offering in the academies of New York state between 1825 and 1860. He found that in 1830 universal history was offered in 44 academies, Roman antiquities in 8, and Grecian antiquities in 47. In 1847 universal history was taught in 98, Roman in 18, and Greek in 59. From this it can be seen that the offering of history had become rather common in academies by 1850, but that much attention was given to classical history. In 1889–1890 the percent of public and private secondary school students in the U.S. taking history (other than U.S.) was 27.8, and in 1899–1900 it was 37.8. This means that if history was offered only in one or two of the four years, nearly all students would have taken at least one course. Stout found that most high schools of the mid-west offered either world history or ancient and modern between 1860 and 1900. In fact, he found that world history in some form was offered more than twice as frequently as United States history.

The writer's collection of history books (other than U.S.) contains more than 200 copies published before 1900. Of these about 80 are general world histories with varied titles. About 100 deal with ancient, Grecian, Roman, English, or French history. The remainder deal with the history of various countries and areas. When one considers that nearly 60 of these books dealt with ancient, Grecian, and Roman history, and that nearly every world history contained considerable treatment of ancient history, it can be concluded that much attention was given to the teaching of ancient or classical history in American schools before 1900. Thus the classical tradition influenced the nature of the early American secondary school curriculum, not merely through the teaching of Latin and Greek, but also in the teaching of history.

## A. *World History Textbooks Before 1850*

*Alexander Fraser Tytler.* Tytler was a Professor of History at the University of Edinburgh. For his work he prepared "Outlines of a Course of Lectures on General History." Soon he decided to compose and enlarge his notes as an aid for his students. These labors resulted in the *Elements of General History, Ancient and Modern* published in 1801. It was not long before the book began to be republished in the U.S., usually with certain changes by some American editors. For example, the 1809 edition was corrected and enlarged by the Rev. Dr. Holmes. Francis Nichols claimed title to the 1813 American edition, which was based on the fifth British edition. S. G. Goodrich secured the copyright for the 1821 edition, which contained a chronological table of 82 pages, and 22 pages of questions in the back prepared by Thomas Robbins. The 1824 edition was copyrighted by Isaac Hill, which contained some material added by Edward Nares of England, and "additions and alterations by an American Gentleman." The 1851 edition was copyrighted by John F. Brown and claimed to be the 195th edition. The latter two books claimed to be "adapted for the use of schools and academies."

From the foregoing it can be seen that Tytler's *Elements* became very popular in America. All of the writer's nine copies were rather large books bound in leather. The earlier editions devoted about 150 pages to ancient history, 200 pages to modern history, and from 25 to 35 pages to the history of the Jews. Folding maps were also included. The later editions, due to the use of smaller print, covered ancient history in 105 pages and the modern in 125. The 1821 edition omitted the treatment of Jewish history. The two later editions used about 200 pages each for the treatment of further modern history from 1700 to 1815. All of the editions contained a chronological table varying from 40 to 82 pages. The two later books also contained examination questions in the back. The 1851 edition included 1520 questions. The Tytler books set a pattern for other world histories.

*Caleb Bingham* (1757–1819). Bingham, who was the author of several very popular early American readers, published *A Historical Grammar* for use in "schools and academies" in 1802. This book was originally written in France, then translated by Lucy Peacock, and "revised, corrected, and greatly enlarged" by Bingham. The pre-Christian era was presented in eight periods, and the Christian era in six. The 186 pages of text appeared in catechetical or question-and-answer form about the historical events during these periods. An abridged chronology relative to the arts and sciences consumed 21 pages, followed by 20 pages listing eminent and remakable persons appeared in the back. The book was only half the size of Tytler's *Elements of General History*.

*Benjamin Tucker.* In 1806 Tucker published a *Sacred and Profane History Epitomized with a Continuation of Modern History.* This book devoted 64 pages to ancient, 65 to medieval, and 155 to modern history. Fifty pages were given to Greek and Roman civilization, and 46 pages to sacred and ecclesiastical history. In 1822 Tucker published a revised and enlarged edition with the title changed to *An Epitome of Ancient and Modern History*. Part I dealt with ancient history, sacred and profane, from the creation to the fall of the Roman Empire. Part II dealt with modern history, covering the feudal system, the Crusades, chivalry, the Reformation, the Revival of Learning, and some modern history of the leading countries of Europe, Asia, Africa, and America. In the back there appeared a chronological table of remarkable events, discoveries, and inventions covering nearly 40 pages. The material was all presented in catechetical form. He claimed this form to be "best calculated to impress and familiarize the minds of pupils with the subject."

*Samuel Whelpley.* In 1814 Whelpley published *A Compend of History from the Earliest Times.* This edition devoted about two-thirds of its space to ancient history. About 95 pages were spent on Greek civilization and 125 on Roman. Later he saw the need of giving fuller treatment to modern history. So in 1815 he published Volumes I and II in one book. Volume I of 222 pages covered history to the Empire of Charlemagne. The textual matter of Volume II, dealing with modern times, covered 210 pages. In addition, in the back other matters were given treatment, such as the importance of historical knowledge, the credibility of Mosaic history, sources of knowledge of ancient history, and several kinds of chronological tables. Too, it included a folded Imperial and Biographical Chart. The 1826 edition was its ninth. Joseph Emerson in 1818 published separately a booklet of *Questions Adapted to Whelpley's Compend of History.*

*Rev. David Blair.* In the 1820's the *Outlines of Chronology, Ancient and Modern* was published. Its fourth edition appeared in 1828. This was a small book of 231 pages. Its material was presented in ten periods. It was attractively printed and well organized with the subsections numbered for guidance in study. In the back in real small type there appeared 30 pages of questions for examination.

*J. E. Worcester* (1784–1865). In 1826 Worcester published his *Elements of History, Ancient and Modern* with historical tables and charts. He stated that these should help the study of history, as maps do for geography. About 100 pages were given to the ancient times, only 22 pages to the middle ages, and 165 pages to modern times. There was a section on Ecclesiastial History near the back. Why it was there is puzzling. More than 25 pages in the back were devoted to many historical charts or tables. The paragraphs throughout the book were numbered. In 1849 this book was revised and enlarged. It contained 60 pages of questions in the back. Reference was made in it that it was adopted in Boston, Worcester, Salem, Cambridge, and Roxbury, and that Harvard freshmen were required to take an examination on it for admission. Worcester's *Elements* appeared in many editions even as late as 1869.

In 1827 Worcester published *An Epitome of History.* This was a small book of 135 pages. It had parts on ancient, medieval, modern, and American history.

*Q.* What was the name of the firſt king of Egypt ?

*A.* He was called *Menes*, and was, it is conjectured, Mifraim, the ſon of *Ham*, one of the ſons of Noah.

*Q.* What other events occur in this period ?

*A.* The conſtruction of the Egyptian Pyramids, which are reckoned among the ſeven wonders of the world, and are the only remains of thoſe wonders that ſtill exiſt.

*Q.* What other empire flouriſhed in this period ?

*A.* The empire of China, which, by a long ſucceſſion of kings, has been preſerved till the preſent day ; and contains, according to the opinion of ſome judicious writers, at leaſt one third of all the inhabitants on the globe.

*Q.* Who was its founder?

*A.* He was called *Fohi\**.

*Q.* Was idolatry eſtabliſhed during this period ?

*A.* The children of Noah, in the beginning of it, preſerved the worſhip of the true God ; but afterwards the morals of men became altogether corrupt, and ſuperſtition introduced idolatry.

---

## THIRD PERIOD.

FROM THE CALLING OF ABRAHAM TO THE LAW GIVEN
BY MOSES.——431 YEARS.

*Q.* Why did God call Abraham ?

*A.* To preſerve him and his deſcendants from the idolatry that was univerſally diffuſed throughout the world.

*Q.* What were the remarkable events that occurred during this period ?

*A.* The birth of *Iſhmael*, from whom deſcend the people called Arabs ; that of Iſaac, Jacob, and Eſau, with ſeveral other remarkable events recorded in the holy Scriptures ; ſuch as the ſelling of Joſeph by his brethren ; the removal of Jacob into Egypt ; the perſecution of the Iſraelites under Pharaoh, and their retreat out of Egypt.

\* The Chineſe reckon much earlier, and pretend to have exiſted, not only antecedent to the deluge, but even to the creation ; nothing certain, however, appears in their annals till the time of Fohi.

25  A page from Caleb Bingham's *A Historical Grammer of Universal History*, 1802. Note the catechetical method of teaching

AN

# EPITOME

*of*

# ANCIENT AND MODERN HISTORY.

*INTENDED FOR THE USE OF SCHOOLS.*

### PART I.

ANCIENT HISTORY, SACRED AND PROFANE, FROM THE CREATION
TO THE FALL OF THE ROMAN EMPIRE.

### PART II.

MODERN HISTORY, OR A CONTINUATION OF GENERAL EVENTS
TO THE PRESENT TIME: WITH AN APPENDIX,

CONTAINING

*An Account of the Feudal System, the Crusades, Chivalry,
the Reformation, and the Revival of Learning.*

To the whole is added,

A CHRONOLOGICAL TABLE OF REMARKABLE EVENTS, &c. FROM
THE CREATION TO THE YEAR 1822.

## BY BENJAMIN TUCKER,

AUTHOR OF THE IMPROVED EDITIONS OF BLAIR'S GRAMMAR
OF CHEMISTRY.

A NEW EDITION,
GREATLY IMPROVED AND ENLARGED.

••••◦◉◦••••

# PHILADELPHIA:

PUBLISHED AND SOLD BY D. HOGAN, 255, MARKET ST.
J. Anderson, Printer.

## 1822.

26  Title-page from Tucker's *Epitome*, 1822

Throughout the paragraphs were numbered. At the bottom of the pages there were questions relating to the text rather than in the back. This treatise was virtually an abstract of his larger work. It soon appeared in other editions.

*Dionysius Lardner and John Frost.* Lardner wrote the *Outlines of History* in England. This, he said, was written primarily as a reference book with an emphasis on the political aspects of history. However, Frost recognized its possibilities as a regular school textbook for America. So in 1831 he published it in Philadelphia as the *Outlines of Universal History.* He somewhat expanded the brief treatment about America and changed other features. This text devoted 116 pages to ancient, 127 to medieval, and 104 to modern history. Several tables and an index followed. It was one of the first world histories to contain an index. Then 86 pages of questions for the examination of students arranged by chapters concluded the book. Lardner's books appeared in several editions here. The 1832 American edition was bound in green leather.

*S. G. Goodrich* (1793–1860). Goodrich wrote most of his earlier books under the pen name of Peter Parley. His explanation for this was because, when he first began to write children's books, he was in his 20's. Yet he attempted to write as a grandfather addressing young children. Thus the would-be elderly Peter Parley wrote for children. He soon became the most prolific textbook writer in America. He eventually wrote at least 84 text and reading books for children. These included readers, literatures, histories, spelling books, geographies, and science books. The writer's collection contains 27 copies of his United States histories and 23 other histories.

In 1832 he began to prepare a series of attractive history books. He began with *The First Book of History* "for Children and Youth by the Author of Peter Parley's Tales." By 1850 it had appeared in nearly 300 editions. *The Second Book of History* was also published in 1832, and *The Third Book* in 1835. All of these appeared in many editions, often with revisions. The *First* was recopyrighted in 1837, 1848, and 1852; the *Second* in 1835, and 1851. All of these were printed in sizes similar to geographies. Most of their pages were 5 1/2 by 7 inches and printed in double column. Like most of Goodrich's books, they contained many pictures. These also included many maps and the 1856 edition even contained some colored maps.

What of the content? *The First Book* dealt with the individual States of our union, and individually with many Latin American countries, together with the West Indies. The earlier editions had 84 brief chapters, while the 1852 edition had 107. The reason for the increase was that there were more states in

Q

the Union then. *The Second Book* dealt with the modern history of Europe, Africa, and Asia in 93 brief chapters. Questions appeared at the bottom of most pages of the *First* and *Second* books. *The Third Book* dealt mainly with ancient history in connection with ancient geography. This book was designed to be a sequel to the other two books. The first 18 chapters dealt with the ancient Greeks, and then more than 50 chapters with Roman history. Other chapters covered ancient Egypt, Libya, Babylonia, Assyria, Chaldea, Syria, Phoenicia, and the Hebrews. The paragraphs in all three books were numbered to aid the pupil in study. It is not certain now at which grade level these books were used most commonly. Each contained roughly 200 rather large pages with small type in double columns, which meant that each contained considerable content.

In 1837 Goodrich published a *Common School History,* which reached the ninth edition by 1841. After an introduction it covered the history of a number of countries of Asia, Africa, Europe, America, and Oceania. In all it contained 191 brief chapters, and had 25 pages of questions in the back but no index. In 1849 it was recopyrighted with a number of revisions. One was to place the questions at the bottom of the textual pages. In 1858 it was again recopyrighted with an added title, *A Pictorial History of the World.* Its content was changed only slightly, but an index of eleven pages was added. It was again revised in 1866 and continued to appear at least until 1879.

Also in 1837 Goodrich produced his *Universal History on the Basis of Geography.* This contained two volumes bound in one book. Volume I covered mainly the more ancient history of Asia, Africa, and Europe in 380 pages, and Volume II covered the later history of Europe, and also America and Oceania in 374 pages. It also appeared in reprints.

From the discussion of all these histories it must be evident that Goodrich was a prolific writer. However, an examination of these books reveals a great deal of repetition and duplication. Evidently he must have engaged much help to produce so many books in such numerous fields. Their popularity may be attributed to a number of features. Among these was his ability to write in terms that children could understand. The chapters and lessons were brief. Also, more than any author of his period, he included many attractive pictures and maps. It is clear that his history books were widely used.

*Emma Hart Willard* (1787–1870). Mrs. Willard was one of the most distinguished of the women educators in America before 1850. After teaching in several New England academies she was persuaded to become the head of the newly founded Troy Female Seminary in 1821, which was referred to as the early "Vassar of New York state." She travelled widely to help spread the revival of common schools in America. She also became the writer of popular textbooks, particularly in the fields of history and geography. Her younger sister, Mrs. Elmira Lincoln Phelps, also wrote popular textbooks, particularly in several fields of science.

In 1837 Mrs. Willard published a *Universal History*. In 1844 it was recopyrighted as a *Universal History in Perspective*. This became very popular. The 1850 edition was the tenth, and it continued to appear at least until 1879. She demonstrated keen pedagogical sense in her textbooks. In the history books she developed interesting time charts and maps. She attempted to combine the ethnographical and the chronological approaches with the aid of charts and maps, so that students could get a clearer understanding of developments in history. The 1844 edition began with a detailed chronological table and index of 16 pages. It also included a large folded historic chart. Part I began with creation and went to the birth of Christ, being divided into six sub-periods. Part II then went to the discovery of America, being divided into five subperiods. Lastly, Part III covered history to 1843, being divided into nine subperiods. The subperiods were numbered with Roman numerals, and the paragraphs with Arabic numerals. The subperiods were further divided into what may be called sections, of which there were 1842 in the entire book. Furthermore, there were characterizing comments and topic titles on the margin of the pages of the textual material, and questions at the bottom of the pages. There were also many interesting pictures and maps throughout the book. Thus the students were greatly aided and guided in the study of history. The 1850 edition contained 494 pages.

*Other world histories before 1850.* In addition to the books here discussed many other less popular ones were published before 1850. The following may be mentioned: John Payne's *An Epitome of History* (1795), John Gough's *A Collection of Narrative Pieces from Ancient and Modern History* (1801), Lucy Peacock's *Historical Grammar* (1802), John Robinson's *An Easy Grammar of History* (1807), D. Fraser's *A Compendium of the History of All Nations* (1807), William Mavor's *The Catechism of Universal History* (1815), Munroe and Francis' *The Elements of Ancient and Universal History* (1818), Frederick Butler's *Sketches of Universal History, Sacred and Profane* (1818), Abbe Millot's *Elements of General History* (1823), Edward Quin's *A Universal History from Creation to A. D. 1828* (1828), Albert Wells' *A Compendium of General History* (1828), Royal Robbins' *The*

*World Displayed in Its History and Geography* (1830), William Sullivan's *Historical Class Book* (1833), G. P. Putnam's *Introduction and Index to Universal History* (1833), J. L. Blake's *A View of the World* (1834), Thomas Keightley's *Outlines of Universal History* (1835), Samuel Perkins' *The World as It Is* (1836), Martin J. Kerney's *A Compendium of Ancient and Modern History* (1845), C. Barth's *A General History of the World* (1847), Charles J. Hendee's *The First Book of History* (1848), and Richard G. Parker's *Outlines of General History* (1848).

### B. *World History Textbooks, 1850–1900*

A NUMBER of the histories first published before 1850 continued to circulate during this period, particularly books by Goodrich, Worcester, and by Mrs. Willard. In this section attention shall be given only those first published after 1850. Of these only a few seem to have gained very wide popularity. These will be given some attention.

*Marcius Willson* (1813–1905). In 1854 Willson, who earlier had published a popular American history textbook, published his *Outlines of History*. This was a large book of 561 pages of textual material, which presented history into ancient and modern times. It was divided at A.D. 1. More than a hundred pages were devoted to Grecian history and even more to Roman, but only 86 pages to the middle ages. In the back there were 18 colored maps and a geographical index. A rather detailed table of contents appeared in the beginning of the book, but no historic index anywhere. The paragraphs were numbered, and interesting supplementary comments appeared at the bottom of many pages. It continued to appear for more than a decade.

*John J. Anderson* (1821–1906). Anderson, who also published several popular American history books, in 1869 produced *A Manual of General History*. It was intended for "use of academies, high-schools, and families." He claimed that this book was prepared with great care on the narrative plan. It was divided into three parts, the ancient period extending roughly to 400, and the middle ages to about 1500. It was well organized, and included questions at the bottom of the pages, chronological tables at the end of sections, a number of colored maps, and an index in the back. It was rather attractively printed. It was much smaller than Willson's text. It was expanded and recopyrighted in 1874 and again in 1882, thus appearing in a number of editions.

*William Swinton* (1833–92). Swinton wrote textbooks in the fields of spelling, reading, grammar, geography, English composition, and American history. In 1874 he published his *Outlines of the World's History*. It covered ancient, medieval, and modern history. He claimed that in writing it he kept certain fundamental questions in mind. For example, what did each of the nations covered contribute to the "common stock of civilization?" In "what *forms* did the mind of the race express itself: in religion, war, law-making, political organization, literature, art?" What was the "actual *life of the people* themselves,—their condition as regards political freedom, education, physical well-being, food, dress, trade, society, etc.?" What have been the great "*steps in human progress?*" The five sections of the book dealt with the ancient oriental monarchies, the history of Greece, the history of Rome, medieval history, and modern history. This outline was somewhat inconsistent in that three of the sections dealt with eras while two dealt with national civilizations. Numerous pictures and maps were included. It appeared in a number of editions.

*The Barnes History.* In 1883 the A. S. Barnes & Co. published *A Brief History of Ancient, Medieval, and Modern Peoples.* Most of this book was written by Mrs. J. Dorman Steele, whose husband wrote very popular books in several fields of science. Mrs. Steele in several ways gave this book a woman's touch. Political history, which commonly received dominant attention in most history books, was condensed so that literature, religion, architecture, philosophy, and so on, could be given treatment. She said, "It is as important to know *something* about Plato as *all* about Caesar." Manners, customs, and scenes of real life representing the people of history were given "semi-romantic" treatment. It was an attractive and well organized book. It included 240 illustrations and 34 maps. The textual material consisted of 600 pages, to which an appendix of 32 pages was added, consisting of 460 Historical Recreations (questions and exercises), and an index. Many interesting comments and references appeared in fine print as footnotes. Nevertheless, the book did not become as popular as the Barnes *History of the United States.* Apparently, it was too different than other world history books to become real popular.

*Mary D. Sheldon.* She, like Mrs. Steele, attempted to write a different kind of book than the usual. In 1885 she published her *Studies in General History.* She acknowledged that this book was "not a history, but a collection of historical materials." She covered the usual nations and periods commonly treated in such histories. However, each chapter or section was not presented in straight narrative form, but rather in parts or exercises. For example, the "Study on Egypt" consisted of: Historical sources and authorities; organization; leading events, works, and names; list of objects found in tombs; and illustrative extracts from Egyptian literature. Throughout the book contained original quotations from the writings of famous men. Forty illustrations and 23 maps were included. Likely under the guidance of a good teacher this was a good book, although unusual. It appeared in several editions.

*Phillip Van Ness Myers* (1846–1937). In 1886 Myers published a *Medieval and Modern History*. He also published an *Ancient History*. Apparently these did not become very popular as separate volumes, so in 1889 he published *A General History* "for Colleges and High Schools," which virtually combined the two. This book immediately became popular. In the preface he acknowledged his indebtedness to more than twenty other listed historians, whose writings he used as sources for help. The book was divided into ancient history, ending with the fall of Rome in 476, covering 370 pages; and medieval and modern history covering 361 pages. Evidently Myers was more interested in the beginnings of our civilization than in the modern times. The book was well organized into parts, periods, chapters, and clearly identified sections. It was well illustrated with many very interesting pictures and colored maps. In the back there was an index and pronouncing vocabulary of 27 pages. The book was slightly revised and recopyrighted in 1906, 1917, and 1921. It evidently was one of the most popular of world histories at the turn of the century. The writer well remembers the book as the one he studied in school.

*Other world history textbooks, 1850–1900.* Among the other world history textbooks published during this period the following may be mentioned: H. White's *Elements of Universal History* (1850), Pierce C. Grace's *Outlines of History* (1851), George Weber's *Outlines of Universal History* (1853), Francis Bowen and M. Behr's *Outlines of Universal History* (1853), J. L. Blake's *A View of the World* (1857), John Barber's *Elements of General History* (1866), T. L. Oldekop's *Mankind in Many Ages* (1866), M. J. Kerney's *A Compendium of Modern History* (1867), Charles K. Adams' *Outlines of Lectures on History* (1870), W. S. Clark's *Elements of History* (1871), John P. Carter's *The Elements of General History* (1871), William Collier's *Outlines of General History* (1873), Edward A. Freeman's *General Sketch of History* (1874), Arthur Gilman's *First Steps in General History* (1874), M. E. Thalheimer's *Outline of General History* (1777), Annie Myrtle's *Historical Sketches* (1878), J. D. Quackenbos's *Illustrated School History of the World* (1879), John MacCarthy's *History of the World* (1882), Charlotte Young's *History of the World* (1882), Carl Ploetz and W. Fillinghast's *Epitome of Ancient, Medieval, and Modern History* (1883), H. M. Cottinger's *Elements of Universal History* (1884), George Park Fisher's *Outlines of Universal History* (1888), John Murray's *Compendium of Ancient and Modern History* (1893), Vincent

S. Walsh's *Nations of the World* (1893), Edgar Sandersons' *History of the World* (1898), and Rand and Mc Nally's *Condensed History of the World* (1899).

## C. *Other History Textbooks*

THE writer's collection contains more than 100 history textbooks which cannot be classified either as American or as world histories. Of these the English, Grecian, Roman, Ancient, and French, appeared most often. In addition there are one or more copies dealing with the history of Europe, Canada, the East, the Reformation, Switzerland, Mexico, Russia, North America, Egypt, and the Bible. Brief treatment will now be given those types that received most frequent attention.

*History of England.* The fact that the collection contains about 40 copies of histories of England attests to the fact that many schools in America must have taught English history. This evidently was true because England was our mother country. One of the earliest popular ones was by Oliver Goldsmith (1788–1874). In 1806 a reprint of Goldsmith's *An Abridgement of the History of England* was published in America. This was a reprint of a stereotyped London edition. It began with the invasion of Julius Caesar and ended with the reign of George III. After brief treatment of Britain, the Saxons, and the invasion by the Danes, a chapter was given each of the kings and queens up to George III. There was no table of contents, index, or any other teaching aid. In 1851 a 55th American edition edited and revised by William C. Taylor was printed in Philadelphia. It included treatment into the reign of Queen Victoria. It was made pedagogically more attractive by numbering the sections, including chronological tables and questions, as well as pictures. William Grimshaw, Pinnock, and others also revised and republished Goldsmith's book.

Another rather popular history of England was Peter Parley's (S.G. Goodrich) *A Pictorial History of England* published in 1845. It was divided into 225 very brief chapters and 444 pages. Their titles were more often topics rather than the reign of kings. Many pictures were included. It continued to appear at least to 1868.

English histories by more than 20 other authors were published here as textbooks. Among those whose books appeared in more than one edition in the chronological order of their appearance were: Herny Hallam, Mrs. Markham, A. B. Berard, John J. Anderson, A. P. Stone, D. H. Montgomery, and possibly others. Nearly all of these books began with the Roman invasion of England and ended near the date of publication.

*Grecian history.* The grasp of the classical tradition held on the secondary school curriculum before 1900 helps explain why so many schools taught Grecian history. Like was true of English history, the most popular early textbook was Dr. Oliver Goldsmith's *Grecian History.* This was reprinted here in 1800. Other editions soon followed. It covered Grecian history from the earliest state to the death of Alexander the Great. Another popular book was Peter Parley's *Tales about Ancient and Modern Greece* published in 1833. This was a rather elementary book with many pictures. It continued to appear for several decades. R. F. Pennell's *Ancient Greece from the Earliest Times to 146 B. C.* (1874), appeared for about two decades. In 1883 The A. S. Barnes and Company published a *Brief History of Greece.* The part which dealt with the political history was written by J. Dorman Steele, and the part dealing with its civilization was written by Mrs. Steele. These parts were followed by readings in Greek history. Other Grecian history textbooks which appeared in more than one edition were prepared by C. D. Cleveland (1831), and likely there were others.

*Roman history.* Roman history likely was frequently taught for the same reason as Grecian. Since the Grecian and Roman history books were smaller than the general world histories, evidently one was taught during the first semester and the other the second. Again the first popular book was Oliver Goldsmith's *Roman History.* The writer's three copies were published in Philadelphia in 1804, in Alexandria in 1818 (3rd ed.), and in Pittsburgh in 1818. Another popular one was S. G. Goodrich's *A Pictorial History of Ancient Rome* (1848). Its contents were presented in 235 brief chapters. Many pictures were included. It continued to appear for at least three decades. Other authors, whose books dealing with Rome appeared in more than one edition, were E. M. Sewell (1849), William Smith (a revision of Gibbon's history (1856), and likely there were others.

*Other histories.* The writer has sixteen ancient history textbooks. Nearly all of these were published before 1850. This fact reflects the traditional influence of paying more attention to the classic past rather than to the more recent historical events. Other books dealt only with medieval or modern history, French history, or with numerous other individual countries.

### D. *Characteristics of World History Textbooks*

*The Books.* The history textbooks (other than U.S.) varied greatly in the nations, regions, and time of coverage. Of the more than 200 in the writer's collection, about 80 are world or universal histories, 16 dealt only with ancient

ADAM AND EVE DRIVEN FROM EDEN.

## CHAPTER XXXVI.—Asia Continued.

*Review of the History of Asia.*

1. LET us now go back and review the history of Asia. In this quarter of the globe the most wonderful events in the history of mankind have happened. Here Adam and Eve were created; here they sinned, and here they were driven from the garden of Eden; and on the banks of the Euphrates all the people dwelt who lived before the flood.

2. It was in Asia that the ark of Noah rested; and

CHAPTER XXXVI.—1-4. What remarkable events have occurred in Asia?

27  A page from a history textbook by Rev. S. G. Goodrich, 1873

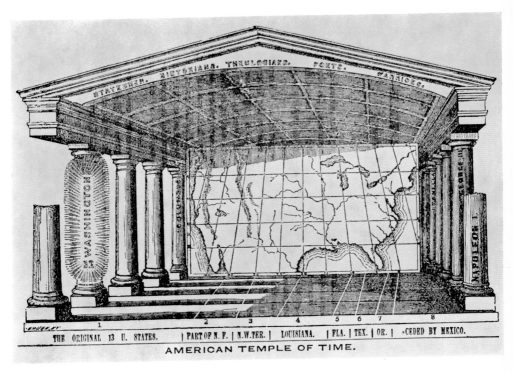

28 An illustration from Emma Willard's *Universal History*, 1845

times, 18 with Grecian and 16 with Roman history, 38 with English and ten with French history, and the others with various other nations and times. Counting the books which dealt with ancient times, together with those of Grecian and Roman history only, in addition to the average 35% of the content in the general world history texts dealing with ancient times, meant that much emphasis in the teaching of history in American secondary schools before 1900 was upon the ancient or classical period of history. This fact, together with the emphasis of the teaching of Latin and Greek, reveals that it took considerable time for American secondary schools to break away from the classical tradition, which has been so strong in European secondary schools.

*Teaching aims.* Most of textbooks contained prefaces. Commonly, if the author had particular aims in mind, they were stated in the preface. Otherwise they must be inferred from an analysis of the contents. Stewart[2] analyzed 45 world history textbooks. He found that authors did not always state clearly the aims for the study of history. Neither was there much unanimity. The aims most commonly mentioned were: History was a source of knowledge to awaken thought and cause intelligent thinking about world affairs; the development of an understanding religious attitude; the inculcation of patriotism; and to present an exhibit of a progressive view of civilization. The earlier books favored the relgious aim more than the later, while the later ones stressed more the political aspects.

*The content.* Table IX taken from Stewart's dissertation shows the percentage distribution of space by topics and by sub-periods. It shows that the earlier books gave more attention to the Far East, Roman history, and the Americas than the later ones. The later books increased their attention to the Dark Ages and Feudalism, the Reformation, and the political and social revolutions. Dawson[3] made a study of the religious content of 95 world histories. He found that the books published in the 1795-1825 period devoted 11.44 per cent to religious content; 1826-1850, 9.68 per cent; 1851-1875, 8.04 per cent; 1876-1899, 8 per cent; and for all the books the per cent was 9.29. This percentage at first appears to be larger than in Stewart's study. However, when one adds the topics of Sacred History, Ecclesiastical History, the Reformation, and what religious content there may have been in the treatment of the Far East of Stewart's study. Their findings would be very similar regarding religious content.

*Methods and teaching aids.* Two of the early histories were written in catechetical form; namely, those by Bingham (1802), and by Tucker (1822). The

TABLE IX: *Percentage Distribution of Subject Matter in the World History Textbooks Published During Four Periods*

| THE CATEGORIES | (AVERAGE PER CENT OF TOTAL SPACE) | | | | |
|---|---|---|---|---|---|
| | 1800 1820 | 1821 1840 | 1841 1860 | 1861 1880 | AVERAGE |
| Ancient Civilization in the Near East Egypt and Tigris-Euphrates Valley | 4.5 | 5.2 | 2.8 | 3.9 | 4.1 |
| Civilization of the Far East—Indian, China, and Japan | 3 5 | 1.1 | .7 | .2 | 1.4 |
| Sacred History or the Hebrews | 5.4 | 4.8 | 3.2 | 3.1 | 4.1 |
| Development of Greek Civilization | 9. | 11.2 | 9.3 | 8.7 | 9.6 |
| Development of Roman Civilization | 17.8 | 19.8 | 13.7 | 12.7 | 16. |
| Ecclesiastical History | 1.7 | 2.3 | 1.7 | 3.1 | 2.2 |
| The Dark Ages and Feudalism | 4.9 | 8. | 8. | 10.5 | 7.8 |
| Medieval Civilization in the Near East Persia Arabic Civilization—Mohammedanism | 1.5 | 3.2 | 2.1 | .7 | 1.9 |
| The Crusades | 1.2 | 1.8 | 1.8 | 3.3 | 2. |
| Renaissance or Revival of Learning | 4.1 | .4 | 1.8 | 1.9 | 2. |
| The Protestant Reformation | 1.5 | .4 | 2.3 | 2.8 | 1.8 |
| The Rise of Nationalism in Europe | 26. | 23. | 27.5 | 26.6 | 25.8 |
| North America and the United States, and South America | 16. | 8.5 | 10.4 | 9.2 | 11. |
| The Era of Political and Social Revolutions | 2.9 | 10.3 | 14.7 | 13.3 | 10.3 |
| Number of Textbooks | 12. | 14. | 9. | 10. | 11.2 |

others were written in narrative or descriptive form. However, most of the later ones presented the content with chapter or sectional headings, topical headings, and numbered paragraphs. All these aids tended to assist the student to keep his mind on the topics. Stewart found that only two of the first fourteen books contained questions, but 18 of the next 31 included them. Dawson found that of his 95 books 79 contained prefaces, 57 introductions, 80 tables of contents, 55 chronological tables, but only 34 had indexes. Only eleven of the first 63 books included indexes. A few also used time charts. Thus the later books were more attractive, organized better, and more teachable than the earlier ones.

The earlier books were factual, the writers merely tending to provide a source of general knowledge. In the second quarter of the 19th century when more books appeared, they gave more attention to political and governmental matters. A few of the books rather early contained considerable social content, but this practice did not prevail until late in the 19th century. Religious content remained rather constant even up to 1900. There was little evidence among the authors that they at all fully conceived or explained the democratic interpretation of history.

---

1 Verna M. Rifenberick, "Relations of Greek Word-Roots and Third Year Latin Vocabulary." (Unpublished Master of Arts Theseis, University of Pittsburgh, 1933).

2 Frank L. Stewart, .. he Development of Secondary School Textbooks in Early American World Histories from 1800 to 1880." (Unpublished doctoral dissertation, University of Pittsburgh, 1953)

3 John H. Dawson, "A Survey of the Religious Content of American World History Textbooks Written Prior to 1900." (Unpublished doctoral dissertation, University of Pittsburgh, 1954)

# Bibliography

ADAMS, Charles K.: *A Manual of Historical Literature*, N.Y., Harper Bros., 1903

ARISTOTLE: *Treatise on Rhetoric*, (Theodore Buckley, Translator), London, Henry G. Bohn, 1846

BINING, Arthur C. and David H.: *Teaching the Social Studies in the Secondary Schools*, N.Y., McGraw Hill Book Co., 1935

BOONE, Richard G.: *Education in the U.S.; Its History from the Earliest Settlements*, New York, D. Appleton & Co., 1889

BRENDEL, F.: "Historical Sketch of the Science of Botany in N. Am. from 1635–1840," *Am. Nat.*, vol. XIII, Dec. 1897

BROWN, Elmer E.: *The Making of Our Middle Schools*, New York, Longmans, Green & Co,. 1902

BROWN, Marion R.: "The History of Zoology in the Secondary Schools of U.S.," *School Science and Mathematics*, vol. II, 1902, pp. 291–9; 256–72

BRUBACHER, John S.: *A History of the Problems of Education*, N.Y., McGraw-Hill Book Co., 1947

BUCKLEY, H.: *A Short History of Physics*, London, 36 Essex Street, 1927

BURRY, Harold E.: "An Analysis of Early American Arithmetic Textbooks Through 1810," (Unpublished doctoral dissertation, University of Pittsburgh, 1958)

CAJORI, Florian: *The Teaching and History of Mathematics in the U.S.*, Washington, D.C., U.S. Bureau of Education, Circulars of Information, No. 3 (1890)

——: *A History of Physics*, N.Y.: MacMillan Co., 1929

CALDWELL, O.W.: "An Investigation of the Teaching of Biological Subjects in Secondary Schools," *School Science and Mathematics*, vol. IX, 1909, pp. 581–97

CARPENTER, Charles: *History of American School Books*, Philadelphia, University of Pennsylvania Press, 1963

CASILE, Bruno A.: "An Analysis of Zoology Textbooks Available for American Secondary Schools Before 1920," (Unpublished doctoral dissertation, University of Pittsburgh, 1953)

CHUBB, Percival: *The Teaching of English*, New York, MacMillan Co., 1902

CLARKE, Frank W.: "A Report on the Teaching of Chemistry and Physics in the U.S.," Washington, Bureau of Ed., No. 6, 1881

254     The Evolution of American Secondary School Textbooks

COULTER, John M.: "Chapters in the History of American Botany," *School Science and Mathematics,* vol. XI, 1911, pp. 814–16

CUNNINGHAM, Margaret S.: "Evolution of the Content of Elementary Plane Geometry from Euclid to the Present," (Master's Thesis, University of Southern California, 1930)

DAWSON, John H.: "A Survey of the Religious Content of American World History Textbooks Written Prior to 1900", (Unpublished Ph.D. dissertation, University of Pittsburgh, 1954)

DODGSON, C. L.: *Euclid and His Modern Rivals,* London, MacMillan, 1885

DOWNING, Elliot R.: *Teaching of Science in the Schools,* Chicago, University of Chicago Press, 1925

DUNMIRE, Burt L.: "The Development of American Literature Textbooks Used in the U.S. from 1870 to 1952," (Unpublished doctoral dissertation, University of Pittsburgh, 1954)

FARBER, Edward.: *The Evolution of Chemistry,* N.Y., Ronald Press, 1952

GRIZZELL, Emit D.: *Origin and Development of the High School in New England Before 1865,* N.Y., MacMillan Co., 1923

HALL-QUEST, Alfred L.: *The Textbook: How to Use It and Judge It,* N.Y., MacMillan Co., 1929

HARRIS, W.T.: "Importance of the Textbook," *Journal of Education,* vol. LXXX, 1914, p. 317

HESS, Glenn C.: "An Analysis of Early American Rhetoric and Composition Textbooks from 1784 to 1870," (Unpublished doctoral dissertation, University of Pittsburgh, 1949)

HOWES, Raymond F. (Ed.): *Historical Studies of Rhetoric and Rhetoricians,* Ithaca, Cornell University Press, 1962

JOHNSON, Clifton: *Old Time Schools and School Books,* N.Y., MacMillan Co., 1904

JONES, P. S.: "Early American Geometry," *The Mathematics Teacher,* XXXVII, (1944) pp. 3–11

KANDEL, I. L.: *History of Secondary Education,* N.Y., Houghton Mifflin Co., 1930

KARPINSKI, Louis C.: *Bibliography of Mathematical Works Printed in Am. Through 1850,* Ann Arbor, Mich., University of Michigan Press, 1940

KELSEY, F.W.: *Latin and Greek in American Education,* New York, MacMillan Co., 1911

KIDDLE, Henry and Alex J. Schern: *The Cyclopedia of Education,* New York E. Steiger, 1877

KING, Angie Turner: "An Analysis of Early Algebra Textbooks Used in American Schools Before 1900," (Unpublished Ph.D. dissertation, University of Pittsburgh, 1955)

LEONARD, Phillip: *Great Men of Science,* N.Y., MacMillan, 1935

LORD, John: *The Life of Emma Willard,* New York, D. Appleton & Co., 1873

MACLEAR, Martha: *The History of the Education of Girls in New York and in New England: 1800–1870,* Harvard University Press, 1926

MAHAFFY, J. P.: *Greek Life and Thought,* New York, MacMillan & Co., 1887

MANGERY, Peter W.: "An Analysis of Chemistry Textbooks Used in American Secondary Schools Before 1890," (Unpublished doctoral dissertation, University of Pittsburgh, 1959)

MARR, Harriet W.: *The Old New England Academies Founded Before 1826,* New York, Comet Press, 1959

MONROE, Paul (Ed.): *A Cyclopedia of Education*, vol. I–V., New York, MacMillan Co., (1913) 1917

——: *Founding of the American Public School System*, N.Y., MacMillan Co., 1940

MOORE, F. J.: *History of Chemistry*, N.Y., McGraw-Hill Book Co., 1939

NEEL, Helen M.: "Analysis of English Literature Textbooks Used in American Secondary Schools Before 1900," (Unpublished doctoral dissertation, University of Pittsburgh, 1954)

PAINTER, F.V.N.: *A History of Education*, N.Y., D. Appleton & Co., 1886

POWERS, S. R.: *A History of Chemistry in the Secondary Schools of the U.S. Prior to 1850*, Minneapolis, University of Minnesota, 1920

REDGROVE, H. S.: *Alchemy: Ancient and Modern*, London, William Rider & Son, 1922

ROORBACH, Agnew O.: *The Development of the Social Studies in American Secondary Education Before 1861*, (Doctoral dissertation, University of Pennsylvania, 1937)

RUSSELL, W. F.: "The Early Teaching of History in Secondary Schools," *History Teacher's Magazine*, vol. v, 1914–5

SANFORD, Vera: *A Short History of Mathematics*, N.Y., Houghton Mifflin Co., 1930

——: *Report of the Committee on Secondary School Studies*, Washington, U.S. Government Printing Office, 1893

SHANK, Paul L.: "The Evolution of Natural Philosophy (Physics) Textbooks Used in American Secondary Schools Before 1880," (Unpublished doctoral dissertation, University of Pittsburgh, 1951)

SIMONS, Lao Genevra: *Bibliography of Early American Textbooks on Algebra*, New York, Yeshiva College, 1936

STAMPER, A.W.: *A History of the Teaching of Elementary Geometry*, N.Y., Teachers College, Columbia University, 1906

STEWART, Frank L.: "The Development of Secondary School Textbooks in Early American World Histories from 1800 to 1880," (Unpublished Ph.D. dissertation, Universtiy of Pittsburgh, 1953)

STOUT, Cyril L.: *Trends of Methods, Contents, and Beliefs in Geography Textbooks 1784–1895*, Nashville, George Peabody College for Teachers, 1937

STOUT, John E.: *The Development of High School Curricula in the North Central States from 1860 to 1918*, Chicago, University of Chicago Press (1921)

THOMAS, Calvin: *Report of the Committee of Twelve of the Modern Language Ass'n. of America* D.C. Heath & Co., 1900

U.S. Bureau of Education: "German Instruction in American Schools," Rep. Com. Ed., 1900–1901, vol. I, pp. 531–708, Washington, U.S. Printing Office

WILSON, John D.: "An Analysis of Plane Geometry Content of Geometry Textbooks Published in the U.S. Before 1900," (Unpublished doctoral dissertation, University of Pittsburgh, 1959)

# Index

R

S